Alfred Tennyson

IN MEMORIAM, MAUD
AND OTHER POEMS

Edited, with an introduction
and notes, by
JOHN D. JUMP
JOHN EDWARD TAYLOR
Professor of English Literature
in the University of Manchester

J. M. Dent & Sons Limited, London
Rowman and Littlefield, Totowa, N.J.

© Introduction and notes
J, M. Dent & Sons Ltd, 1974

Printed in Great Britain by
Biddles Ltd, Guildford, Surrey
and bound at the
Aldine Press . Letchworth . Herts
for

J. M. DENT & SONS LTD
Aldine House . 26 Albemarle Street . London
First published 1974

First published in the United States 1974
by ROWMAN AND LITTLEFIELD, Totowa, New Jersey

Dent edition
Hardback ISBN: 0 460 10044 0
Paperback ISBN: 0 460 11044 6

Rowman and Littlefield edition
Hardback ISBN: 0-87471-592-x
Paperback ISBN: 0-87471-593-8

CONTENTS

INTRODUCTION

I

Dr George Clayton Tennyson, the Rector of Somersby in Lincolnshire, had entered holy orders against his inclination; he found his income insufficient to maintain his large family in what he considered decency; and he bitterly resented the preferment of his younger brother as their wealthy father's heir. Resentment unhinged his mind. He wrecked his health by taking to drink, and drinking tended to make him ungovernably violent. After years of misery, his wife had to insist upon a separation.

Alfred, born in 1809, the third of their children to survive infancy, grew up under the shadow of the family feud and in the gloomy presence of this learned and cultivated but unhappy and demented man. He evidently regarded his father with pity and fear, with anger and love, and at times with plain hostility. Trinity College, Cambridge, where he was admitted late in 1827, must have seemed to offer a haven from domestic storms. But Alfred was bored and lonely there until he met Arthur Henry Hallam in the spring of 1829. The two young men quickly became firm friends. Each could give the other support by his sympathetic understanding of the moods of despondency to which both were subject. They joined the 'Apostles', an informal debating society which included many of the ablest undergraduates among its members; and before the end of the year Hallam fell in love with Tennyson's sister Emily.

Hallam found satisfaction, and greatly assisted his friend, by acting as Tennyson's literary agent. He worked hard to get *Poems, Chiefly Lyrical* (1830) a favourable reception, and but for him Tennyson would not have brought out his second volume, *Poems*, as early as 1832. He praised Tennyson 'as promising fair to be the greatest poet of our generation, perhaps of our century'. Then, in the autumn of 1833, he died suddenly while touring in Austria with his father. Tennyson and his sister lost in Hallam a man whom both loved deeply and who fully returned the love of both. Tennyson's whole life seemed shattered; for a time he wished to die.

Not that Hallam's death was solely responsible for this wish. The circumstances of Tennyson's early life, and possibly hereditary factors, had predisposed him to melancholia. Poems written before as well as after the autumn of 1833 express the desperate loneliness he was always prone to feel and the craving for oblivion to which it constantly led. Shortly before Hallam's death J. W. Croker had produced a brutally sarcastic review of *Poems* (1832; dated 1833), writing with the avowed intention of making another Keats of his victim. Hurt, despondent, and bereaved, Tennyson lasped into the 'ten years' silence' which preceded the launching of his next collection, *Poems* (1842).

Early in this period, in 1834, he fell in love with Rosa Baring of Harrington Hall, near Somersby. Her wealth made her unattainable, and he soon came to see her as a rather commonplace young woman. But he was always to remember vividly the intensity of his brief, thwarted passion. In 1836 he fell in love with Emily Sellwood, a Lincolnshire solicitor's daughter, who was to become his wife after an engagement greatly prolonged and even interrupted by his lack of funds, by her family's anxiety about the mental health of the Tennysons generally, and by her own misgivings regarding his religious faith.

Poems (1842) comprised two volumes: the first contained selected poems, often much revised, from the earlier collections, the second a slightly greater amount of new verse. Both the public and the reviewers responded favourably. But, whereas Tennyson had written much during the greater part of the 'ten years' silence', he wrote little during the years immediately before and after the publication of *Poems* (1842), that broke it. Acute financial problems and the apparent loss of Emily were aggravating his recurrent fierce melancholia. Late in 1843 his friend Edward FitzGerald—subsequently to become famous for *The Rubáiyát of Omar Khayyám*—found him more hopeless than he had ever seen him; and in the following year Tennyson was receiving medical treatment. He continued to be a source of anxiety to his friends until after the publication of *The Princess* (1847).

From about that time, however, things took a turn for the better. Tennyson's financial position improved. A reading of *In Memoriam* in manuscript dispelled Emily's anxiety about his religious faith, and they married in the summer of 1850. Emily was to be a devoted and tireless wife, and their friends soon noted with pleasure the change in Alfred's health and spirits. For some years his reputation as a poet had been growing steadily, and towards the end of 1850 he succeeded William Wordsworth as Poet Laureate.

He believed that he owed this appointment to Prince Albert's liking for *In Memoriam*, which Tennyson had published just before his marriage. Ever since October 1833 when the news of Hallam's death had reached him, he had been composing short lyrics voicing his sense of loss and the thoughts which this inspired. By 1842 there existed about one-half of all that he was to write. Eventually he decided to arrange these lyrics as a long philosophical poem. This poem, *In Memoriam*, was an immediate and resounding success, entering a fifth edition within eighteen months. Not since Byron's years of fame had a new poem received such a welcome.

From 1850 Tennyson enjoyed increasing prosperity and fame. His growing affluence enabled him to buy Farringford, in the Isle of Wight, in 1856, and to build Aldworth, at Blackdown, near Haslemere, in 1868. These were homes in which he found security with his wife and two sons. He entertained distinguished guests: W. E. Gladstone, Benjamin Jowett, and others. From time to time he travelled. The widowed Queen Victoria, influenced no doubt by Albert's regard for Tennyson's writings, entered into friendly correspondence with her Poet Laureate. In 1883 he was raised to the peerage.

One after another, his books augmented his reputation. Admittedly, many reviewers complained that *Maud* (1855) was obscure and morbid. But the reading public did not lose interest, and the first four *Idylls of the King* (1859) and *Enoch Arden* (1864) raised his popularity to such a pitch that a writer in a weekly paper could think it likely that the age would become known as the age of Tennyson. There is no need to review his subsequent publications here. It will suffice to say that, while some of the younger critics from about 1870 were beginning to question his achievement, the public generally continued to hold him in the highest esteem to the end of the century and beyond.

He was a shy, honest, gruffly humorous, sensitive, and deeply emotional man. He made warm and lasting friendships. Even his largely epistolary relationship with his sovereign developed into something of the kind. When the Emperor of Germany cabled to the Queen his condolences on the death of the Poet Laureate in 1892, he was no doubt testifying to Tennyson's tremendous prestige as a poet but he must also have been recognizing the importance of the relationship to Victoria herself.

II

Even as brief a biographical summary as this can leave no one in doubt regarding certain sources of the melancholy which finds

expression in one after another of Tennyson's poems. His deep love
for his home must have made the distresses and frustrations of life
at Somersby almost unbearable. They find an indirect outlet in his
writing. He evokes an oppressive sense of decay in the 'Song'
beginning 'A spirit haunts the year's last hours'; he uses a beautifully
particularized setting to compel his reader to share the loneliness and
dejection of the abandoned woman in 'Mariana'; and in 'The Two
Voices' he confronts the case for escaping the weariness, the fever,
and the fret of life by suicide.

The voice which tempts the speaker to this conclusion seems to
come from within himself. It is a 'still small voice', which does not
so much originate lines of argument as develop disconcertingly those
which the speaker himself advances in trying to resist despair. It
punctures his human pride by pointing out that there must be many
creatures superior to man in a universe that is boundless; it undercuts
his faith in progress by asking what is the significance of progress
along a scale that is infinite; it derides his wish to leave an honourable
name; and it seeks to allay the dread of something after death by
persuading him that the dead are at peace. But the speaker needs to
believe that death does not end all. Despite the voice's insistence upon
the fact of pain, he wants 'More life, and fuller'; and he is
strengthened in this desire by the sight of a happily united family
walking to church. When the sceptical voice dies away, the second
voice of the poem's title cheers the speaker by hinting at a 'hidden
hope' of a divine love.

As this necessarily selective outline will have suggested, the
argument of 'The Two Voices' follows the vagaries of feeling rather
than the routine of logic. The poem's rhyming triplets, which almost
ask for a dubitative pause after each third line, serve well to record
a process of anxious and tentative brooding. Admittedly, 'The Two
Voices' does not achieve the assured success of 'Mariana' or the
'Song'. It is awkward in some places, flat in others; and many
twentieth-century readers have found its churchgoing family too
good to be true. Nevertheless, it does honestly face the issues it
raises, and it is frequently moving and memorable.

Since a draft of it existed three months before Tennyson learned
of Hallam's death, the bereavement cannot have prompted the poem.
Work on it continued for some time, however, so we may assume
that grief at Hallam's death entered into 'The Two Voices' as finally
published. Tennyson himself declared that 'Ulysses' was what he
wrote under the immediate sense of the loss, with the feeling 'that
all had gone by, but that still life must be fought out to the end'.

The speaker in this dramatic monologue has resolved to embark upon a new, perilous, and possibly final voyage. Yet his mood is elegiac; a tone as of mournful acquiescence casts doubt on the strenuousness of his resolution. As a result, we imagine him less as striving, seeking, finding, and refusing to yield than as standing, in the words of a Victorian reviewer, 'for ever a listless and melancholy figure on the shore'. The ambiguity of the portrait springs from Tennyson's utter honesty. Life had indeed to be fought out to the end, but by one whom grief had immobilized and in whom early experience had implanted a longing for oblivion. 'Ulysses' is one of the most complex and poignant of his shorter pieces.

The work that most readily brings Hallam to mind is *In Memoriam*. Critics have sometimes exaggerated the degree of unity that resulted when Tennyson arranged almost a gross of short lyrics to form this long philosophical poem. Admittedly it opens with the first crushing onset of grief, and it closes with the marriage of a sister of the poet. 'It was meant to be a kind of *Divina Commedia*, ending with happiness', stated Tennyson. Its three Christmas passages, implying a fictional span of almost exactly three years between the opening and the close, can be read as marking clear stages in the mourner's emotional and spiritual recovery: the first Christmas Eve falls 'sadly' (xxx), the second 'calmly' (lxxviii), and the third 'strangely' (cv). Lyrics marking other anniversaries serve this purpose, too. But when all has been said we must let Tennyson remind us that the lyrics 'were written at many different places, and as the phases of our intercourse came to my memory and suggested them. I did not write them with any view of weaving them into a whole, or for publication, until I found that I had written so many.'

This did not prevent him from distinguishing nine natural groups of lyrics in *In Memoriam* as finally shaped. A list of the nine, with some indication of their leading subjects or themes, will take us about as far as it seems reasonable to go in trying to see the poem as a strictly organized whole:

1 Grief at the news of Hallam's death overwhelms the mourner (i–viii).

2 In imagination, he follows the ship that is bringing home his friend's body for burial (ix–xx).

3 He recalls the four years of friendship he and the dead man had known (xxi–xxvii).

4 The pain of loss would be insupportable but for the hope of survival after death (xxviii–xlix).

5 Needing to believe in personal immortality and in the enduring

value of human endeavour, the mourner longs for his friend to
approach and sustain him (l–lviii).

6 His reliance upon Hallam's spirit continues despite the extent
of their separation (lix–lxxi).

7 Though his grief is growing calmer, his dependence persists, and
he still begs his friend's spirit to come to him. From about this
point, springtime imagery tends to displace autumn and winter
imagery. A fleeting mystical experience, recorded in xcv, forms
the climax and turning-point of the poem (lxxii–xcviii).

8 The mourner's departure from the childhood home which
Hallam had visited signalizes a fresh start (xcix–ciii).

9 The New Year hymn, cvi, further emphasizing this, leads to a
series of affectionate and admiring recollections of his friend and
to confident assertions of faith in the divine love (civ–cxxxi).
This faith is the theme also of the prologue, which Tennyson
wrote late but used to introduce the entire poem. A lyric on his
sister's wedding forms the epilogue.

The need to believe in survival after death and in the enduring
value of human endeavour had prevailed by the end of *The Two
Voices*. In the fifth group of lyrics composing *In Memoriam*, Tennyson
reaffirms it in face of the appalling fact that not only individuals like
Hallam but whole species of living creatures have been ruthlessly and
arbitrarily swept away in the long course of time. The reaffirmation
is cruelly difficult. What rôle can mind or spirit have had in the
process traced by the geologists? Does not this process invite ex-
planation in purely material or physical terms? Only 'faintly', in
defiance of the evidence, can Tennyson 'trust the larger hope'. This,
at all events, is as far as he can go in the first half of *In Memoriam*.

In the final group of lyrics he achieves a more confident assertion
of faith. He rejects materialism as cripplingly reductive. Men cannot
be satisfactorily explained as 'wholly brain' or mere 'cunning casts
in clay'. Moreover, the evolutionary process moves towards the
fulfilment of a providential plan; it is bringing into being 'a higher
race', which was anticipated in Hallam. This providential plan
implies a loving God. Experience of the kind recorded in xcv enables
the poet to affirm his belief in the divine love. Simply and firmly, he
can declare, 'I have felt.'

So the poem as a whole traces the gradual alleviation of the pain
of bereavement and the eventual confirmation of an intuitive faith in
the 'Strong Son of God, immortal Love'. But while we are actually
reading it we pay less heed to these processes than to the particular
phases of thought and feeling captured in the separate lyrics. Tenny-

son's stanza-form lends itself exactly to this presentation of a series of intellectual and emotional states, each one of which in turn appears to be almost immutable. The four lines composing the *In Memoriam* stanza are all iambic tetrameters. The second and third derive firmness and emphasis from their couplet rhyming. While the first and fourth, thanks to the rhymes which link them, seem to wrap around the couplet, their separation from each other weakens the conclusiveness of the fourth. The stanza turns on itself, encloses itself, pauses in earnest reflection, yet seems always to hint at resumption.

Tennyson's contemporaries had found much to admire in the short pieces published by 1842. Yet some even of the friendliest of them were not completely satisfied. They looked for something more strenuous and sustained. They wanted him to write a long poem, to handle an important contemporary subject, to show a deeper human sympathy, and to preach sound doctrine. Tennyson had responded with *The Princess* (1847), a fanciful contribution to the current discussion of women's education. Ironically, the poetic romance which forms the main part of this work has kept its appeal less well than have the exquisite and moving lyrics which are supposedly incidental to it. But with *In Memoriam* Tennyson solved his problem by shaping a long prophetic poem, as demanded by his critics, from the short personal lyrics that came more naturally to him.

III

Maud (1855) is another long poem made up of short lyrics. These purport to be the dramatic utterances of a young man whose distresses broadly resemble those of Tennyson himself: his father, wronged, resentful, and finally unbalanced, appears to have committed suicide; his mother has been lonely and unhappy; the wealth and social standing of Maud's family constitute as great a barrier to his union with her as those of Rosa Baring's family did to her union with Tennyson; bitter experience had made Tennyson quite as angrily aware of financial malpractices as his hero was to be; and when his hero expresses the grief of bereavement and the longing for reunion with a dead lover in the lyric beginning 'O that 'twere possible' (II.iv) he is elaborating lines that Tennyson had written immediately after Hallam's death. Was the happily married and successful Poet Laureate perhaps trying to come to terms through a fictional plot with the pains and grievances of his own earlier life?

He called the poem 'a little *Hamlet*'. Like the prince, its hero has been deprived of his inheritance by the man whom he holds responsible for his father's death. He sees this man as representative of a whole Mammon-worshipping age. Denouncing it in the manner of Thomas Carlyle or Charles Kingsley, he resolves to bury himself in himself (I.i).

He then sets eyes on this man's daughter, Maud, for the first time since childhood. He tries to dismiss her from his mind as 'Faultily faultless, icily regular, splendidly null' (I.ii). But he cannot forget her looks—though he thinks her proud—and he is captivated by her voice when she sings 'A passionate ballad gallant and gay,/A martial song like a trumpet's call' (I.v). Delighted when Maud shows him friendship, he nevertheless suspects 'some coquettish deceit' (I.vi).

Maud's brother, a selfish and arrogant young dandy with a genuine affection for his sister, is the principal obstacle to their developing relationship. Although their fathers have pledged long ago that the hero and Maud shall become man and wife, the brother wishes to marry her to the effete grandson of a wealthy, ruthless mine-owner.

But Maud and the hero draw together in love. Her acceptance of him is marked by the grave and beautiful lyric, 'I have led her home' (I.xviii). In this, a steady, assured, and customary iambic rhythm prevails for the first time at any length in a poem mainly characterized by hectic and throbbing anapaestic, or mixed anapaestic and iambic, patterns. The hero swears 'to bury/All this dead body of hate' (I.xix). The famous lyric in which he waits eagerly, impatiently, feverishly for her to leave the dance at the Hall, her home, and join him in the garden marks the climax of the poem (I.xxii).

The hero's fortunes now resemble Romeo's more closely than Hamlet's. Just as Romeo fights with Juliet's kinsman Tybalt and is banished, so the hero fights with Maud's brother and goes into exile. There are extenuating circumstances: the brother acts in defiance of the fathers' pledge and of the lovers' mutual affection; he calls the hero a liar and strikes him in the presence of his 'grinning' rival (II.i); and he receives his wound in a formal duel, after which he admits, 'The fault was mine' (II.i). Maud's death follows quickly on this calamity.

The hero retains two clear images of her. One shows her as she appeared when he was a happy accepted lover; the other shows her as she appeared when she uttered her 'passionate cry' (II.i) of grief at the bloodshed. This second image becomes the 'phantom' that haunts him in his exile and madness, a symbol of his guilt. His madness is powerfully rendered in a lyric, II.v, which incorporates disordered reminiscences of all that has gone before.

Part III associates his recovery of his reason, and the final disappearance of the 'phantom', with his ceasing to bury himself in himself and instead devoting himself to a great cause. 'It is better to fight for the good than to rail at the ill' (III.vi).

This is on the whole the hero's version of what happens in *Maud*. Does the poem present any alternative version? A play allows different characters to take different views of what is going on— Lear's differs from Cordelia's, and hers from Goneril's and Regan's— but *Maud* is not a play. All the lyrics come from the hero's mouth. In such dramatic monologues as 'My Last Duchess', 'Andrea del Sarto', and 'The Bishop Orders his Tomb', Browning allows his characters to give their own accounts of things, but at the same time, by permitting a little over-insistence, for example, or by briefly releasing passions which the characters strive to repress, he implies alternative accounts which the reader may share with him. In this sense, Tennyson's lyrics are hardly dramatic at all. If we were to learn that the poem had not been written by Tennyson but by a young man who had himself loved Maud, shot and perhaps killed her brother, and enlisted in the army, we should find this only too easy to believe.

Does this matter? May we not read the poem as a series of lyrics expressing the changing moods of an isolated, unhappy, angry, neurotic young man; who is lifted out of his misery when he finds his love returned but is plunged into even deeper misery when circumstances lead him to wreck that love; and who emerges from his consequent madness only when he finds a great and noble cause which he can serve?

That 'great and noble cause' troubles many readers. They cannot view the Crimean War in that light. With the wisdom of hindsight, they can see that it was unnecessary; and they know that it was going to be mismanaged. But we can hardly blame the hero, or Tennyson, for not knowing all this at the time. What matters in the poem is that the hero is devoting himself to what he believes to be a struggle against falsehood and tyranny.

It is plausible enough, psychologically speaking, that he should be able to overcome his personal grief and guilt by achieving solidarity with others in such a movement. Moreover, he believes that the war will do for the nation something comparable with what he expects military service will do for himself. In the opening lyric and later

he has castigated contemporary selfishness and greed. He has de-
nounced the evils permitted or even encouraged by Victorian
capitalism, and he has protested against the materialism of the age.
He now trusts that the challenge of war will elicit in Englishmen a
stronger sense of solidarity with, and of responsibility towards, one
another and so lead them to eliminate these evils. Much of his
criticism of the aggressive individualism of his time is justified; and
both then and later men have urgently needed a strong sense of
collective purpose. However, war seems an intolerably ruthless,
destructive, and wasteful way of supplying this want, and one that
can hardly supply it permanently.

Yet we scrutinize the poem in vain for any recognition by Tenny-
son that this is so. He is apparently content that the war should be
fought to cure his hero's neurosis and to raise standards of behaviour
in commerce and industry. In short, he seems to have surrendered his
poem to his hero. Understandably, there were contemporaries who
criticized Tennyson for identifying with his hero's bellicosity while
sitting safely at home in the Isle of Wight.

Tennyson seems to identify not merely with his hero's bellicosity
but with all his hero's changing and often passionate moods. As a
result, *Maud* is not only a poem about a somewhat feverish hero; it is
a somewhat feverish poem about such a hero. It is a skilfully planned
series of personal lyrics written in an assumed character. This charac-
ter is not dramatically projected. We are left to judge for ourselves
the reliability of his testimony; we receive little or no guidance from
the poem itself.

But his changing and often passionate moods are rendered with a
marvellous intimacy and persuasiveness. *Maud* may hardly deserve
the subtitle, *A Monodrama*. It is, however, a compelling, moving,
exciting, lyrical sequence.

Tennyson cast several of his finest shorter poems in the form of
dramatic monologues. In most of them, as in *Maud*, there is little
point in trying to distinguish between what the character says and
what the poem says. This is evidently the case with 'Ulysses'; and
in 'Tithonus', also commenced shortly after Hallam's death, Tenny-
son places in a suitable speaker's mouth his own recognition that
there are terms on which even immortality would become a curse
and would produce a longing for extinction. 'Ulysses' and 'Tithonus'
are two of the subtlest, richest, and most truly personal of his poems.

But they hardly aspire to be 'dramatic' in the sense in which 'St.
Simeon Stylites' may be so described. In this, the speaker has sought
salvation by mortifying the flesh. For thirty years he has confined

himself to the top of a high pillar; he has grown emaciated, deformed, diseased; but he has, he hopes, acquired a degree of sanctity sufficient to qualify him to be a miraculous healer on earth and one of the blessed hereafter. Tennyson allows him to grow over-insistent in his pleading. Argumentatively, he asks Christ who, if not he, may be saved: 'Who may be made a saint, if I fail here?' He boasts that 'no one, even among the saints,/May match his pains with mine'. Though he thanks God for 'His bounty' in making him an 'example to mankind,/Which few can reach to', his words inadvertently disclose his arrogant assumption that he has by his own effort 'reached' the state to which he is ostensibly thanking God for raising him.

By such touches, Tennyson makes his poem convey meanings which Simeon does not intend. As we read, we see Simeon both through his own eyes and through those of an independent observer. His monologue is dramatic in the sense in which one hesitates to apply the term to *Maud* or 'Ulysses' or 'Tithonus'. To say this is not to decry these three works and others like them; it is merely to define the kind of success characteristic of these more subjective monologues.

IV

The grotesque traits in the portrait of Simeon may serve to remind us that Tennyson's writings exhibit a considerable variety both in content and in form. His melancholia and his efforts to dispel the fears it aroused, dominate most of the poems reviewed so far. *Maud* is not alone in bringing home to us how acute was his awareness of the sub-rational forces, both in the individual and in the world generally, that make for madness, violence, and destruction, and how earnestly he strove to understand and to manage these forces within his own life. The complement of this painful awareness is a craving for stability, security, and peace of mind. This can be expressed mawkishly, as in the evocation of 'settled bliss' at the end of 'The Miller's Daughter'. But it can equally be communicated with serene finality by the compellingly suggestive detail of a landscape, as when he speaks of the knolls 'where, couch'd at ease,/The white kine glimmer'd, and the trees/Laid their dark arms about the field' (*In Memoriam*, xcv) or of 'The pillar'd dusk of sounding sycamores' ('Audley Court').

His poetic renderings of natural phenomena are rarely less than brilliant. Patient and sensitive observation is served in them by his supreme skill in the handling of words, by what Walt Whitman called his 'finest verbalism'. During his later years, readers noted the conjunction of such verbalism with a gentle sadness and tenderness and spoke of him as the English Virgil. During his earlier years, its manifestation in such poems as 'Mariana', the 'Song' ('A spirit haunts the year's last hours'), 'The Lady of Shalott', and 'The Lotos-Eaters' led them to regard him as the successor to John Keats. His language in these is rich, deliberate, incantatory. 'The Lady of Shalott' shows how readily it can give access to that mediaeval dream-world which attracted so many nineteenth-century writers and painters.

Though Tennyson mediaevalizes in several early lyrical poems, his most distinguished achievement in that direction is an epic fragment, 'Morte d'Arthur'. In this, a poet who longed for settled ways comes to terms, through an Arthur who is dying, or passing to Avilion, with the irresistible and often violent processes of change. The fragment is haunting, poignant, and compelling.

Tennyson knew that many critics were currently demanding poems about contemporary life. So in self-defence he enclosed his fragment in what amounted to an apology, 'The Epic'. Gradually conquering his timidity, he returned to the Arthurian material in middle age and eventually produced what many Victorians thought his masterpiece, *Idylls of the King*. Like *In Memoriam* and *Maud*, this is a long work built up from relatively short, separate items. Four of these appeared in 1859: 'Enid', 'Vivien', 'Elaine', and 'Guinevere'. Readers understandably saw them simply as four cabinet pictures related to the Arthurian legends. As picture followed picture during the next quarter-century, however, it became clear that there was what Tennyson called 'an allegorical or perhaps rather a parabolic drift' designed to unite them into a single whole. Thanks to this, the complete set of twelve *Idylls* offers an elaborate treatment of the struggle in human life between soul and sense.

The first of the *Idylls* as finally arranged, 'The Coming of Arthur', opens the cycle with appropriate hints and ambiguities. 'Merlin and Vivien' and 'The Holy Grail' are among the most successful of those that follow. The finest of all is the last, 'The Passing of Arthur', which incorporates 'Morte d'Arthur' almost without alteration.

At the opposite extreme from the *Idylls*, with their collective aspiration to something like epic status, stand the songs and short lyrics in *The Princess*. These are among Tennyson's most delicate and evocative creations; here if anywhere, art aspires towards the condition of music. In particular, 'Tears, idle tears', 'Now sleeps the crimson petal', and 'Come down, O maid' call both for high praise and for a confession that critical analysis cannot go very far towards explaining their charm. Equally fine achievements occur elsewhere. Many examples could be taken from *In Memoriam* and *Maud*. But two independent lyrics will suffice to complete this review: 'Break, break, break' expresses with poignant indirectness the poet's desolation at Hallam's death; and 'Crossing the Bar' sums up with simple dignity the outcome of a lifetime's brooding on faith and doubt.

Many of his shorter poems are neither songs nor song-like lyrics. 'To E. FitzGerald' is an urbane and cordial Horatian ode; 'Northern Farmer—Old Style' and 'Northern Farmer—New Style' are humorous and racy dialect poems; the satirical impulse which contributes to them leads in 'A Character' to a cool scrutiny of the victim's polished self-esteem; a similar satirical impulse enables the hero of *Maud* sharply to characterize his lover's overbearing brother (I.xiii); the vigorous rhetoric of 'The Charge of the Light Brigade', a poem on which Tennyson did not particularly pride himself, would shame most other Poets Laureate; and 'Vastness' shows him late in his career resorting again to the denunciatory, prophetic tones already heard in 'Locksley Hall' and in several sections of *Maud*.

But 'Vastness' within itself exemplifies the variety of Tennyson's work. After a thirty-five-line Jeremiad, he breaks off, pauses, and quietly concludes, 'Peace, let it be! for I loved him, and love him for ever: the dead are not dead but alive.' Here, as in 'In the Valley of Cauteretz', the elderly poet can for the moment think of nothing but the greatly loved friend who died when they were both young and who has been present to him ever since.

V

A short essay such as this can deal only very selectively with the considerable body of verse that I have been invited to introduce and annotate. I have chosen to concentrate mainly upon the two major poems, *In Memoriam* and *Maud*, while at the same time mentioning briefly, and as far as possible characterizing, a large number of the shorter pieces. Like all other recent writers on Tennyson, I owe a great deal to Christopher Ricks. His copiously annotated edition, *The Poems of Tennyson* (Longmans, 1969), is indispensable; and his biographical and critical study, *Tennyson* (Macmillan, 1972), is an outstanding work of its kind. No doubt I owe much also to other authors who figure in my biography, but I feel that my debt to the two works of Ricks calls for the special acknowledgement which I now make.

John D. Jump, 1974.

SELECT BIBLIOGRAPHY

TEXTS

The Poems of Tennyson, ed. Christopher Ricks (1969). Longman's Annotated English Poets. The first complete and fully annotated edition of the poems. Excludes the plays apart from the juvenile *Devil and the Lady*.

Tennyson: Poems and Plays, ed. T. Herbert Warren, revised by Frederick Page (1953). Oxford Standard Authors. Includes all the plays of Tennyson's mature years.

BIOGRAPHICAL STUDIES

Tennyson, Charles, *Alfred Tennyson* (1949). The first to reveal the truth about Tennyson's early life.

Tennyson, Hallam, Lord, *Alfred Lord Tennyson: A Memoir*, 2 vols. (1897).

CRITICAL STUDIES

Bradley, A. C., *A Commentary on Tennyson's 'In Memoriam'* (1901; revised 1902, 1930).

Buckley, Jerome Hamilton, *Tennyson: The Growth of a Poet* (Cambridge, Mass., 1960).

Gransden, K. W., *Tennyson: 'In Memoriam'* (1964). Studies in English Literature.

Hunt, John Dixon (ed.), *Tennyson, 'In Memoriam': A Casebook* (1970). Reprints excerpts from contemporary reviews as well as longer articles by T. S. Eliot, Graham Hough, and others.

Johnson, E. D. H., *The Alien Vision of Victorian Poetry: Sources of the Poetic Imagination in Tennyson, Browning, and Arnold* (Princeton, 1952).

Jump, John D. (ed.), *Tennyson: The Critical Heritage* (1967). Reprints 35 contemporary evaluations of Tennyson's poetry, nearly half of them in their entirety.

Killham, John (ed.), *Critical Essays on the Poetry of Tennyson* (1960). Contains essays by G. M. Young, Arthur J. Carr, H. M. McLuhan, W. W. Robson, and others.

Nicolson, Harold, *Tennyson: Aspects of his Life, Character, and Poetry* (1923). The best biographical-and-critical study from the early part of the twentieth century.

Palmer, D. J. (ed.), *Tennyson* (1973). Writers and their Background. Nine new essays on different aspects of Tennyson's work, followed by a useful Select Bibliography.

Rader, Ralph Wilson, *Tennyson's 'Maud': The Biographical Genesis* (Berkeley, 1963).

Ricks, Christopher, *Tennyson* (1972). The best biographical-and-critical study from the later years of the twentieth century.

Sinfield, Alan, *The Language of Tennyson's 'In Memoriam'* (Oxford, 1971).

Southam, B. C., *Tennyson* (1971). Writers and their Work.

Tillotson, Kathleen, 'Tennyson's Serial Poem', in Geoffrey and Kathleen Tillotson, *Mid-Victorian Studies*, 1965. An account of the evolution and reception of the *Idylls of the King*.

MARIANA

'Mariana in the moated grange.'
Measure for Measure.

WITH blackest moss the flower-plots
    Were thickly crusted, one and all:
The rusted nails fell from the knots
    That held the pear to the gable-wall.
The broken sheds look'd sad and strange:
    Unlifted was the clinking latch;
    Weeded and worn the ancient thatch
Upon the lonely moated grange.
        She only said, 'My life is dreary,
            He cometh not,' she said;
        She said, 'I am aweary, aweary,
            I would that I were dead!'

Her tears fell with the dews at even;
    Her tears fell ere the dews were dried;
She could not look on the sweet heaven,
    Either at morn or eventide.
After the flitting of the bats,
    When thickest dark did trance the sky,
    She drew her casement-curtain by,
And glanced athwart the glooming flats.
        She only said, 'The night is dreary,
            He cometh not,' she said;
        She said, 'I am aweary, aweary,
            I would that I were dead!'

Upon the middle of the night,
    Waking she heard the night-fowl crow:
The cock sung out an hour ere light:
    From the dark fen the oxen's low
Came to her: without hope of change,
    In sleep she seem'd to walk forlorn,
    Till cold winds woke the gray-eyed morn
About the lonely moated grange.
        She only said, 'The day is dreary,
            He cometh not,' she said;
        She said, 'I am aweary, aweary,
            I would that I were dead!'

About a stone-cast from the wall
    A sluice with blacken'd waters slept,
And o'er it many, round and small,
    The cluster'd marish-mosses crept.

10

20

30

40

I

Hard by a poplar shook alway,
   All silver-green with gnarled bark:
For leagues no other tree did mark
The level waste, the rounding gray.
     She only said, ' My life is dreary,
       He cometh not,' she said;
     She said, ' I am aweary, aweary,
       I would that I were dead ! '

And ever when the moon was low,
   And the shrill winds were up and away,   *50*
In the white curtain, to and fro,
   She saw the gusty shadow sway.
But when the moon was very low,
   And wild winds bound within their cell,
The shadow of the poplar fell
Upon her bed, across her brow.
     She only said, ' The night is dreary,
       He cometh not,' she said;
     She said, ' I am aweary, aweary,
       I would that I were dead ! '   *60*

All day within the dreamy house,
   The doors upon their hinges creak'd;
The blue fly sung in the pane; the mouse
   Behind the mouldering wainscot shriek'd,
Or from the crevice peer'd about.
   Old faces glimmer'd thro' the doors,
   Old footsteps trod the upper floors,
Old voices called her from without.
     She only said, ' My life is dreary,
       He cometh not,' she said;   *70*
     She said, ' I am aweary, aweary,
       I would that I were dead ! '

The sparrow's chirrup on the roof,
   The slow clock ticking, and the sound
Which to the wooing wind aloof
   The poplar made, did all confound
Her sense; but most she loathed the hour
   When the thick-moted sunbeam lay
   Athwart the chambers, and the day
Was sloping toward his western bower.   *80*
     Then, said she, ' I am very dreary,
       He will not come,' she said;
     She wept, ' I am aweary, aweary,
       Oh God, that I were dead ! '

SONG

A SPIRIT haunts the year's last hours
Dwelling amid these yellowing bowers:
    To himself he talks;
For at eventide, listening earnestly,
At his work you may hear him sob and sigh
    In the walks;
    Earthward he boweth the heavy stalks
Of the mouldering flowers:
    Heavily hangs the broad sunflower
      Over its grave i' the earth so chilly;   *10*
    Heavily hangs the hollyhock,
      Heavily hangs the tiger-lily.

The air is damp, and hush'd, and close,
As a sick man's room when he taketh repose
    An hour before death;
My very heart faints and my whole soul grieves
At the moist rich smell of the rotting leaves,
    And the breath
    Of the fading edges of box beneath,
And the year's last rose.   *20*
    Heavily hangs the broad sunflower
      Over its grave i' the earth so chilly;
    Heavily hangs the hollyhock,
      Heavily hangs the tiger-lily.

A CHARACTER

WITH a half-glance upon the sky
At night he said, ' The wanderings
Of this most intricate Universe
Teach me the nothingness of things.'
Yet could not all creation pierce
Beyond the bottom of his eye.

He spake of beauty: that the dull
Saw no divinity in grass,
Life in dead stones, or spirit in air;
Then looking as 'twere in a glass,   *10*
He smooth'd his chin and sleek'd his hair,
And said the earth was beautiful.

He spake of virtue : not the gods
More purely, when they wish to charm
Pallas and Juno sitting by :
And with a sweeping of the arm,
And a lack-lustre dead-blue eye,
Devolved his rounded periods.

Most delicately hour by hour
He canvass'd human mysteries,   20
And trod on silk, as if the winds
Blew his own praises in his eyes,
And stood aloof from other minds
In impotence of fancied power.

With lips depress'd as he were meek,
Himself unto himself he sold :
Upon himself himself did feed :
Quiet, dispassionate, and cold,
And other than his form of creed,
With chisell'd features clear and sleek.   30

THE LADY OF SHALOTT

PART I

On either side the river lie
Long fields of barley and of rye,
That clothe the wold and meet the sky;
And thro' the field the road runs by
　　　To many-tower'd Camelot;
And up and down the people go,
Gazing where the lilies blow
Round an island there below,
　　　The island of Shalott.

Willows whiten, aspens quiver,　　　　　　　　*10*
Little breezes dusk and shiver
Thro' the wave that runs for ever
By the island in the river
　　　Flowing down to Camelot.
Four gray walls, and four gray towers,
Overlook a space of flowers,
And the silent isle imbowers
　　　The Lady of Shalott.

By the margin, willow-veil'd,
Slide the heavy barges trail'd　　　　　　　　*20*
By slow horses; and unhail'd
The shallop flitteth silken-sail'd
　　　Skimming down to Camelot:
But who hath seen her wave her hand?
Or at the casement seen her stand?
Or is she known in all the land,
　　　The Lady of Shalott?

Only reapers, reaping early
In among the bearded barley,
Hear a song that echoes cheerly　　　　　　　*30*
From the river winding clearly
　　　Down to tower'd Camelot:
And by the moon the reaper weary,
Piling sheaves in uplands airy,
Listening, whispers ' 'Tis the fairy
　　　Lady of Shalott.'

PART II

There she weaves by night and day
A magic web with colours gay.
She has heard a whisper say,
A curse is on her if she stay　　　　　　　　*40*
　　　To look down to Camelot.

She knows not what the curse may be,
And so she weaveth steadily,
And little other care hath she,
    The Lady of Shalott.

And moving thro' a mirror clear
That hangs before her all the year,
Shadows of the world appear.
There she sees the highway near
    Winding down to Camelot: 50
There the river eddy whirls,
And there the surly village-churls,
And the red cloaks of market girls,
    Pass onward from Shalott.

Sometimes a troop of damsels glad,
An abbot on an ambling pad,
Sometimes a curly shepherd-lad,
Or long-hair'd page in crimson clad,
    Goes by to tower'd Camelot;
And sometimes thro' the mirror blue   60
The knights come riding two and two:
She hath no loyal knight and true,
    The Lady of Shalott.

But in her web she still delights
To weave the mirror's magic sights,
For often thro' the silent nights
A funeral, with plumes and lights
    And music, went to Camelot:
Or when the moon was overhead,
Came two young lovers lately wed;   70
' I am half sick of shadows,' said
    The Lady of Shalott.

PART III

A BOW-SHOT from her bower-eaves,
He rode between the barley-sheaves,
The sun came dazzling thro' the leaves,
And flamed upon the brazen greaves
    Of bold Sir Lancelot.
A red-cross knight for ever kneel'd
To a lady in his shield,
That sparkled on the yellow field,   80
    Beside remote Shalott.

The gemmy bridle glitter'd free,
Like to some branch of stars we see
Hung in the golden Galaxy.

The bridle bells rang merrily
      As he rode down to Camelot:
And from his blazon'd baldric slung
A mighty silver bugle hung,
And as he rode his armour rung,
      Beside remote Shalott.   *90*

All in the blue unclouded weather
Thick-jewell'd shone the saddle-leather,
The helmet and the helmet-feather
Burn'd like one burning flame together,
      As he rode down to Camelot.
As often thro' the purple night,
Below the starry clusters bright,
Some bearded meteor, trailing light,
      Moves over still Shalott.

His broad clear brow in sunlight glow'd;   *100*
On burnished hooves his war-horse trode;
From underneath his helmet flow'd
His coal-black curls as on he rode,
      As he rode down to Camelot.
From the bank and from the river
He flash'd into the crystal mirror,
' Tirra lirra,' by the river
      Sang Sir Lancelot.

She left the web, she left the loom,
She made three paces thro' the room,   *110*
She saw the water-lily bloom,
She saw the helmet and the plume,
      She look'd down to Camelot.
Out flew the web and floated wide;
The mirror crack'd from side to side;
' The curse is come upon me,' cried
      The Lady of Shalott.

PART IV

In the stormy east-wind straining,
The pale yellow woods were waning,
The broad stream in his banks complaining,   *120*
Heavily the low sky raining
      Over tower'd Camelot;
Down she came and found a boat
Beneath a willow left afloat,
And round about the prow she wrote
      The Lady of Shalott.

And down the river's dim expanse
Like some bold seër in a trance,
Seeing all his own mischance—
With a glassy countenance   *130*
    Did she look to Camelot.
And at the closing of the day
She loosed the chain, and down she lay;
The broad stream bore her far away,
    The Lady of Shalott.

Lying, robed in snowy white
That loosely flew to left and right—
The leaves upon her falling light—
Thro' the noises of the night
    She floated down to Camelot: *140*
And as the boat-head wound along
The willowy hills and fields among,
They heard her singing her last song,
    The Lady of Shalott.

Heard a carol, mournful, holy,
Chanted loudly, chanted lowly,
Till her blood was frozen slowly,
And her eyes were darken'd wholly,
    Turn'd to tower'd Camelot.
For ere she reach'd upon the tide   *150*
The first house by the water-side,
Singing in her song she died,
    The Lady of Shalott.

Under tower and balcony,
By garden-wall and gallery,
A gleaming shape she floated by,
Dead-pale between the houses high,
    Silent into Camelot.
Out upon the wharfs they came,
Knight and burgher, lord and dame,   *160*
And round the prow they read her name,
    The Lady of Shalott.

Who is this? and what is here?
And in the lighted palace near
Died the sound of royal cheer;
And they cross'd themselves for fear,
    All the knights at Camelot:
But Lancelot mused a little space;
He said, ' She has a lovely face;
God in his mercy lend her grace,   *170*
    The Lady of Shalott.'

THE MILLER'S DAUGHTER

I SEE the wealthy miller yet,
  His double chin, his portly size,
And who that knew him could forget
  The busy wrinkles round his eyes?
The slow wise smile that, round about
  His dusty forehead drily curl'd,
Seem'd half-within and half-without,
  And full of dealings with the world?

In yonder chair I see him sit,
  Three fingers round the old silver cup—   10
I see his gray eyes twinkle yet
  At his own jest—gray eyes lit up
With summer lightnings of a soul
  So full of summer warmth, so glad,
So healthy, sound, and clear and whole,
  His memory scarce can make me sad.

Yet fill my glass: give me one kiss:
  My own sweet Alice, we must die.
There's somewhat in this world amiss
  Shall be unriddled by and by.   20
There's somewhat flows to us in life,
  But more is taken quite away.
Pray, Alice, pray, my darling wife,
  That we may die the self-same day.

Have I not found a happy earth?
  I least should breathe a thought of pain.
Would God renew me from my birth
  I'd almost live my life again.
So sweet it seems with thee to walk,
  And once again to woo thee mine—   30
It seems in after-dinner talk
  Across the walnuts and the wine—

To be the long and listless boy
  Late-left an orphan of the squire,
Where this old mansion mounted high
  Looks down upon the village spire:
For even here, where I and you
  Have lived and loved alone so long,
Each morn my sleep was broken thro'
  By some wild skylark's matin song.   40

And oft I heard the tender dove
　　In firry woodlands making moan;
But ere I saw your eyes, my love,
　　I had no motion of my own.
For scarce my life with fancy play'd
　　Before I dream'd that pleasant dream—
Still hither thither idly sway'd
　　Like those long mosses in the stream.

Or from the bridge I lean'd to hear
　　The milldam rushing down with noise,　　　*50*
And see the minnows everywhere
　　In crystal eddies glance and poise,
The tall flag-flowers when they sprung
　　Below the range of stepping-stones,
Or those three chestnuts near, that hung
　　In masses thick with milky cones.

But, Alice, what an hour was that,
　　When after roving in the woods
('Twas April then), I came and sat
　　Below the chestnuts, when their buds　　　*60*
Were glistening to the breezy blue;
　　And on the slope, an absent fool,
I cast me down, nor thought of you,
　　But angled in the higher pool.

A love-song I had somewhere read,
　　An echo from a measured strain,
Beat time to nothing in my head
　　From some odd corner of the brain.
It haunted me, the morning long,
　　With weary sameness in the rhymes,　　　*70*
The phantom of a silent song,
　　That went and came a thousand times.

Then leapt a trout.　In lazy mood
　　I watch'd the little circles die;
They past into the level flood,
　　And there a vision caught my eye;
The reflex of a beauteous form,
　　A glowing arm, a gleaming neck,
As when a sunbeam wavers warm
　　Within the dark and dimpled beck.　　　*80*

For you remember, you had set,
　　That morning, on the casement-edge
A long green box of mignonette,
　　And you were leaning from the ledge

And when I raised my eyes, above
  They met with two so full and bright—
Such eyes! I swear to you, my love,
  That these have never lost their light.

I loved, and love dispell'd the fear
  That I should die an early death: *90*
For love possess'd the atmosphere,
  And fill'd the breast with purer breath.
My mother thought, What ails the boy?
  For I was alter'd, and began
To move about the house with joy,
  And with the certain step of man.

I loved the brimming wave that swam
  Thro' quiet meadows round the mill,
The sleepy pool above the dam,
  The pool beneath it never still,   *100*
The meal-sacks on the whiten'd floor,
  The dark round of the dripping wheel,
The very air about the door
  Made misty with the floating meal.

And oft in ramblings on the wold,
  When April nights began to blow,
And April's crescent glimmer'd cold,
  I saw the village lights below;
I knew your taper far away,
  And full at heart of trembling hope,   *110*
From off the wold I came, and lay
  Upon the freshly-flower'd slope.

The deep brook groan'd beneath the mill;
  And 'by that lamp,' I thought, 'she sits!'
The white chalk-quarry from the hill
  Gleam'd to the flying moon by fits
' O that I were beside her now!
  O will she answer if I call?
O would she give me vow for vow,
  Sweet Alice, if I told her all?'   *120*

Sometimes I saw you sit and spin;
  And, in the pauses of the wind,
Sometimes I heard you sing within;
  Sometimes your shadow cross'd the blind.
At last you rose and moved the light,
  And the long shadow of the chair
Flitted across into the night,
  And all the casement darken'd there.

But when at last I dared to speak,
    The lanes, you know, were white with may,   *130*
Your ripe lips moved not, but your cheek
    Flush'd like the coming of the day;
And so it was—half-sly, half-shy,
    You would, and would not, little one!
Although I pleaded tenderly,
    And you and I were all alone.

And slowly was my mother brought
    To yield consent to my desire:
She wish'd me happy, but she thought
    I might have look'd a little higher;   *140*
And I was young—too young to wed:
    ' Yet must I love her for your sake;
Go fetch your Alice here,' she said:
    Her eyelid quiver'd as she spake.

And down I went to fetch my bride:
    But, Alice, you were ill at ease;
This dress and that by turns you tried,
    Too fearful that you should not please.
I loved you better for your fears,
    I knew you could not look but well;   *150*
And dews, that would have fall'n in tears,
    I kiss'd away before they fell.

I watch'd the little flutterings,
    The doubt my mother would not see;
She spoke at large of many things,
    And at the last she spoke of me;
And turning look'd upon your face,
    As near this door you sat apart,
And rose, and, with a silent grace
    Approaching, press'd you heart to heart.   *160*

Ah, well—but sing the foolish song
    I gave you, Alice, on the day
When, arm in arm, we went along,
    A pensive pair, and you were gay
With bridal flowers—that I may seem,
    As in the nights of old, to lie
Beside the mill-wheel in the stream,
    While those full chestnuts whisper by.

It is the miller's daughter,
  And she is grown so dear, so dear,
That I would be the jewel
  That trembles in her ear:
For hid in ringlets day and night,
I'd touch her neck so warm and white.   *170*

And I would be the girdle
  About her dainty dainty waist,
And her heart would beat against me,
  In sorrow and in rest:
And I should know if it beat right,
I'd clasp it round so close and tight.   *180*

And I would be the necklace,
  And all day long to fall and rise
Upon her balmy bosom,
  With her laughter or her sighs,
And I would lie so light, so light,
I scarce should be unclasp'd at night.

A trifle, sweet! which true love spells—
  True love interprets—right alone.
His light upon the letter dwells,
  For all the spirit is his own.   *190*
So, if I waste words now, in truth
  You must blame Love. His early rage
Had force to make me rhyme in youth,
  And makes me talk too much in age.

And now those vivid hours are gone,
  Like mine own life to me thou art,
Where Past and Present, wound in one,
  Do make a garland for the heart:
So sing that other song I made,
  Half-anger'd with my happy lot,   *200*
The day, when in the chestnut shade
  I found the blue Forget-me-not.

    Love that hath us in the net,
    Can he pass, and we forget?
    Many suns arise and set.
    Many a chance the years beget.
    Love the gift is Love the debt.
        Even so.
    Love is hurt with jar and fret.
    Love is made a vague regret.   *210*

Eyes with idle tears are wet.
Idle habit links us yet.
What is love? for we forget:
    Ah, no! no!

Look thro' mine eyes with thine.   True wife,
    Round my true heart thine arms entwine
My other dearer life in life,
    Look thro' my very soul with thine!
Untouch'd with any shade of years,
    May those kind eyes for ever dwell!   220
They have not shed a many tears,
    Dear eyes, since first I knew them well.

Yet tears they shed: they had their part
    Of sorrow: for when time was ripe,
The still affection of the heart
    Became an outward breathing type,
That into stillness past again,
    And left a want unknown before;
Although the loss had brought us pain,
    That loss but made us love the more,   230

With farther lookings on.   The kiss,
    The woven arms, seem but to be
Weak symbols of the settled bliss,
    The comfort, I have found in thee:
But that God bless thee, dear—who wrought
    Two spirits to one equal mind—
With blessings beyond hope or thought,
    With blessings which no words can find.

Arise, and let us wander forth,
    To yon old mill across the wolds;   240
For look, the sunset, south and north,
    Winds all the vale in rosy folds,
And fires your narrow casement glass,
    Touching the sullen pool below:
On the chalk-hill the bearded grass
    Is dry and dewless.   Let us go.

ŒNONE

THERE lies a vale in Ida, lovelier
Than all the valleys of Ionian hills.
The swimming vapour slopes athwart the glen,
Puts forth an arm, and creeps from pine to pine,
And loiters, slowly drawn.   On either hand
The lawns and meadow-ledges midway down
Hang rich in flowers, and far below them roars
The long brook falling thro' the clov'n ravine
In cataract after cataract to the sea.
Behind the valley topmost Gargarus   *10*
Stands up and takes the morning : but in front
The gorges, opening wide apart, reveal
Troas and Ilion's column'd citadel,
The crown of Troas.
            Hither came at noon
Mournful Œnone, wandering forlorn
Of Paris, once her playmate on the hills.
Her cheek had lost the rose, and round her neck
Floated her hair or seem'd to float in rest.
She, leaning on a fragment twined with vine,
Sang to the stillness, till the mountainshade   *20*
Sloped downward to her seat from the upper cliff.

   ' O mother Ida, many-fountain'd Ida,
Dear mother Ida, harken ere I die.
For now the noonday quiet holds the hill :
The grasshopper is silent in the grass :
The lizard, with his shadow on the stone,
Rests like a shadow, and the winds are dead.
The purple flower droops : the golden bee
Is lily-cradled : I alone awake.
My eyes are full of tears, my heart of love,   *30*
My heart is breaking, and my eyes are dim,
And I am all aweary of my life.

   ' O mother Ida, many-fountain'd Ida,
Dear mother Ida, harken ere I die.
Hear me, O Earth, hear me, O Hills, O Caves
That house the cold crown'd snake !   O mountain brooks,
I am the daughter of a River-God,
Hear me, for I will speak, and build up all
My sorrow with my song, as yonder walls
Rose slowly to a music slowly breathed,   *40*
A cloud that gather'd shape : for it may be
That, while I speak of it, a little while
My heart may wander from its deeper woe.

' O mother Ida, many-fountain'd Ida,
Dear mother Ida, harken ere I die.
I waited underneath the dawning hills,
Aloft the mountain lawn was dewy-dark,
And dewy-dark aloft the mountain pine:
Beautiful Paris, evil-hearted Paris,
Leading a jet-black goat white-horn'd, white-hooved,   *50*
Came up from reedy Simois all alone.

' O mother Ida, harken ere I die.
Far-off the torrent call'd me from the cleft:
Far up the solitary morning smote
The streaks of virgin snow.   With down-dropt eyes
I sat alone: white-breasted like a star
Fronting the dawn he moved; a leopard skin
Droop'd from his shoulder, but his sunny hair
Cluster'd about his temples like a God's:
And his cheek brighten'd as the foam-bow brightens   *60*
When the wind blows the foam, and all my heart
Went forth to embrace him coming ere he came.

' Dear mother Ida, harken ere I die.
He smiled, and opening out his milk-white palm
Disclosed a fruit of pure Hesperian gold,
That smelt ambrosially and while I look'd
And listen'd, the full-flowing river of speech
Came down upon my heart.
                                        ' " My own Œnone,
Beautiful-brow'd Œnone, my own soul,
Behold this fruit, whose gleaming rind ingrav'n   *70*
' For the most fair,' would seem to award it thine,
As lovelier than whatever Oread haunt
The knolls of Ida, loveliest in all grace
Of movement, and the charm of married brows."

' Dear mother Ida, harken ere I die.
He prest the blossom of his lips to mine,
And added " This was cast upon the board,
When all the full-faced presence of the Gods
Ranged in the halls of Peleus; whereupon
Rose feud, with question unto whom 'twere due: *80*
But light-foot Iris brought it yester-eve,
Delivering, that to me, by common voice
Elected umpire, Herè comes to-day,
Pallas and Aphroditè, claiming each
This meed of fairest.   Thou, within the cave
Behind yon whispering tuft of oldest pine,
Mayst well behold them unbeheld, unheard
Hear all, and see thy Paris judge of Gods."

' Dear mother Ida, harken ere I die.
It was the deep midnoon: one silvery cloud   *90*
Had lost his way between the piney sides
Of this long glen.   Then to the bower they came,
Naked they came to that smooth-swarded bower,
And at their feet the crocus brake like fire,
Violet, amaracus, and asphodel,
Lotos and lilies: and a wind arose,
And overhead the wandering ivy and vine,
This way and that, in many a wild festoon
Ran riot, garlanding the gnarled boughs
With bunch and berry and flower thro' and thro'.   *100*

' O mother Ida, harken ere I die.
On the tree-tops a crested peacock lit,
And o'er him flow'd a golden cloud, and lean'd
Upon him, slowly dropping fragrant dew.
Then first I heard the voice of her, to whom
Coming thro' Heaven, like a light that grows
Larger and clearer, with one mind the Gods
Rise up for reverence.   She to Paris made
Proffer of royal power, ample rule
Unquestion'd, overflowing revenue   *110*
Wherewith to embellish state, " from many a vale
And river-sunder'd champaign clothed with corn,
Or labour'd mine undrainable of ore.
Honour," she said, " and homage, tax and toll,
From many an inland town and haven large,
Mast-throng'd beneath her shadowing citadel
In glassy bays among her tallest towers."

' O mother Ida, harken ere I die.
Still she spake on and still she spake of power,
" Which in all action is the end of all;   *120*
Power fitted to the season; wisdom-bred
And throned of wisdom—from all neighbour crowns
Alliance and allegiance, till thy hand
Fail from the sceptre-staff.   Such boon from me,
From me, Heaven's Queen, Paris, to thee king-born,
A shepherd all thy life but yet king-born,
Should come most welcome, seeing men, in power
Only, are likest gods, who have attain'd
Rest in a happy place and quiet seats
Above the thunder, with undying bliss   *130*
In knowledge of their own supremacy."

' Dear mother Ida, harken ere I die.
She ceased, and Paris held the costly fruit
Out at arm's-length, so much the thought of power

Flatter'd his spirit; but Pallas where she stood
Somewhat apart, her clear and bared limbs
O'erthwarted with the brazen-headed spear
Upon her pearly shoulder leaning cold,
The while, above, her full and earnest eye
Over her snow-cold breast and angry cheek   *140*
Kept watch, waiting decision, made reply.

    ' " Self-reverence, self-knowledge, self-control,
These three alone lead life to sovereign power.
Yet not for power (power of herself
Would come uncall'd for) but to live by law,
Acting the law we live by without fear;
And, because right is right, to follow right
Were wisdom in the scorn of consequence."

    ' Dear mother Ida, harken ere I die.
Again she said: " I woo thee not with gifts.   *150*
Sequel of guerdon could not alter me
To fairer.   Judge thou me by what I am,
So shalt thou find me fairest.
               Yet, indeed,
If gazing on divinity disrobed
Thy mortal eyes are frail to judge of fair,
Unbias'd by self-profit, oh! rest thee sure
That I shall love thee well and cleave to thee,
So that my vigour, wedded to thy blood,
Shall strike within thy pulses, like a God's,
To push thee forward thro' a life of shocks,   *160*
Dangers, and deeds, until endurance grow
Sinew'd with action, and the full-grown will,
Circled thro' all experiences, pure law,
Commeasure perfect freedom."
            ' Here she ceas'd,
And Paris ponder'd, and I cried, " O Paris,
Give it to Pallas! " but he heard me not,
Or hearing would not hear me, woe is me!

    ' O mother Ida, many-fountain'd Ida,
Dear mother Ida, harken ere I die.
Idalian Aphroditè beautiful,   *170*
Fresh as the foam, new-bathed in Paphian wells,
With rosy slender fingers backward drew
From her warm brows and bosom her deep hair
Ambrosial, golden round her lucid throat
And shoulder: from the violets her light foot
Shone rosy-white, and o'er her rounded form
Between the shadows of the vine-bunches
Floated the glowing sunlights, as she moved.

' Dear mother Ida, harken ere I die.
She with a subtle smile in her mild eyes,   *180*
The herald of her triumph, drawing nigh
Half-whisper'd in his ear, " I promise thee
The fairest and most loving wife in Greece,"
She spoke and laugh'd : I shut my sight for fear :
But when I look'd, Paris had raised his arm,
And I beheld great Herè's angry eyes,
As she withdrew into the golden cloud,
And I was left alone within the bower;
And from that time to this I am alone,
And I shall be alone until I die.   *190*

' Yet, mother Ida, harken ere I die.
Fairest—why fairest wife? am I not fair?
My love hath told me so a thousand times.
Methinks I must be fair, for yesterday,
When I past by, a wild and wanton pard,
Eyed like the evening star, with playful tail
Crouch'd fawning in the weed.   Most loving is she?
Ah me, my mountain shepherd, that my arms
Were wound about thee, and my hot lips prest
Close, close to thine in that quick-falling dew   *200*
Of fruitful kisses, thick as Autumn rains
Flash in the pools of whirling Simois.

' O mother, hear me yet before I die.
They came, they cut away my tallest pines,
My tall dark pines, that plumed the craggy ledge
High over the blue gorge, and all between
The snowy peak and snow-white cataract
Foster'd the callow eaglet—from beneath
Whose thick mysterious boughs in the dark morn
The panther's roar came muffled, while I sat   *210*
Low in the valley.   Never, never more
Shall lone Œnone see the morning mist
Sweep thro' them; never see them overlaid
With narrow moon-lit slips of silver cloud,
Between the loud stream and the trembling stars.

' O mother, hear me yet before I die.
I wish that somewhere in the ruin'd folds,
Among the fragments tumbled from the glens,
Or the dry thickets, I could meet with her
The Abominable, that uninvited came   *220*
Into the fair Peleïan banquet-hall,
And cast the golden fruit upon the board,
And bred this change; that I might speak my mind,
And tell her to her face how much I hate
Her presence, hated both of Gods and men.

' O mother, hear me yet before I die.
Hath he not sworn his love a thousand times,
In this green valley, under this green hill,
Ev'n on this hand, and sitting on this stone?
Seal'd it with kisses? water'd it with tears?   *230*
O happy tears, and how unlike to these!
O happy Heaven, how canst thou see my face?
O happy earth, how canst thou bear my weight?
O death, death, death, thou ever-floating cloud,
There are enough unhappy on this earth,
Pass by the happy souls, that love to live:
I pray thee, pass before my light of life,
And shadow all my soul, that I may die.
Thou weighest heavy on the heart within,
Weigh heavy on my eyelids: let me die.   *240*

' O mother, hear me yet before I die.
I will not die alone, for fiery thoughts
Do shape themselves within me, more and more,
Whereof I catch the issue, as I hear
Dead sounds at night come from the inmost hills,
Like footsteps upon wool. I dimly see
My far-off doubtful purpose, as a mother
Conjectures of the features of her child
Ere it is born: her child!—a shudder comes
Across me: never child be born of me,   *250*
Unblest, to vex me with his father's eyes!

' O mother, hear me yet before I die.
Hear me, O earth. I will not die alone,
Lest their shrill happy laughter come to me
Walking the cold and starless road of Death
Uncomforted, leaving my ancient love
With the Greek woman. I will rise and go
Down into Troy, and ere the stars come forth
Talk with the wild Cassandra, for she says
A fire dances before her, and a sound   *260*
Rings ever in her ears of armed men.
What this may be I know not, but I know
That, wheresoe'er I am by night and day,
All earth and air seem only burning fire.'

THE SISTERS

WE were two daughters of one race:
She was the fairest in the face:
   The wind is blowing in turret and tree.
They were together, and she fell;
Therefore revenge became me well.
   O the Earl was fair to see!

She died: she went to burning flame:
She mix'd her ancient blood with shame.
   The wind is howling in turret and tree.
Whole weeks and months, and early and late,   *10*
To win his love I lay in wait:
   O the Earl was fair to see!

I made a feast; I bad him come;
I won his love, I brought him home.
   The wind is roaring in turret and tree.
And after supper, on a bed,
Upon my lap he laid his head:
   O the Earl was fair to see!

I kiss'd his eyelids into rest:
His ruddy cheek upon my breast.   *20*
   The wind is raging in turret and tree.
I hated him with the hate of hell,
But I loved his beauty passing well.
   O the Earl was fair to see!

I rose up in the silent night:
I made my dagger sharp and bright.
   The wind is raving in turret and tree.
As half-asleep his breath he drew,
Three times I stabb'd him thro' and thro'.
   O the Earl was fair to see!   *30*

I curl'd and comb'd his comely head,
He look'd so grand when he was dead.
   The wind is blowing in turret and tree.
I wrapt his body in the sheet,
And laid him at his mother's feet.
   O the Earl was fair to see!

THE LOTOS-EATERS

' Courage ! ' he said, and pointed toward the land,
' This mounting wave will roll us shoreward soon.'
In the afternoon they came unto a land
In which it seemed always afternoon.
All round the coast the languid air did swoon,
Breathing like one that hath a weary dream.
Full-faced above the valley stood the moon;
And like a downward smoke, the slender stream
Along the cliff to fall and pause and fall did seem.

A land of streams ! some, like a downward smoke   *10*
Slow-dropping veils of thinnest lawn, did go;
And some thro' wavering lights and shadows broke,
Rolling a slumbrous sheet of foam below.
They saw the gleaming river seaward flow
From the inner land : far off, three mountain-tops,
Three silent pinnacles of aged snow,
Stood sunset-flush'd : and, dew'd with showery drops,
Up-clomb the shadowy pine above the woven copse.

The charmed sunset linger'd low adown
In the red West : thro' mountain clefts the dale   *20*
Was seen far inland, and the yellow down
Border'd with palm, and many a winding vale
And meadow, set with slender galingale;
A land where all things always seem'd the same !
And round about the keel with faces pale,
Dark faces pale against that rosy flame,
The mild-eyed melancholy Lotos-eaters came.

Branches they bore of that enchanted stem,
Laden with flower and fruit, whereof they gave
To each, but whoso did receive of them,   *30*
And taste, to him the gushing of the wave
Far far away did seem to mourn and rave
On alien shores; and if his fellow spake,
His voice was thin, as voices from the grave;
And deep-asleep he seem'd, yet all awake,
And music in his ears his beating heart did make.

They sat them down upon the yellow sand,
Between the sun and moon upon the shore;
And sweet it was to dream of Fatherland,
Of child, and wife, and slave; but evermore   *40*
Most weary seem'd the sea, weary the oar,

Weary the wandering fields of barren foam.
Then some one said, ' We will return no more ';
And all at once they sang, ' Our island home
Is far beyond the wave; we will no longer roam.'

CHORIC SONG

THERE is sweet music here that softer falls
Than petals from blown roses on the grass,
Or night-dews on still waters between walls
Of shadowy granite, in a gleaming pass;
Music that gentlier on the spirit lies,   *50*
Than tir'd eyelids upon tir'd eyes;
Music that brings sweet sleep down from the blissful skies.
Here are cool mosses deep,
And thro' the moss the ivies creep,
And in the stream the long-leaved flowers weep,
And from the craggy ledge the poppy hangs in sleep.

Why are we weigh'd upon with heaviness,
And utterly consumed with sharp distress,
While all things else have rest from weariness?
All things have rest: why should we toil alone,   *60*
We only toil, who are the first of things,
And make perpetual moan,
Still from one sorrow to another thrown:
Nor ever fold our wings,
And cease from wanderings,
Nor steep our brows in slumber's holy balm;
Nor harken what the inner spirit sings,
' There is no joy but calm ! '
Why should we only toil, the roof and crown of things?

Lo ! in the middle of the wood,   *70*
The folded leaf is woo'd from out the bud
With winds upon the branch, and there
Grows green and broad, and takes no care,
Sun-steep'd at noon, and in the moon
Nightly dew-fed; and turning yellow
Falls, and floats adown the air.
Lo ! sweeten'd with the summer light,
The full-juiced apple, waxing over-mellow,
Drops in a silent autumn night.
All its allotted length of days,   *80*
The flower ripens in its place,
Ripens and fades, and falls, and hath no toil,
Fast-rooted in the fruitful soil.

Hateful is the dark-blue sky,
Vaulted o'er the dark-blue sea.
Death is the end of life; ah, why
Should life all labour be?
Let us alone.   Time driveth onward fast,
And in a little while our lips are dumb.
Let us alone.   What is it that will last?   *90*
All things are taken from us, and become
Portions and parcels of the dreadful Past.
Let us alone.   What pleasure can we have
To war with evil?   Is there any peace
In ever climbing up the climbing wave?
All things have rest, and ripen toward the grave
In silence; ripen, fall and cease;
Give us long rest or death, dark death, or dreamful ease.

How sweet it were, hearing the downward stream,
With half-shut eyes ever to seem   *100*
Falling asleep in a half-dream!
To dream and dream, like yonder amber light,
Which will not leave the myrrh-bush on the height;
To hear each other's whisper'd speech;
Eating the Lotos day by day,
To watch the crisping ripples on the beach,
And tender curving lines of creamy spray;
To lend our hearts and spirits wholly
To the influence of mild-minded melancholy;
To muse and brood and live again in memory,   *110*
With those old faces of our infancy
Heap'd over with a mound of grass,
Two handfuls of white dust, shut in an urn of brass!

Dear is the memory of our wedded lives,
And dear the last embraces of our wives
And their warm tears: but all hath suffer'd change:
For surely now our household hearths are cold:
Our sons inherit us: our looks are strange:
And we should come like ghosts to trouble joy.
Or else the island princes over-bold   *120*
Have eat our substance, and the minstrel sings
Before them of the ten years' war in Troy,
And our great deeds, as half-forgotten things.
Is there confusion in the little isle?
Let what is broken so remain.
The Gods are hard to reconcile:
'Tis hard to settle order once again.
There *is* confusion worse than death,
Trouble on trouble, pain on pain,

Long labour unto aged breath, 130
Sore task to hearts worn out by many wars
And eyes grown dim with gazing on the pilot-stars.

But, propt on beds of amaranth and moly,
How sweet (while warm airs lull us, blowing lowly)
With half-dropt eyelid still,
Beneath a heaven dark and holy,
To watch the long bright river drawing slowly
His waters from the purple hill—
To hear the dewy echoes calling
From cave to cave thro' the thick-twined vine— 140
To watch the emerald-colour'd water falling
Thro' many a wov'n acanthus-wreath divine!
Only to hear and see the far-off sparkling brine,
Only to hear were sweet, stretch'd out beneath the pine.

The Lotos blooms below the barren peak;
The Lotos blows by every winding creek:
All day the wind breathes low with mellower tone:
Thro' every hollow cave and alley lone
Round and round the spicy downs the yellow Lotos-dust is blown.
We have had enough of action, and of motion we, 150
Roll'd to starboard, roll'd to larboard, when the surge was seething free,
Where the wallowing monster spouted his foam-fountains in the sea.
Let us swear an oath, and keep it with an equal mind,
In the hollow Lotos-land to live and lie reclined
On the hills like Gods together, careless of mankind.
For they lie beside their nectar, and the bolts are hurl'd
Far below them in the valleys, and the clouds are lightly curl'd
Round their golden houses, girdled with the gleaming world:
Where they smile in secret, looking over wasted lands,
Blight and famine, plague and earthquake, roaring deeps and fiery sands, 160
Clanging fights, and flaming towns, and sinking ships, and praying
hands.
But they smile, they find a music centred in a doleful song
Steaming up, a lamentation and an ancient tale of wrong,
Like a tale of little meaning tho' the words are strong;
Chanted from an ill-used race of men that cleave the soil,
Sow the seed, and reap the harvest with enduring toil,
Storing yearly little dues of wheat, and wine and oil;
Till they perish and they suffer—some, 'tis whisper'd—down in hell
Suffer endless anguish, others in Elysian valleys dwell,
Resting weary limbs at last on beds of asphodel. 170
Surely, surely, slumber is more sweet than toil, the shore
Than labour in the deep mid-ocean, wind and wave and oar;
Oh rest ye, brother mariners, we will not wander more.

THE TWO VOICES

A STILL small voice spake unto me,
' Thou art so full of misery,
Were it not better not to be? '

Then to the still small voice I said;
' Let me not cast in endless shade
What is so wonderfully made.'

To which the voice did urge reply;
' To-day I saw the dragon-fly
Come from the wells where he did lie.

' An inner impulse rent the veil   10
Of his old husk: from head to tail
Came out clear plates of sapphire mail.

' He dried his wings: like gauze they grew:
Thro' crofts and pastures wet with dew
A living flash of light he flew.'

I said, ' When first the world began,
Young Nature thro' five cycles ran,
And in the sixth she moulded man.

' She gave him mind, the lordliest
Proportion, and, above the rest,   20
Dominion in the head and breast.'

Thereto the silent voice replied;
' Self-blinded are you by your pride:
Look up thro' night: the world is wide.

' This truth within thy mind rehearse,
That in a boundless universe
Is boundless better, boundless worse.

' Think you this mould of hopes and fears
Could find no statelier than his peers
In yonder hundred million spheres? '   30

It spake, moreover, in my mind:
' Tho' thou wert scatter'd to the wind,
Yet is there plenty of the kind.'

Then did my response clearer fall:
' No compound of this earthly ball
Is like another, all in all.'

To which he answer'd scoffingly;
' Good soul! suppose I grant it thee,
Who'll weep for thy deficiency?

' Or will one beam be less intense,   *40*
When thy peculiar difference
Is cancell'd in the world of sense?'

I would have said, ' Thou canst not know,'
But my full heart, that work'd below,
Rain'd thro' my sight its overflow.

Again the voice spake unto me:
' Thou art so steep'd in misery,
Surely 'twere better not to be.

' Thine anguish will not let thee sleep,
Nor any train of reason keep: *50*
Thou canst not think, but thou wilt weep.'

I said, ' The years with change advance:
If I make dark my countenance,
I shut my life from happier chance.

' Some turn this sickness yet might take,
Ev'n yet.'   But he: ' What drug can make
A wither'd palsy cease to shake?'

I wept, ' Tho' I should die, I know
That all about the thorn will blow
In tufts of rosy-tinted snow;   *60*

' And men, thro' novel spheres of thought
Still moving after truth long sought,
Will learn new things when I am not.'

' Yet,' said the secret voice, ' some time,
Sooner or later, will gray prime
Make thy grass hoar with early rime.

' Not less swift souls that yearn for light,
Rapt after heaven's starry flight,
Would sweep the tracts of day and night.

' Not less the bee would range her cells,   *70*
The furzy prickle fire the dells,
The foxglove cluster dappled bells.'

I said that ' all the years invent;
Each month is various to present
The world with some development.

' Were this not well, to bide mine hour,
Tho' watching from a ruin'd tower
How grows the day of human power ? '

' The highest-mounted mind,' he said,
' Still sees the sacred morning spread   *80*
The silent summit overhead.

' Will thirty seasons render plain
Those lonely lights that still remain,
Just breaking over land and main ?

' Or make that morn, from his cold crown
And crystal silence creeping down,
Flood with full daylight glebe and town?

' Forerun thy peers, thy time, and let
Thy feet, millenniums hence, be set
In midst of knowledge, dream'd not yet.   *90*

' Thou hast not gain'd a real height,
Nor art thou nearer to the light,
Because the scale is infinite.

' 'Twere better not to breathe or speak,
Than cry for strength, remaining weak,
And seem to find, but still to seek.

' Moreover, but to seem to find
Asks what thou lackest, thought resign'd,
A healthy frame, a quiet mind.'

I said, ' When I am gone away,   *100*
" He dared not tarry," men will say,
Doing dishonour to my clay.'

' This is more vile,' he made reply,
' To breathe and loathe, to live and sigh,
Than once from dread of pain to die.

' Sick art thou—a divided will
Still heaping on the fear of ill
The fear of men, a coward still.

' Do men love thee?   Art thou so bound
To men, that how thy name may sound   *110*
Will vex thee lying underground?

' The memory of the wither'd leaf
In endless time is scarce more brief
Than of the garner'd Autumn-sheaf.

' Go, vexed Spirit, sleep in trust;
The right ear, that is fill'd with dust,
Hears little of the false or just.'

' Hard task, to pluck resolve,' I cried,
' From emptiness and the waste wide
Of that abyss, or scornful pride!   *120*

' Nay—rather yet that I could raise
One hope that warm'd me in the days
While still I yearn'd for human praise.

' When, wide in soul and bold of tongue,
Among the tents I paused and sung,
The distant battle flash'd and rung.

' I sung the joyful Pæan clear,
And, sitting, burnish'd without fear
The brand, the buckler, and the spear—

' Waiting to strive a happy strife,   *130*
To war with falsehood to the knife,
And not to lose the good of life—

' Some hidden principle to move,
To put together, part and prove,
And mete the bounds of hate and love—

' As far as might be, to carve out
Free space for every human doubt,
That the whole mind might orb about—

' To search thro' all I felt or saw,
The springs of life, the depths of awe,   *140*
And reach the law within the law:

' At least, not rotting like a weed,
But, having sown some generous seed,
Fruitful of further thought and deed,

' To pass, when Life her light withdraws,
Not void of righteous self-applause,
Nor in a merely selfish cause—

' In some good cause, not in mine own,
To perish, wept for, honour'd, known,
And like a warrior overthrown;   *150*

' Whose eyes are dim with glorious tears,
When, soil'd with noble dust, he hears
His country's war-song thrill his ears :

' Then dying of a mortal stroke,
What time the foeman's line is broke,
And all the war is roll'd in smoke.'

' Yea ! ' said the voice, ' thy dream was good,
While thou abodest in the bud.
It was the stirring of the blood.

' If Nature put not forth her power   *160*
About the opening of the flower,
Who is it that could live an hour ?

' Then comes the check, the change, the fall,
Pain rises up, old pleasures pall.
There is one remedy for all.

' Yet hadst thou, thro' enduring pain,
Link'd month to month with such a chain
Of knitted purport, all were vain.

' Thou hadst not between death and birth
Dissolved the riddle of the ear.h.   *170*
So were thy labour little-worth.

' That men with knowledge merely play'd,
I told thee—hardly nigher made,
Tho' scaling slow from grade to grade;

' Much less this dreamer, deaf and blind,
Named man, may hope some truth to find,
That bears relation to the mind.

' For every worm beneath the moon
Draws different threads, and late and soon
Spins, toiling out his own cocoon.   *180*

' Cry, faint not : either Truth is born
Beyond the polar gleam forlorn,
Or in the gateways of the morn.

' Cry, faint not, climb : the summits slope
Beyond the furthest flights of hope,
Wrapt in dense cloud from base to cope.

' Sometimes a little corner shines,
As over rainy mist inclines
A gleaming crag with belts of pines.

' I will go forward, sayest thou,   *190*
I shall not fail to find her now.
Look up, the fold is on her brow.

' If straight thy track, or if oblique,
Thou know'st not.   Shadows thou dost strike,
Embracing cloud, Ixion-like ;

' And owning but a little more
Than beasts, abidest lame and poor,
Calling thyself a little lower

' Than angels.   Cease to wail and brawl !
Why inch by inch to darkness crawl ?   *200*
There is one remedy for all.'

' O dull, one-sided voice,' said I,
' Wilt thou make everything a lie,
To flatter me that I may die ?

' I know that age to age succeeds,
Blowing a noise of tongues and deeds,
A dust of systems and of creeds.

' I cannot hide that some have striven,
Achieving calm, to whom was given
The joy that mixes man with Heaven :   *210*

' Who, rowing hard against the stream,
Saw distant gates of Eden gleam,
And did not dream it was a dream ;

' But heard, by secret transport led,
Ev'n in the charnels of the dead,
The murmur of the fountain-head—

' Which did accomplish their desire,
Bore and forbore, and did not tire,
Like Stephen, an unquenched fire.

' He heeded not reviling tones,   220
Nor sold his heart to idle moans,
Tho' cursed and scorn'd, and bruised with stones:

' But looking upward, full of grace,
He pray'd, and from a happy place
God's glory smote him on the face.'

The sullen answer slid betwixt:
' Not that the grounds of hope were fix'd,
The elements were kindlier mix'd.'

I said, ' I toil beneath the curse,
But, knowing not the universe,   230
I fear to slide from bad to worse.

' And that, in seeking to undo
One riddle, and to find the true,
I knit a hundred others new:

' Or that this anguish fleeting hence,
Unmanacled from bonds of sense,
Be fix'd and froz'n to permanence:

' For I go, weak from suffering here:
Naked I go, and void of cheer:
What is it that I may not fear?'   240

' Consider well,' the voice replied,
' His face, that two hours since hath died;
Wilt thou find passion, pain or pride?

' Will he obey when one commands?
Or answer should one press his hands?
He answers not, nor understands.

' His palms are folded on his breast:
There is no other thing express'd
But long disquiet merged in rest.

' His lips are very mild and meek :   *250*
Tho' one should smite him on the cheek,
And on the mouth, he will not speak.

' His little daughter, whose sweet face
He kiss'd, taking his last embrace,
Becomes dishonour to her race—

' His sons grow up that bear his name,
Some grow to honour, some to shame,—
But he is chill to praise or blame.

' He will not hear the north-wind rave,
Nor, moaning, household shelter crave   *260*
From winter rains that beat his grave.

' High up the vapours fold and swim :
About him broods the twilight dim :
The place he knew forgetteth him.'

' If all be dark, vague voice,' I said,
' These things are wrapt in doubt and dread,
Nor canst thou show the dead are dead.

' The sap dries up : the plant declines.
A deeper tale my heart divines.
Know I not Death? the outward signs?   *270*

' I found him when my years were few;
A shadow on the graves I knew,
And darkness in the village yew.

' From grave to grave the shadow crept :
In her still place the morning wept :
Touch'd by his feet the daisy slept.

' The simple senses crown'd his head :
" Omega ! thou art Lord," they said,
" We find no motion in the dead."

' Why, if man rot in dreamless ease,   *280*
Should that plain fact, as taught by these,
Not make him sure that he shall cease?

' Who forged that other influence,
That heat of inward evidence,
By which he doubts against the sense?

' He owns the fatal gift of eyes,
That read his spirit blindly wise,
Not simple as a thing that dies.

' Here sits he shaping wings to fly :
His heart forebodes a mystery :   *290*
He names the name Eternity.

' That type of Perfect in his mind
In Nature can he nowhere find.
He sows himself on every wind.

' He seems to hear a Heavenly Friend,
And thro' thick veils to apprehend
A labour working to an end.

' The end and the beginning vex
His reason : many things perplex,
With motions, checks, and counterchecks.   *300*

' He knows a baseness in his blood
At such strange war with something good,
He may not do the thing he would.

' Heaven opens inward, chasms yawn,
Vast images in glimmering dawn,
Half shown, are broken and withdrawn.

' Ah ! sure within him and without,
Could his dark wisdom find it out,
There must be answer to his doubt,

' But thou canst answer not again.   *310*
With thine own weapon art thou slain,
Or thou wilt answer but in vain.

' The doubt would rest, I dare not solve.
In the same circle we revolve.
Assurance only breeds resolve.'

As when a billow, blown against,
Falls back, the voice with which I fenced
A little ceased, but recommenced.

' Where wert thou when thy father play'd
In his free field, and pastime made,   *320*
A merry boy in sun and shade ?

' A merry boy they call'd him then,
He sat upon the knees of men
In days that never come again.

' Before the little ducts began
To feed thy bones with lime, and ran
Their course, till thou wert also man:

' Who took a wife, who rear'd his race,
Whose wrinkles gather'd on his face,
Whose troubles number with his days: 330

' A life of nothings, nothing-worth,
From that first nothing ere his birth
To that last nothing under earth!'

' These words,' I said, ' are like the rest;
No certain clearness, but at best
A vague suspicion of the breast:

' But if I grant, thou mightst defend
The thesis which thy words intend—
That to begin implies to end;

' Yet how should I for certain hold,   340
Because my memory is so cold,
That I first was in human mould?

' I cannot make this matter plain,
But I would shoot, howe'er in vain,
A random arrow from the brain.

' It may be that no life is found,
Which only to one engine bound
Falls off, but cycles always round.

' As old mythologies relate,
Some draught of Lethe might await   350
The slipping thro' from state to state.

' As here we find in trances, men
Forget the dream that happens then,
Until they fall in trance again.

' So might we, if our state were such
As one before, remember much,
For those two likes might meet and touch.

' But, if I lapsed from nobler place,
Some legend of a fallen race
Alone might hint of my disgrace;   *360*

' Some vague emotion of delight
In gazing up an 'Alpine height,
Some yearning toward the lamps of night;

' Or if thro' lower lives I came—
'Tho' all experience past became
Consolidate in mind and frame—

' I might forget my weaker lot;
For is not our first year forgot?
The haunts of memory echo not.

' And men, whose reason long was blind,   *370*
From cells of madness unconfined,
Oft lose whole years of darker mind.

' Much more, if first I floated free,
As naked essence, must I be
Incompetent of memory:

' For memory dealing but with time,
And he with matter, could she climb
Beyond her own material prime?

' Moreover, something is or seems,
That touches me with mystic gleams,   *380*
Like glimpses of forgotten dreams—

' Of something felt, like something here;
Of something done, I know not where;
Such as no language may declare.'

The still voice laugh'd.   ' I talk,' said he,
' Not with thy dreams.   Suffice it thee
Thy pain is a reality.'

' But thou,' said I, ' hast missed thy mark,
Who sought'st to wreck my mortal ark,
By making all the horizon dark.   *390*

' Why not set forth, if I should do
This rashness, that which might ensue
With this old soul in organs new?

' Whatever crazy sorrow saith,
No life that breathes with human breath
Has ever truly long'd for death.

' 'Tis life, whereof our nerves are scant,
Oh life, not death, for which we pant;
More life, and fuller, that I want.'

I ceased, and sat as one forlorn.   *400*
Then said the voice, in quiet scorn,
' Behold, it is the Sabbath morn.'

And I arose, and I released
The casement, and the light increased
With freshness in the dawning east.

Like soften'd airs that blowing steal,
When meres begin to uncongeal,
The sweet church bells began to peal.

On to God's house the people prest :
Passing the place where each must rest,   *410*
Each enter'd like a welcome guest.

One walk'd between his wife and child,
With measured footfall firm and mild,
And now and then he gravely smiled.

The prudent partner of his blood
Lean'd on him, faithful, gentle, good,
Wearing the rose of womanhood.

And in their double love secure,
The little maiden walk'd demure,   *420*
Pacing with downward eyelids pure.

These three made unity so sweet,
My frozen heart began to beat,
Remembering its ancient heat.

I blest them, and they wander'd on :
I spoke, but answer came there none :
The dull and bitter voice was gone.

A second voice was at mine ear,
A little whisper silver-clear,
A murmur, ' Be of better cheer.'

As from some blissful neighbourhood,   *430*
A notice faintly understood,
' I see the end, and know the good.'

A little hint to solace woe,
A hint, a whisper breathing low,
' I may not speak of what I know.'

Like an Æolian harp that wakes
No certain air, but overtakes
Far thought with music that it makes:

Such seem'd the whisper at my side:
' What is it thou knowest, sweet voice? ' I cried.   *440*
' A hidden hope,' the voice replied:

So heavenly-toned, that in that hour
From out my sullen heart a power
Broke, like the rainbow from the shower,

To feel, altho' no tongue can prove,
That every cloud, that spreads above
And veileth love, itself is love.

And forth into the fields I went,
And Nature's living motion lent
The pulse of hope to discontent.   *450*

I wonder'd at the bounteous hours,
The slow result of winter showers:
You scarce could see the grass for flowers.

I wonder'd, while I paced along:
The woods were fill'd so full with song,
There seem'd no room for sense of wrong;

And all so variously wrought,
I marvell'd how the mind was brought
To anchor by one gloomy thought;

And wherefore rather I made choice   *460*
To commune with that barren voice,
Than him that said, ' Rejoice! Rejoice! '

ST. SIMEON STYLITES

ALTHO' I be the basest of mankind,
From scalp to sole one slough and crust of sin,
Unfit for earth, unfit for heaven, scarce meet
For troops of devils, mad with blasphemy,
I will not cease to grasp the hope I hold
Of saintdom, and to clamour, mourn and sob,
Battering the gates of heaven with storms of prayer,
Have mercy, Lord, and take away my sin.

   Let this avail, just, dreadful, mighty God,
This not be all in vain, that thrice ten years,   *10*
Thrice multiplied by superhuman pangs,
In hungers and in thirsts, fevers and cold,
In coughs, aches, stitches, ulcerous throes and cramps,
A sign betwixt the meadow and the cloud,
Patient on this tall pillar I have borne
Rain, wind, frost, heat, hail, damp, and sleet, and snow;
And I had hoped that ere this period closed
Thou wouldst have caught me up into Thy rest,
Denying not these weather-beaten limbs
The meed of saints, the white robe and the palm.   *20*

   O take the meaning, Lord: I do not breathe,
Not whisper, any murmur of complaint.
Pain heap'd ten-hundred-fold to this, were still
Less burthen, by ten-hundred-fold, to bear,
Than were those lead-like tons of sin, that crush'd
My spirit flat before Thee.

               O Lord, Lord,
Thou knowest I bore this better at the first,
For I was strong and hale of body then;
And tho' my teeth, which now are dropt away,
Would chatter with the cold, and all my beard   *30*
Was tagg'd with icy fringes in the moon,
I drown'd the whoopings of the owl with sound
Of pious hymns and psalms, and sometimes saw
An angel stand and watch me, as I sang.
Now am I feeble grown; my end draws nigh;
I hope my end draws nigh: half deaf I am,
So that I scarce can hear the people hum
About the column's base, and almost blind,
And scarce can recognise the fields I know;
And both my thighs are rotted with the dew;   *40*
Yet cease I not to clamour and to cry,

While my stiff spine can hold my weary head,
Till all my limbs drop piecemeal from the stone,
Have mercy, mercy: take away my sin.
  O Jesus, if Thou wilt not save my soul,
Who may be saved? who is it may be saved?
Who may be made a saint, if I fail here?
Show me the man hath suffer'd more than I.
For did not all Thy martyrs die one death?
For either they were stoned, or crucified,   *50*
Or burn'd in fire, or boil'd in oil, or sawn
In twain beneath the ribs; but I die here
To-day, and whole years long, a life of death.
Bear witness, if I could have found a way
(And heedfully I sifted all my thought)
More slowly-painful to subdue this home
Of sin, my flesh, which I despise and hate,
I had not stinted practice, O my God.
  For not alone this pillar-punishment,
Not this alone I bore: but while I lived   *60*
In the white convent down the valley there,
For many weeks about my loins I wore
The rope that haled the buckets from the well,
Twisted as tight as I could knot the noose;
And spake not of it to a single soul,
Until the ulcer, eating thro' my skin,
Betray'd my secret penance, so that all
My brethren marvell'd greatly. More than this
I bore, whereof, O God, Thou knowest all.
  Three winters, that my soul might grow to Thee,   *70*
I lived up there on yonder mountain side.
My right leg chain'd into the crag, I lay
Pent in a roofless close of ragged stones;
Inswathed sometimes in wandering mist, and twice
Black'd with Thy branding thunder, and sometimes
Sucking the damps for drink, and eating not,
Except the spare chance-gift of those that came
To touch my body and be heal'd, and live:
And they say then that I work'd miracles,
Whereof my fame is loud amongst mankind,   *80*
Cured lameness, palsies, cancers. Thou, O God,
Knowest alone whether this was or no.
Have mercy, mercy! cover all my sin.
  Then, that I might be more alone with Thee,
Three years I lived upon a pillar, high
Six cubits, and three years on one of twelve;
And twice three years I crouch'd on one that rose
Twenty by measure; last of all, I grew
Twice ten long weary weary years to this,
That numbers forty cubits from the soil.   *90*

I think that I have borne as much as this—
Or else I dream—and for so long a time,
If I may measure time by yon slow light,
And this high dial, which my sorrow crowns—
So much—even so.

          And yet I know not well,
For that the evil ones come here, and say,
' Fall down, O Simeon : thou hast suffer'd long
For ages and for ages ! ' then they prate
Of penances I cannot have gone thro',
Perplexing me with lies; and oft I fall,   *100*
Maybe for months, in such blind lethargies
That Heaven, and Earth, and Time are choked.

                        But yet
Bethink Thee, Lord, while Thou and all the saints
Enjoy themselves in heaven, and men on earth
House in the shade of comfortable roofs,
Sit with their wives by fires, eat wholesome food,
And wear warm clothes, and even beasts have stalls,
I, 'tween the spring and downfall of the light,
Bow down one thousand and two hundred times,
To Christ, the Virgin Mother, and the saints;   *110*
Or in the night, after a little sleep,
I wake : the chill stars sparkle; I am wet
With drenching dews, or stiff with crackling frost.
I wear an undress'd goatskin on my back;
A grazing iron collar grinds my neck;
And in my weak, lean arms I lift the cross,
And strive and wrestle with Thee till I die :
O mercy, mercy ! wash away my sin.

  O Lord, thou knowest what a man I am;
A sinful man, conceived and born in sin :   *120*
'Tis their own doing; this is none of mine;
Lay it not to me. Am I to blame for this,
That here come those that worship me ? Ha ! ha !
They think that I am somewhat. What am I ?
The silly people take me for a saint,
And bring me offerings of fruit and flowers :
And I, in truth (Thou wilt bear witness here)
Have all in all endured as much, and more
Than many just and holy men, whose names
Are register'd and calendar'd for saints.   *130*

  Good people, you do ill to kneel to me.
What is it I can have done to merit this?
I am a sinner viler than you all.
It may be I have wrought some miracles,
And cured some halt and maim'd; but what of that?
It may be, no one, even among the saints,
May match his pains with mine; but what of that?

Yet do not rise; for you may look on me,
And in your looking you may kneel to God.
Speak! is there any of you halt or maim'd?   *140*
I think you know I have some power with Heaven
From my long penance: let him speak his wish.
    Yes, I can heal him. Power goes forth from me.
They say that they are heal'd. Ah, hark! they shout
' St. Simeon Stylites.' Why, if so,
God reaps a harvest in me. O my soul,
God reaps a harvest in thee. If this be,
Can I work miracles and not be saved?
This is not told of any. They were saints.
It cannot be but that I shall be saved;   *150*
Yea, crown'd a saint. They shout, ' Behold a saint! '
And lower voices saint me from above.
Courage, St. Simeon! This dull chrysalis
Cracks into shining wings, and hope ere death
Spreads more and more and more, that God hath now
Sponged and made blank of crimeful record all
My mortal archives.
              O my sons, my sons,
I, Simeon of the pillar, by surname
Stylites, among men; I, Simeon,
The watcher on the column till the end;   *160*
I, Simeon, whose brain the sunshine bakes;
I, whose bald brows in silent hours become
Unnaturally hoar with rime, do now
From my high nest of penance here proclaim
That Pontius and Iscariot by my side
Show'd like fair seraphs. On the coals I lay,
A vessel full of sin: all hell beneath
Made me boil over. Devils pluck'd my sleeve,
Abaddon and Asmodeus caught at me.
I smote them with the cross; they swarm'd again.   *170*
In bed like monstrous apes they crush'd my chest:
They flapp'd my light out as I read: I saw
Their faces grow between me and my book;
With colt-like whinny and with hoggish whine
They burst my prayer. Yet this way was left,
And by this way I 'scaped them. Mortify
Your flesh, like me, with scourges and with thorns;
Smite, shrink not, spare not. If it may be, fast
Whole Lents, and pray. I hardly, with slow steps,
With slow, faint steps, and much exceeding pain,   *180*
Have scrambled past those pits of fire, that still
Sing in mine ears. But yield not me the praise:
God only thro' His bounty hath thought fit,
Among the powers and princes of this world,
To make me an example to mankind,

Which few can reach to.   Yet I do not say
But that a time may come—yea, even now,
Now, now, his footsteps smite the threshold stairs
Of life—I say, that time is at the doors
When you may worship me without reproach;   *190*
For I will leave my relics in your land,
And you may carve a shrine about my dust,
And burn a fragrant lamp before my bones,
When I am gather'd to the glorious saints.
    While I spake then, a sting of shrewdest pain
Ran shrivelling thro' me, and a cloudlike change,
In passing, with a grosser film made thick
These heavy, horny eyes.   The end! the end!
Surely the end!   What's here? a shape, a shade,
A flash of light.   Is that the angel there   *200*
That holds a crown?   Come, blessed brother, come.
I know thy glittering face.   I waited long;
My brows are ready.   What! deny it now?
Nay, draw, draw, draw nigh.   So I clutch it.   Christ!
'Tis gone: 'tis here again; the crown! the crown!
So now 'tis fitted on and grows to me,
And from it melt the dews of Paradise,
Sweet! sweet! spikenard, and balm, and frankincense.
Ah! let me not be fool'd, sweet saints: I trust
That I am whole, and clean, and meet for Heaven.   *210*
    Speak, if there be a priest, a man of God,
Among you there, and let him presently
Approach, and lean a ladder on the shaft,
And climbing up into my airy home,
Deliver me the blessed sacrament;
For by the warning of the Holy Ghost,
I prophesy that I shall die to-night,
A quarter before twelve.
                But Thou, O Lord,
Aid all this foolish people; let them take
Example, pattern: lead them to Thy light.   *220*

ULYSSES

It little profits that an idle king,
By this still hearth, among these barren crags,
Match'd with an aged wife, I mete and dole
Unequal laws unto a savage race,
That hoard, and sleep, and feed, and know not me.
I cannot rest from travel: I will drink
Life to the lees: all times I have enjoy'd
Greatly, have suffer'd greatly, both with those
That loved me, and alone; on shore, and when
Thro' scudding drifts the rainy Hyades   *10*
Vext the dim sea: I am become a name;
For always roaming with a hungry heart
Much have I seen and known; cities of men
And manners, climates, councils, governments,
Myself not least, but honour'd of them all;
And drunk delight of battle with my peers,
Far on the ringing plains of windy Troy.
I am a part of all that I have met;
Yet all experience is an arch wherethro'
Gleams that untravell'd world, whose margin fades   *20*
For ever and for ever when I move.
How dull it is to pause, to make an end,
To rust unburnish'd, not to shine in use!
As tho' to breathe were life. Life piled on life
Were all too little, and of one to me
Little remains: but every hour is saved
From that eternal silence, something more,
A bringer of new things; and vile it were
For some three suns to store and hoard myself,
And this gray spirit yearning in desire   *30*
To follow knowledge like a sinking star,
Beyond the utmost bound of human thought.
    This is my son, mine own Telemachus,
To whom I leave the sceptre and the isle—
Well-loved of me, discerning to fulfil
This labour, by slow prudence to make mild
A rugged people, and thro' soft degrees
Subdue them to the useful and the good.
Most blameless is he, centred in the sphere
Of common duties, decent not to fail   *40*
In offices of tenderness, and pay
Meet adoration to my household gods,

When I am gone.   He works his work, I mine.
  There lies the port; the vessel puffs her sail:
There gloom the dark broad seas.   My mariners,
Souls that have toil'd, and wrought, and thought with me—
That ever with a frolic welcome took
The thunder and the sunshine, and opposed
Free hearts, free foreheads—you and I are old;
Old age hath yet his honour and his toil;   50
Death closes all: but something ere the end,
Some work of noble note, may yet be done,
Not unbecoming men that strove with Gods.
The lights begin to twinkle from the rocks:
The long day wanes: the slow moon climbs: the deep
Moans round with many voices.   Come, my friends,
'Tis not too late to seek a newer world.
Push off, and sitting well in order smite
The sounding furrows; for my purpose holds
To sail beyond the sunset, and the baths   60
Of all the western stars, until I die.
It may be that the gulfs will wash us down:
It may be we shall touch the Happy Isles,
And see the great Achilles, whom we knew.
Tho' much is taken, much abides; and tho'
We are not now that strength which in old days
Moved earth and heaven; that which we are, we are;
One equal temper of heroic hearts,
Made weak by time and fate, but strong in will
To strive, to seek, to find, and not to yield.   70

THE EPIC

At Francis Allen's on the Christmas-eve,—
The game of forfeits done—the girls all kiss'd
Beneath the sacred bush and past away—
The parson Holmes, the poet Everard Hall,
The host, and I sat round the wassail-bowl,
Then half-way ebb'd: and there we held a talk,
How all the old honour had from Christmas gone,
Or gone, or dwindled down to some odd games
In some odd nooks like this; till I, tired out
With cutting eights that day upon the pond,   *10*
Where, three times slipping from the outer edge,
I bump'd the ice into three several stars,
Fell in a doze; and half-awake I heard
The parson taking wide and wider sweeps,
Now harping on the church-commissioners,
Now hawking at Geology and schism;
Until I woke, and found him settled down
Upon the general decay of faith
Right thro' the world, ' at home was little left,
And none abroad: there was no anchor, none,   *20*
To hold by.'   Francis, laughing, clapt his hand
On Everard's shoulder, with ' I hold by him.'
' And I,' quoth Everard, ' by the wassail-bowl.'
' Why yes,' I said, ' we knew your gift that way
At college: but another which you had,
I mean of verse (for so we held it then),
What came of that?'   ' You know,' said Frank, ' he burnt
His epic, his King Arthur, some twelve books '—
And then to me demanding why?   ' Oh, sir,
He thought that nothing new was said, or else   *30*
Something so said 'twas nothing—that a truth
Looks freshest in the fashion of the day:
God knows: he has a mint of reasons: ask.
It pleased *me* well enough.'   ' Nay, nay,' said Hall,
' Why take the style of those heroic times?
For nature brings not back the Mastodon,
Nor we those times; and why should any man
Remodel models? these twelve books of mine
Were faint Homeric echoes, nothing-worth,
Mere chaff and draff, much better burnt.'   ' But I,'   *40*
Said Francis, ' pick'd the eleventh from this hearth
And have it: keep a thing, its use will come.
I hoard it as a sugar-plum for Holmes.'
He laugh'd, and I, tho' sleepy, like a horse
That hears the corn-bin open, prick'd my ears;

For I remember'd Everard's college fame
When we were Freshmen : then at my request
He brought it; and the poet little urged,
'But with some prelude of disparagement,
Read, mouthing out his hollow oes and aes,   *50*
Deep-chested music, and to this result.

MORTE D'ARTHUR

So all day long the noise of battle roll'd
Among the mountains by the winter sea;
Until King Arthur's table, man by man,
Had fallen in Lyonnesse about their Lord,
King Arthur : then, because his wound was deep,
The bold Sir Bedivere uplifted him,
Sir Bedivere, the last of all his knights,
And bore him to a chapel nigh the field,
A broken chancel with a broken cross,   *60*
That stood on a dark strait of barren land.
On one side lay the Ocean, and on one
Lay a great water, and the moon was full.
    Then spake King Arthur to Sir Bedivere:
' The sequel of to-day unsolders all
The goodliest fellowship of famous knights
Whereof this world holds record.   Such a sleep
They sleep—the men I loved.   I think that we
Shall never more, at any future time,
Delight our souls with talk of knightly deeds,   *70*
Walking about the gardens and the halls
Of Camelot, as in the days that were.
I perish by this people which I made,—
Tho' Merlin sware that I should come again
To rule once more—but let what will be, be,
I am so deeply smitten thro' the helm
That without help I cannot last till morn.
Thou therefore take my brand Excalibur,
Which was my pride : for thou rememberest how
In those old days, one summer noon, an arm   *80*
Rose up from out the bosom of the lake,
Clothed in white samite, mystic, wonderful,
Holding the sword—and how I row'd across
And took it, and have worn it, like a king :
And, wheresoever I am sung or told
In aftertime, this also shall be known :
But now delay not : take Excalibur,
And fling him far into the middle mere :
Watch what thou seëst, and lightly bring me word.'

To him replied the bold Sir Bedivere: *90*
' It is not meet, Sir King, to leave thee thus,
Aidless, alone, and smitten thro' the helm.
A little thing may harm a wounded man.
Yet I thy hest will all perform at full,
Watch what I see, and lightly bring thee word.'
    So saying, from the ruin'd shrine he stept
And in the moon athwart the place of tombs,
Where lay the mighty bones of ancient men,
Old knights, and over them the sea-wind sang
Shrill, chill, with flakes of foam.   He, stepping down   *100*
By zig-zag paths, and juts of pointed rock,
Came on the shining levels of the lake.
    There drew he forth the brand Excalibur,
And o'er him, drawing it, the winter moon,
Brightening the skirts of a long cloud, ran forth
And sparkled keen with frost against the hilt:
For all the haft twinkled with diamond sparks,
Myriads of topaz-lights, and jacinth-work
Of subtlest jewellery.   He gazed so long
That both his eyes were dazzled, as he stood,   *110*
This way and that dividing the swift mind,
In act to throw: but at the last it seem'd
Better to leave Excalibur conceal'd
There in the many-knotted waterflags,
That whistled stiff and dry about the marge.
So strode he back slow to the wounded King.
    Then spake King Arthur to Sir Bedivere:
' Hast thou perform'd my mission which I gave?
What is it thou hast seen? or what hast heard?'
    And answer made the bold Sir Bedivere: *120*
' I heard the ripple washing in the reeds,
And the wild water lapping on the crag.'
    To whom replied King Arthur, faint and pale:
' Thou hast betray'd thy nature and thy name,
Not rendering true answer, as beseem'd
Thy fëalty, nor like a noble knight:
For surer sign had follow'd, either hand,
Or voice, or else a motion of the mere.
This is a shameful thing for men to lie.
Yet now, I charge thee, quickly go again   *130*
As thou art lief and dear, and do the thing
I bad thee, watch, and lightly bring me word.'
    Then went Sir Bedivere the second time
Across the ridge, and paced beside the mere,
Counting the dewy pebbles, fix'd in thought;
But when he saw the wonder of the hilt,
How curiously and strangely chased, he smote
His palms together, and he cried aloud,

' And if indeed I cast the brand away,
Surely a precious thing, one worthy note,   *140*
Should thus be lost for ever from the earth,
Which might have pleased the eyes of many men.
What good should follow this, if this were done?
What harm, undone? deep harm to disobey,
Seeing obedience is the bond of rule.
Were it well to obey then, if a king demand
An act unprofitable, against himself?
The King is sick, and knows not what he does.
What record, or what relic of my lord
Should be to aftertime, but empty breath   *150*
And rumours of a doubt? but were this kept,
Stored in some treasure-house of mighty kings,
Some one might show it at a joust of arms,
Saying, " King Arthur's sword, Excalibur,
Wrought by the lonely maiden of the Lake.
Nine years she wrought it, sitting in the deeps
Upon the hidden bases of the hills."
So might some old man speak in the aftertime
To all the people, winning reverence.
But now much honour and much fame were lost.'   *160*
    So spake he, clouded with his own conceit,
And hid Excalibur the second time,
And so strode back slow to the wounded King.
    Then spoke King Arthur, breathing heavily :
' What is it thou hast seen? or what hast heard?'
    And answer made the bold Sir Bedivere :
' I heard the water lapping on the crag,
And the long ripple washing in the reeds.'
    To whom replied King Arthur, much in wrath :
' Ah, miserable and unkind, untrue,   *170*
Unknightly, traitor-hearted! Woe is me!
Authority forgets a dying king,
Laid widow'd of the power in his eye
That bow'd the will. I see thee what thou art,
For thou, the latest-left of all my knights
In whom should meet the offices of all,
Thou wouldst betray me for the precious hilt;
Either from lust of gold, or like a girl
Valuing the giddy pleasure of the eyes.
Yet, for a man may fail in duty twice,   *180*
And the third time may prosper, get thee hence :
But, if thou spare to fling Excalibur,
I will arise and slay thee with my hands.'
    Then quickly rose Sir Bedivere, and ran,
And, leaping down the ridges lightly, plunged
Among the bulrush-beds, and clutch'd the sword,
And strongly wheel'd and threw it. The great brand

Made lightnings in the splendour of the moon,
And flashing round and round, and whirl'd in an arch,
Shot like a streamer of the northern morn,   *190*
Seen where the moving isles of winter shock
By night, with noises of the northern sea.
So flash'd and fell the brand Excalibur:
But ere he dipt the surface, rose an arm
Clothed in white samite, mystic, wonderful,
And caught him by the hilt, and brandish'd him
Three times, and drew him under in the mere.
And lightly went the other to the King.
    Then spoke King Arthur, drawing thicker breath:
' Now see I by thine eyes that this is done.   *200*
Speak out: what is it thou hast heard, or seen? '
    And answer made the bold Sir Bedivere:
' Sir King, I closed mine eyelids, lest the gems
Should blind my purpose, for I never saw,
Nor shall see, here or elsewhere, till I die,
Not tho' I live three lives of mortal men,
So great a miracle as yonder hilt.
Then with both hands I flung him, wheeling him;
But when I look'd again, behold an arm,
Clothed in white samite, mystic, wonderful,   *210*
That caught him by the hilt, and brandish'd him
Three times, and drew him under in the mere.'
    And answer made King Arthur, breathing hard:
' My end draws nigh; 'tis time that I were gone.
Make broad thy shoulders to receive my weight,
And bear me to the margin; yet I fear
My wound hath taken cold, and I shall die.'
    So saying, from the pavement he half rose,
Slowly, with pain, reclining on his arm,
And looking wistfully with wide blue eyes   *220*
As in a picture.   Him Sir Bedivere
Remorsefully regarded thro' his tears,
And would have spoken, but he found not words,
Then took with care, and kneeling on one knee,
O'er both his shoulders drew the languid hands,
And rising bore him thro' the place of tombs.
    But, as he walk'd, King Arthur panted hard,
Like one that feels a nightmare on his bed
When all the house is mute.   So sigh'd the King,
Muttering and murmuring at his ear, ' Quick, quick!   *230*
I fear it is too late, and I shall die.'
But the other swiftly strode from ridge to ridge,
Clothed with his breath, and looking, as he walk'd,
Larger than human on the frozen hills.
He heard the deep behind him, and a cry
Before.   His own thought drove him, like a goad.

Dry clash'd his harness in the icy caves
And barren chasms, and all to left and right
The bare black cliff clang'd round him, as he based
His feet on juts of slippery crag that rang   *240*
Sharp-smitten with the dint of armed heels—
And on a sudden, lo! the level lake,
And the long glories of the winter moon.
   Then saw they how there hove a dusky barge,
Dark as a funeral scarf from stem to stern,
Beneath them; and descending they were ware
That all the decks were dense with stately forms
Black-stoled, black-hooded, like a dream—by these
Three Queens with crowns of gold—and from them rose
A cry that shiver'd to the tingling stars,   *250*
And, as it were one voice an agony
Of lamentation, like a wind, that shrills
All night in a waste land, where no one comes,
Or hath come, since the making of the world.
   Then murmur'd Arthur, ' Place me in the barge,'
And to the barge they came. There those three Queens
Put forth their hands, and took the King, and wept.
But she, that rose the tallest of them all
And fairest, laid his head upon her lap,
And loosed the shatter'd casque, and chafed his hands,   *260*
And call'd him by his name, complaining loud,
And dropping bitter tears against his brow
Striped with dark blood: for all his face was white
And colourless, and like the wither'd moon
Smote by the fresh beam of the springing east;
And all his greaves and cuisses dash'd with drops
Of onset; and the light and lustrous curls—
That made his forehead like a rising sun
High from the daïs-throne—were parch'd with dust;
Or, clotted into points and hanging loose,   *270*
Mix'd with the knightly growth that fringed his lips.
So like a shatter'd column lay the King;
Not like that Arthur who, with lance in rest,
From spur to plume a star of tournament,
Shot thro' the lists at Camelot, and charged
Before the eyes of ladies and of kings.
   Then loudly cried the bold Sir Bedivere,
' Ah! my Lord Arthur, whither shall I go?
Where shall I hide my forehead and my eyes?
For now I see the true old times are dead,   *280*
When every morning brought a noble chance,
And every chance brought out a noble knight.
Such times have been not since the light that led
The holy Elders with the gift of myrrh.
But now the whole ROUND TABLE is dissolved

Which was an image of the mighty world;
And I, the last, go forth companionless,
And the days darken round me, and the years,
Among new men, strange faces, other minds.'
    And slowly answered Arthur from the barge: *290*
' The old order changeth, yielding place to new,
And God fulfils Himself in many ways,
Lest one good custom should corrupt the world.
Comfort thyself: what comfort is in me?
I have lived my life, and that which I have done
May He within Himself make pure! but thou,
If thou shouldst never see my face again,
Pray for my soul. More things are wrought by prayer
Than this world dreams of. Wherefore, let thy voice,
Rise like a fountain for me night and day.   *300*
For what are men better than sheep or goats
That nourish a blind life within the brain,
If, knowing God, they lift not hands of prayer
Both for themselves and those who call them friend?
For so the whole round earth is every way
Bound by gold chains about the feet of God.
But now farewell. I am going a long way
With these thou seëst—if indeed I go—
(For all my mind is clouded with a doubt)
To the island-valley of Avilion;   *310*
Where falls not hail, or rain, or any snow,
Nor ever wind blows loudly; but it lies
Deep-meadow'd, happy, fair with orchard-lawns
And bowery hollows crown'd with summer sea,
Where I will heal me of my grievous wound.'
    So said he, and the barge with oar and sail
Moved from the brink, like some full-breasted swan
That, fluting a wild carol ere her death,
Ruffles her pure cold plume, and takes the flood
With swarthy webs. Long stood Sir Bedivere   *320*
Revolving many memories, till the hull
Look'd one black dot against the verge of dawn,
And on the mere the wailing died away.

HERE ended Hall, and our last light, that long
Had wink'd and threaten'd darkness, flared and fell:
At which the Parson, sent to sleep with sound,
And waked with silence, grunted ' Good!' but we
Sat rapt: it was the tone with which he read—
Perhaps some modern touches here and there
Redeem'd it from the charge of nothingness—   *330*
Or else we loved the man, and prized his work;
I know not: but we sitting, as I said,
The cock crew loud; as at that time of year

The lusty bird takes every hour for dawn :
Then Francis, muttering, like a man ill-used,
' There now—that's nothing ! ' drew a little back,
And drove his heel into the smoulder'd log,
That sent a blast of sparkles up the flue :
And so to bed ; where yet in sleep I seem'd
To sail with Arthur under looming shores,   *340*
Point after point ; till on to dawn, when dreams
Begin to feel the truth and stir of day,
To me, methought, who waited with a crowd,
There came a bark that, blowing forward, bore
King Arthur, like a modern gentleman
Of stateliest port ; and all the people cried,
' Arthur is come again : he cannot die.'
Then those that stood upon the hills behind
Repeated—' Come again, and thrice as fair ; '
And, further inland, voices echo'd—' Come   *350*
With all good things, and war shall be no more.'
At this a hundred bells began to peal,
That with the sound I woke, and heard indeed
The clear church-bells ring in the Christmas-morn.

'BREAK, BREAK, BREAK . . .'

BREAK, break, break,
  On thy cold gray stones, O Sea!
And I would that my tongue could utter
  The thoughts that arise in me.

O well for the fisherman's boy,
  That he shouts with his sister at play!
O well for the sailor lad,
  That he sings in his boat on the bay!

And the stately ships go on
  To their haven under the hill;   *10*
But O for the touch of a vanish'd hand,
  And the sound of a voice that is still!

Break, break, break,
  At the foot of thy crags, O Sea!
But the tender grace of a day that is dead
  Will never come back to me.

AMPHION

My father left a park to me,
  But it is wild and barren,
A garden too with scarce a tree,
  And waster than a warren:
Yet say the neighbours when they call,
  It is not bad but good land,
And in it is the germ of all
  That grows within the woodland.

O had I lived when song was great
  In days of old Amphion,   *10*
And ta'en my fiddle to the gate,
  Nor cared for seed or scion!
And had I lived when song was great,
  And legs of trees were limber,
And ta'en my fiddle to the gate,
  And fiddled in the timber!

'Tis said he had a tuneful tongue,
  Such happy intonation,
Wherever he sat down and sung
  He left a small plantation;   *20*
Wherever in a lonely grove
  He set up his forlorn pipes,
The gouty oak began to move,
  And flounder into hornpipes.

The mountain stirr'd its bushy crown,
  And, as tradition teaches,
Young ashes pirouetted down
  Coquetting with young beeches;
And briony-vine and ivy-wreath
  Ran forward to his rhyming,   *30*
And from the valleys underneath
  Came little copses climbing.

The linden broke her ranks and rent
  The woodbine wreaths that bind her,
And down the middle, buzz! she went
  With all her bees behind her:
The poplars, in long order due,
  With cypress promenaded,
The shock-head willows two and two
  By rivers gallopaded.   *40*

Came wet-shod alder from the wave,
 Came yews, a dismal coterie;
Each puck'd his one foot from the grave
 Poussetting with a sloe-tree:
Old elms came breaking from the vine,
 The vine stream'd out to follow,
And, sweating rosin, plump'd the pine
 From many a cloudy hollow.

And wasn't it a sight to see,
 When, ere his song was ended,   *50*
Like some great landslip, tree by tree,
 The country-side descended;
And shepherds from the mountain-eaves
 Look'd down, half-pleased, half-frighten'd,
As dash'd about the drunken leaves
 The random sunshine lighten'd!

Oh, nature first was fresh to men,
 And wanton without measure;
So youthful and so flexile then,
 You moved her at your pleasure.   *60*
Twang out, my fiddle! shake the twigs!
 And make her dance attendance;
Blow, flute, and stir the stiff-set sprigs,
 And scirrhous roots and tendons.

'Tis vain! in such a brassy age
 I could not move a thistle;
The very sparrows in the hedge
 Scarce answer to my whistle;
Or at the most, when three-parts-sick
 With strumming and with scraping,   *70*
A jackass heehaws from the rick,
 The passive oxen gaping.

But what is that I hear? a sound
 Like sleepy counsel pleading;
O Lord!—'tis in my neighbour's ground,
 The modern Muses reading.
They read Botanic Treatises,
 And Works on Gardening thro' there,
And Methods of transplanting trees
 To look as if they grew there.   *80*

The wither'd Misses! how they prose
 O'er books of travell'd seamen,
And show you slips of all that grows
 From England to Van Diemen.

They read in arbours clipt and cut,
  And alleys, faded places,
By squares of tropic summer shut
  And warm'd in crystal cases.

But these, tho' fed with careful dirt,
  Are neither green nor sappy;   *90*
Half-conscious of the garden-squirt,
  The spindlings look unhappy.
Better to me the meanest weed
  That blows upon its mountain,
The vilest herb that runs to seed
  Beside its native fountain.

And I must work thro' months of toil,
  And years of cultivation,
Upon my proper patch of soil
  To grow my own plantation.   *100*
I'll take the showers as they fall,
  I will not vex my bosom:
Enough if at the end of all
  A little garden blossom.

LOCKSLEY HALL

COMRADES, leave me here a little, while as yet 'tis early morn:
Leave me here, and when you want me, sound upon the bugle-horn.

'Tis the place, and all around it, as of old, the curlews call,
Dreary gleams about the moorland flying over Locksley Hall;

Locksley Hall, that in the distance overlooks the sandy tracts,
And the hollow ocean-ridges roaring into cataracts.

Many a night from yonder ivied casement, ere I went to rest,
Did I look on great Orion sloping slowly to the West.

Many a night I saw the Pleiads, rising thro' the mellow shade,
Glitter like a swarm of fire-flies tangled in a silver braid.   *10*

Here about the beach I wander'd, nourishing a youth sublime
With the fairy tales of science, and the long result of Time;

When the centuries behind me like a fruitful land reposed;
When I clung to all the present for the promise that it closed:

When I dipt into the future far as human eye could see;
Saw the Vision of the world, and all the wonder that would be.——

In the Spring a fuller crimson comes upon the robin's breast;
In the Spring the wanton lapwing gets himself another crest;

In the Spring a livelier iris changes on the burnish'd dove;
In the Spring a young man's fancy lightly turns to thoughts of love.   *20*

Then her cheek was pale and thinner than should be for one so young,
And her eyes on all my motions with a mute observance hung.

And I said, ' My cousin Amy, speak, and speak the truth to me,
Trust me, cousin, all the current of my being sets to thee.'

On her pallid cheek and forehead came a colour and a light,
As I have seen the rosy red flushing in the northern night.

And she turn'd—her bosom shaken with a sudden storm of sighs—
All the spirit deeply dawning in the dark of hazel eyes—

Saying, ' I have hid my feelings, fearing they should do me wrong ; '
Saying, ' Dost thou love me, cousin ? ' weeping, ' I have loved thee
　　long.'　　　　　　　　　　　　　　　　　　　　　　　　　*30*

Love took up the glass of Time, and turn'd it in his glowing hands ;
Every moment, lightly shaken, ran itself in golden sands.

Love took up the harp of Life, and smote on all the chords with might ;
Smote the chord of Self, that, trembling, pass'd in music out of sight.

Many a morning on the moorland did we hear the copses ring,
And her whisper throng'd my pulses with the fullness of the Spring.

Many an evening by the waters did we watch the stately ships,
And our spirits rush'd together at the touching of the lips.

O my cousin, shallow-hearted ! O my Amy, mine no more !
O the dreary, dreary moorland ! O the barren, barren shore !　　*40*

Falser than all fancy fathoms, falser than all songs have sung,
Puppet to a father's threat, and servile to a shrewish tongue !

Is it well to wish thee happy ?—having known me—to decline
On a range of lower feelings and a narrower heart than mine !

Yet it shall be : thou shalt lower to his level day by day,
What is fine within thee growing coarse to sympathise with clay.

As the husband is, the wife is : thou art mated with a clown,
And the grossness of his nature will have weight to drag thee down.

He will hold thee, when his passion shall have spent its novel force,
Something better than his dog, a little dearer than his horse.　　*50*

What is this ? his eyes are heavy : think not they are glazed with wine.
Go to him : it is thy duty : kiss him : take his hand in thine.

It may be my lord is weary, that his brain is overwrought :
Soothe him with thy finer fancies, touch him with thy lighter thought.

He will answer to the purpose, easy things to understand—
Better thou wert dead before me, tho' I slew thee with my hand !

Better thou and I were lying, hidden from the heart's disgrace,
Roll'd in one another's arms, and silent in a last embrace.

Cursed be the social wants that sin against the strength of youth !
Cursed be the social lies that warp us from the living truth !   60

Cursed be the sickly forms that err from honest Nature's rule !
Cursed be the gold that gilds the straiten'd forehead of the fool !

Well—'tis well that I should bluster !—Hadst thou less unworthy
          proved—
Would to God—for I had loved thee more than ever wife was loved.

Am I mad, that I should cherish that which bears but bitter fruit ?
I will pluck it from my bosom, tho' my heart be at the root.

Never, tho' my mortal summers to such length of years should come
As the many-winter'd crow that leads the clanging rookery home.

Where is comfort ? in division of the records of the mind ?
Can I part her from herself, and love her, as I knew her, kind ?   70

I remember one that perish'd : sweetly did she speak and move :
Such a one do I remember, whom to look at was to love.

Can I think of her as dead, and love her for the love she bore ?
No—she never loved me truly : love is love for evermore.

Comfort ? comfort scorn'd of devils ! this is truth the poet sings,
That a sorrow's crown of sorrow is remembering happier things.

Drug thy memories, lest thou learn it, lest thy heart be put to proof,
In the dead unhappy night, and when the rain is on the roof.

Like a dog, he hunts in dreams, and thou art staring at the wall,
Where the dying night-lamp flickers, and the shadows rise and fall. 80

Then a hand shall pass before thee, pointing to his drunken sleep,
To thy widow'd marriage-pillows, to the tears that thou wilt weep.

Thou shalt hear the 'Never, never,' whisper'd by the phantom years,
And a song from out the distance in the ringing of thine ears;

And an eye shall vex thee, looking ancient kindness on thy pain.
Turn thee, turn thee on thy pillow : get thee to thy rest again.

Nay, but Nature brings thee solace; for a tender voice will cry.
'Tis a purer life than thine; a lip to drain thy trouble dry.

Baby lips will laugh me down: my latest rival brings thee rest.
Baby fingers, waxen touches, press me from the mother's breast.　*90*

O, the child too clothes the father with a dearness not his due.
Half is thine and half is his: it will be worthy of the two.

O, I see thee old and formal, fitted to thy petty part,
With a little hoard of maxims preaching down a daughter's heart.

'They were dangerous guides the feelings—she herself was not
　exempt—
Truly, she herself had suffer'd'—Perish in thy self-contempt!

Overlive it—lower yet—be happy! wherefore should I care?
I myself must mix with action, lest I wither by despair.

What is that which I should turn to, lighting upon days like these?
Every door is barr'd with gold, and opens but to golden keys.　*100*

Every gate is throng'd with suitors, all the markets overflow.
I have but an angry fancy: what is that which I should do?

I had been content to perish, falling on the foeman's ground,
When the ranks are roll'd in vapour, and the winds are laid with sound.

But the jingling of the guinea helps the hurt that Honour feels,
And the nations do but murmur, snarling at each other's heels.

Can I but relive in sadness? I will turn that earlier page.
Hide me from my deep emotion, O thou wondrous Mother-Age!

Make me feel the wild pulsation that I felt before the strife,
When I heard my days before me, and the tumult of my life;　*110*

Yearning for the large excitement that the coming years would yield,
Eager-hearted as a boy when first he leaves his father's field,

And at night along the dusky highway near and nearer drawn,
Sees in heaven the light of London flaring like a dreary dawn;

And his spirit leaps within him to be gone before him then,
Underneath the light he looks at, in among the throngs of men:

Men, my brothers, men the workers, ever reaping something new:
That which they have done but earnest of the things that they shall do:

For I dipt into the future, far as human eye could see,
Saw the Vision of the world, and all the wonder that would be;   *120*

Saw the heavens fill with commerce, argosies of magic sails,
Pilots of the purple twilight, dropping down with costly bales;

Heard the heavens fill with shouting, and there rain'd a ghastly dew
From the nations' airy navies grappling in the central blue;

Far along the world-wide whisper of the south-wind rushing warm,
With the standards of the peoples plunging thro' the thunder-storm;

Till the war-drum throbb'd no longer, and the battle-flags were furl'd
In the Parliament of man, the Federation of the world.

There the common sense of most shall hold a fretful realm in awe,
And the kindly earth shall slumber, lapt in universal law.   *130*

So I triumph'd ere my passion sweeping thro' me left me dry,
Left me with the palsied heart, and left me with the jaundiced eye;

Eye, to which all order festers, all things here are out of joint:
Science moves, but slowly slowly, creeping on from point to point:

Slowly comes a hungry people, as a lion creeping nigher,
Glares at one that nods and winks behind a slowly-dying fire.

Yet I doubt not thro' the ages one increasing purpose runs,
And the thoughts of men are widen'd with the process of the suns.

What is that to him that reaps not harvest of his youthful joys,
Tho' the deep heart of existence beat for ever like a boy's?   *140*

Knowledge comes, but wisdom lingers, and I linger on the shore,
And the individual withers, and the world is more and more.

Knowledge comes, but wisdom lingers, and he bears a laden breast,
Full of sad experience, moving toward the stillness of his rest.

Hark, my merry comrades call me, sounding on the bugle-horn,
They to whom my foolish passion were a target for their scorn:

Shall it not be scorn to me to harp on such a moulder'd string?
I am shamed thro' all my nature to have loved so slight a thing.

Weakness to be wroth with weakness! woman's pleasure, woman's
    pain—
Nature made them blinder motions bounded in a shallower brain: *150*

Woman is the lesser man, and all thy passions, match'd with mine,
Are as moonlight unto sunlight, and as water unto wine—

Here at least, where nature sickens, nothing.   Ah, for some retreat
Deep in yonder shining Orient, where my life began to beat;

Where in wild Mahratta-battle fell my father evil-starr'd;—
I was left a trampled orphan, and a selfish uncle's ward.

Or to burst all links of habit—there to wander far away,
On from island unto island at the gateways of the day.

Larger constellations burning, mellow moons and happy skies,
Breadths of tropic shade and palms in cluster, knots of Paradise.   *160*

Never comes the trader, never floats an European flag,
Slides the bird o'er lustrous woodland, swings the trailer from the
    crag;

Droops the heavy-blossom'd bower, hangs the heavy-fruited tree—
Summer isles of Eden lying in dark-purple spheres of sea.

There methinks would be enjoyment more than in this march of mind,
In the steamship, in the railway, in the thoughts that shake mankind.

There the passions cramp'd no longer shall have scope and breathing
    space;
I will take some savage woman, she shall rear my dusky race.

Iron jointed, supple-sinew'd, they shall dive, and they shall run,
Catch the wild goat by the hair, and hurl their lances in the sun;   *170*

Whistle back the parrot's call, and leap the rainbows of the brooks,
Not with blinded eyesight poring over miserable books—

Fool, again the dream, the fancy! but I *know* my words are wild,
But I count the gray barbarian lower than the Christian child.

I, to herd with narrow foreheads, vacant of our glorious gains,
Like a beast with lower pleasures, like a beast with lower pains!

Mated with a squalid savage—what to me were sun or clime?
I the heir of all the ages, in the foremost files of time—

I that rather held it better men should perish one by one,
Than that earth should stand at gaze like Joshua's moon in Ajalon ! *180*

Not in vain the distance beacons.   Forward, forward let us range,
Let the great world spin for ever down the ringing grooves of change.

Thro' the shadow of the globe we sweep into the younger day :
Better fifty years of Europe than a cycle of Cathay.

Mother-Age (for mine I knew not) help me as when life begun :
Rift the hills, and roll the waters, flash the lightnings, weigh the Sun.

O, I see the crescent promise of my spirit hath not set.
Ancient founts of inspiration well thro' all my fancy yet.

Howsoever these things be, a long farewell to Locksley Hall !
Now for me the woods may wither, now for me the roof-tree fall. *190*

Comes a vapour from the margin, blackening over heath and holt,
Cramming all the blast before it, in its breast a thunderbolt.

Let it fall on Locksley Hall, with rain or hail, or fire or snow ;
For the mighty wind arises, roaring seaward, and I go.

THE VISION OF SIN

I HAD a vision when the night was late:
A youth came riding toward a palace-gate.
He rode a horse with wings, that would have flown,
But that his heavy rider kept him down.
And from the palace came a child of sin,
And took him by the curls, and led him in,
Where sat a company with heated eyes,
Expecting when a fountain should arise:
A sleepy light upon their brows and lips—
As when the sun, a crescent of eclipse,   10
Dreams over lake and lawn, and isles and capes—
Suffused them, sitting, lying, languid shapes,
By heaps of gourds, and skins of wine, and piles of grapes.

Then methought I heard a mellow sound,
Gathering up from all the lower ground;
Narrowing in to where they sat assembled
Low voluptuous music winding trembled,
Wov'n in circles: they that heard it sigh'd,
Panted hand-in-hand with faces pale,
Swung themselves, and in low tones replied;   20
Till the fountain spouted, showering wide
Sleet of diamond-drift and pearly hail;
Then the music touch'd the gates and died;
Rose again from where it seem'd to fail,
Storm'd in orbs of song, a growing gale;
Till thronging in and in, to where they waited,
As 'twere a hundred-throated nightingale,
The strong tempestuous treble throbb'd and palpitated;
Ran into its giddiest whirl of sound,
Caught the sparkles, and in circles,   30
Purple gauzes, golden hazes, liquid mazes,
Flung the torrent rainbow round:
Then they started from their places,
Moved with violence, changed in hue,
Caught each other with wild grimaces,
Half-invisible to the view,
Wheeling with precipitate paces
To the melody, till they flew,
Hair, and eyes, and limbs, and faces,
Twisted hard in fierce embraces,   40
Like to Furies, like to Graces,
Dash'd together in blinding dew:
Till, kill'd with some luxurious agony,

The nerve-dissolving melody
Flutter'd headlong from the sky.

And then I look'd up toward a mountain-tract,
That girt the region with high cliff and lawn:
I saw that every morning, far withdrawn
Beyond the darkness and the cataract,
God made Himself an awful rose of dawn,   50
Unheeded: and detaching, fold by fold,
From those still heights, and, slowly drawing near,
A vapour heavy, hueless, formless, cold,
Came floating on for many a month and year,
Unheeded: and I thought I would have spoken,
And warn'd that madman ere it grew too late:
But, as in dreams, I could not. Mine was broken,
When that cold vapour touch'd the palace gate,
And link'd again. I saw within my head
A gray and gap-tooth'd man as lean as death,   60
Who slowly rode across a wither'd heath,
And lighted at a ruin'd inn, and said:

    ' Wrinkled ostler, grim and thin!
       Here is custom come your way;
    Take my brute, and lead him in,
       Stuff his ribs with mouldy hay.

    ' Bitter barmaid, waning fast!
       See that sheets are on my bed;
    What! the flower of life is past:
       It is long before you wed.   70

    ' Slip-shod waiter, lank and sour,
       At the Dragon on the heath!
    Let us have a quiet hour,
       Let us hob-and-nob with Death.

    ' I am old, but let me drink;
       Bring me spices, bring me wine;
    I remember, when I think,
       That my youth was half divine.

    ' Wine is good for shrivell'd lips,
       When a blanket wraps the day,   80
    When the rotten woodland drips,
       And the leaf is stamp'd in clay.

' Sit thee down, and have no shame,
 Cheek by jowl, and knee by knee:
What care I for any name?
 What for order or degree?

' Let me screw thee up a peg:
 Let me loose thy tongue with wine:
Callest thou that thing a leg?
 Which is thinnest? thine or mine?   *90*

' Thou shalt not be saved by works:
 Thou hast been a sinner too:
Ruin'd trunks on wither'd forks,
 Empty scarecrows, I and you!

' Fill the cup, and fill the can:
 Have a rouse before the morn:
Every moment dies a man,
 Every moment one is born.

' We are men of ruin'd blood;
 Therefore comes it we are wise.   *100*
Fish are we that love the mud,
 Rising to no fancy-flies.

' Name and fame! to fly sublime
 Thro' the courts, the camps, the schools,
Is to be the ball of Time,
 Bandied by the hands of fools.

' Friendship!—to be two in one—
 Let the canting liar pack!
Well I know, when I am gone,
 How she mouths behind my back.   *110*

' Virtue!—to be good and just—
 Every heart, when sifted well,
Is a clot of warmer dust,
 Mix'd with cunning sparks of hell.

' O! we two as well can look
 Whited thought and cleanly life
As the priest, above his book
 Leering at his neighbour's wife.

' Fill the cup, and fill the can:
 Have a rouse before the morn: *120*
Every moment dies a man,
 Every moment one is born.

' Drink, and let the parties rave:
    They are fill'd with idle spleen;
Rising, falling, like a wave,
    For they know not what they mean.

' He that roars for liberty
    Faster binds a tyrant's power;
And the tyrant's cruel glee
    Forces on the freër hour.   *130*

' Fill the can, and fill the cup:
    All the windy ways of men
Are but dust that rises up,
    And is lightly laid again.

' Greet her with applausive breath,
    Freedom, gaily doth she tread;
In her right a civic wreath,
    In her left a human head.

' No, I love not what is new;
    She is of an ancient house: *140*
And I think we know the hue
    Of that cap upon her brows.

' Let her go ! her thirst she slakes
    Where the bloody conduit runs,
Then her sweetest meal she makes
    On the first-born of her sons.

' Drink to lofty hopes that cool—
    Visions of a perfect State:
Drink we, last, the public fool,
    Frantic love and frantic hate.   *150*

' Chant me now some wicked stave,
    Till thy drooping courage rise,
And the glow-worm of the grave
    Glimmer in thy rheumy eyes.

' Fear not thou to loose thy tongue;
    Set thy hoary fancies free;
What is loathsome to the young
    Savours well to thee and me.

' Change, reverting to the years,
    When thy nerves could understand   *160*
What there is in loving tears,
    And the warmth of hand in hand.

' Tell me tales of thy first love—
  April hopes, the fools of chance;
Till the graves begin to move,
  And the dead begin to dance.

' Fill the can, and fill the cup:
  All the windy ways of men
Are but dust that rises up,
  And is lightly laid again.   *170*

' Trooping from their mouldy dens
  The chap-fallen circle spreads:
Welcome, fellow-citizens,
  Hollow hearts and empty heads!

' You are bones, and what of that?
  Every face, however full,
Padded round with flesh and fat,
  Is but modell'd on a skull.

' Death is king, and Vivat Rex!
  Tread a measure on the stones,   *180*
Madam—if I know your sex,
  From the fashion of your bones.

' No, I cannot praise the fire
  In your eye—nor yet your lip:
All the more do I admire
  Joints of cunning workmanship.

' Lo! God's likeness—the ground-plan—
  Neither modell'd, glazed, nor framed:
Buss me, thou rough sketch of man,
  Far too naked to be shamed!   *190*

' Drink to Fortune, drink to Chance,
  While we keep a little breath!
Drink to heavy Ignorance!
  Hob-and-nob with brother Death!

' Thou art mazed, the night is long,
  And the longer night is near:
What! I am not all as wrong
  As a bitter jest is dear.

' Youthful hopes, by scores, to all,
  When the locks are crisp and curl'd;   *200*
Unto me my maudlin gall
  And my mockeries of the world.

' Fill the cup, and fill the can :
    Mingle madness, mingle scorn !
Dregs of life, and lees of man :
    Yet we will not die forlorn.'

The voice grew faint : there came a further change :
Once more uprose the mystic mountain-range :
Below were men and horses pierced with worms,
And slowly quickening into lower forms;   *210*
By shards and scurf of salt, and scum of dross,
Old plash of rains, and refuse patch'd with moss.
Then some one spake : ' Behold ! it was a crime
Of sense avenged by sense that wore with time.'
Another said : ' The crime of sense became
The crime of malice, and is equal blame.'
And one : ' He had not wholly quench'd his power;
A little grain of conscience made him sour.'
At last I heard a voice upon the slope
Cry to the summit, ' Is there any hope ? '   *220*
To which an answer peal'd from that high land,
But in a tongue no man could understand;
And on the glimmering limit far withdrawn
God made Himself an awful rose of dawn.

'AS THRO' THE LAND ...'

As thro' the land at eve we went,
    And pluck'd the ripen'd ears,
We fell out, my wife and I,
O we fell out I know not why,
    And kiss'd again with tears.
And blessings on the falling out
      That all the more endears,
When we fall out with those we love
      And kiss again with tears!
For when we came where lies the child   *10*
    We lost in other years,
There above the little grave,
O there above the little grave,
    We kiss'd again with tears.

'SWEET AND LOW ...'

Sweet and low, sweet and low,
    Wind of the western sea,
Low, low, breathe and blow,
    Wind of the western sea!
Over the rolling waters go,
Come from the dying moon, and blow,
    Blow him again to me;
While my little one, while my pretty one, sleeps.

Sleep and rest, sleep and rest,
    Father will come to thee soon;   *10*
Rest, rest, on mother's breast,
    Father will come to thee soon;
Father will come to his babe in the nest,
Silver sails all out of the west
    Under the silver moon:
Sleep, my little one, sleep, my pretty one, sleep.

'THE SPLENDOUR FALLS ...'

The splendour falls on castle walls
    And snowy summits old in story:
The long light shakes across the lakes,
    And the wild cataract leaps in glory.
Blow, bugle, blow, set the wild echoes flying,
Blow, bugle; answer, echoes, dying, dying, dying.
    O hark, O hear! how thin and clear,
      And thinner, clearer, farther going!
    O sweet and far from cliff and scar
      The horns of Elfland faintly blowing!   *10*
Blow, let us hear the purple glens replying:
Blow, bugle; answer, echoes, dying, dying, dying.

O love, they die in yon rich sky,
  They faint on hill or field or river:
Our echoes roll from soul to soul,
  And grow for ever and for ever.
Blow, bugle, blow, set the wild echoes flying,
And answer, echoes, answer, dying, dying, dying.

'TEARS, IDLE TEARS . . .'

' Tears, idle tears, I know not what they mean,
Tears from the depth of some divine despair
Rise in the heart, and gather to the eyes,
In looking on the happy Autumn-fields,
And thinking of the days that are no more.

' Fresh as the first beam glittering on a sail,
That brings our friends up from the underworld,
Sad as the last which reddens over one
That sinks with all we love below the verge;
So sad, so fresh, the days that are no more.   *10*

' Ah, sad and strange as in dark summer dawns
The earliest pipe of half-awaken'd birds
To dying ears, when unto dying eyes
The casement slowly grows a glimmering square;
So sad, so strange, the days that are no more.

' Dear as remember'd kisses after death,
And sweet as those by hopeless fancy feign'd
On lips that are for others; deep as love,
Deep as first love, and wild with all regret;
O Death in Life, the days that are no more.'   *10*

'HOME THEY BROUGHT HER WARRIOR . . .'

Home they brought her warrior dead:
  She nor swoon'd, nor utter'd cry:
All her maidens, watching, said,
  ' She must weep or she will die.'

Then they praised him, soft and low,
  Call'd him worthy to be loved,
Truest friend and noblest foe;
  Yet she neither spoke nor moved.

Stole a maiden from her place,
  Lightly to the warrior stept,   *10*
Took the face-cloth from the face;
  Yet she neither moved nor wept.

Rose a nurse of ninety years,
  Set his child upon her knee—
Like summer tempest came her tears—
  ' Sweet my child, I live for thee.'

'ASK ME NO MORE . . .'

Ask me no more: the moon may draw the sea;
  The cloud may stoop from heaven and take the shape
  With fold to fold, of mountain or of cape;
But O too fond, when have I answer'd thee?
          Ask me no more.

Ask me no more: what answer should I give?
  I love not hollow cheek or faded eye:
  Yet, O·my friend, I will not have thee die!
Ask me no more, lest I should bid thee live;
          Ask me no more.   *10*

Ask me no more: thy fate and mine are seal'd:
  I strove against the stream and all in vain:
  Let the great river take me to the main:
No more, dear love, for at a touch I yield;
          Ask me no more.

'NOW SLEEPS THE CRIMSON PETAL . . .'

  ' Now sleeps the crimson petal, now the white;
Nor waves the cypress in the palace walk;
Nor winks the gold fin in the porphyry font:
The fire-fly wakens: waken thou with me.

  Now droops the milkwhite peacock like a ghost,
And like a ghost she glimmers on to me.

  Now lies the Earth all Danaë to the stars,
And all thy heart lies open unto me.

  Now slides the silent meteor on, and leaves
A shining furrow, as thy thoughts in me.   *10*

  Now folds the lily all her sweetness up,
And slips into the bosom of the lake:
So fold thyself, my dearest, thou, and slip
Into my bosom and be lost in me.'

'COME DOWN, O MAID . . .'

  ' Come down, O maid, from yonder mountain height:
What pleasure lives in height (the shepherd sang)
In height and cold, the splendour of the hills?
But cease to move so near the Heavens, and cease
To glide a sunbeam by the blasted Pine,
To sit a star upon the sparkling spire;
And come, for Love is of the valley, come,
For Love is of the valley, come thou down

And find him; by the happy threshold, he,
Or hand in hand with Plenty in the maize,   *10*
Or red with spirted purple of the vats,
Or foxlike in the vine; nor cares to walk
With Death and Morning on the silver horns,
Nor wilt thou snare him in the white ravine,
Nor find him dropt upon the firths of ice,
That huddling slant in furrow-cloven falls
To roll the torrent out of dusky doors:
But follow; let the torrent dance thee down
To find him in the valley; let the wild
Lean-headed Eagles yelp alone, and leave   *20*
The monstrous ledges there to slope, and spill
Their thousand wreaths of dangling water-smoke,
That like a broken purpose waste in air:
So waste not thou; but come; for all the vales
Await thee; azure pillars of the hearth
Arise to thee; the children call, and I
Thy shepherd pipe, and sweet is every sound,
Sweeter thy voice, but every sound is sweet;
Myriads of rivulets hurrying thro' the lawn,
The moan of doves in immemorial elms,   *30*
And murmuring of innumerable bees.'

IN MEMORIAM A. H. H.

OBIT MDCCCXXXIII

STRONG Son of God, immortal Love,
    Whom we, that have not seen thy face,
    By faith, and faith alone, embrace,
Believing where we cannot prove;

Thine are these orbs of light and shade;
    Thou madest Life in man and brute;
    Thou madest Death; and lo, Thy foot
Is on the skull which Thou hast made.

Thou wilt not leave us in the dust:
    Thou madest man, he knows not why,   *10*
    He thinks he was not made to die;
And Thou hast made him: Thou art just.

Thou seemest human and divine,
    The highest, holiest manhood, Thou:
    Our wills are ours, we know not how;
Our wills are ours, to make them Thine.

Our little systems have their day;
    They have their day and cease to be:
    They are but broken lights of Thee,
And Thou, O Lord, art more than they.   *20*

We have but faith: we cannot know;
    For knowledge is of things we see;
    And yet we trust it comes from Thee,
A beam in darkness: let it grow.

Let knowledge grow from more to more,
    But more of reverence in us dwell;
    That mind and soul, according well,
May make one music as before,

But vaster. We are fools and slight;
    We mock Thee when we do not fear: *30*
    But help thy foolish ones to bear;
Help Thy vain worlds to bear thy light.

Forgive what seem'd my sin in me;
    What seem'd my worth since I began;
    For merit lives from man to man,
And not from man, O Lord, to Thee.

Forgive my grief for one removed,
    Thy creature, whom I found so fair.
    I trust he lives in Thee, and there
I find him worthier to be loved.   *40*

Forgive these wild and wandering cries,
    Confusions of a wasted youth;
    Forgive them where they fail in truth,
And in Thy wisdom make me wise.

               1849.

I

I HELD it truth, with him who sings
    To one clear harp in divers tones,
    That men may rise on stepping-stones
Of their dead selves to higher things.

But who shall so forecast the years
    And find in loss a gain to match?
    Or reach a hand thro' time to catch
The far-off interest of tears?

Let Love clasp Grief lest both be drown'd,
    Let darkness keep her raven gloss: *10*
    Ah, sweeter to be drunk with loss,
To dance with death, to beat the ground,

Than that the victor Hours should scorn
    The long result of love, and boast,
    ' Behold the man that loved and lost,
But all he was is overworn.'

II

Old Yew, which graspest at the stones
    That name the under-lying dead,
    Thy fibres net the dreamless head,
Thy roots are wrapt about the bones.

The seasons bring the flower again,
    And bring the firstling to the flock;
    And in the dusk of thee, the clock
Beats out the little lives of men.

O not for thee the glow, the bloom,
    Who changest not in any gale,   *10*
    Nor branding summer suns avail
To touch thy thousand years of gloom:

And gazing on thee, sullen tree,
 Sick for thy stubborn hardihood,
 I seem to fail from out my blood
And grow incorporate into thee.

III

O Sorrow, cruel fellowship,
 O Priestess in the vaults of Death,
 O sweet and bitter in a breath,
What whispers from thy lying lip?

' The stars,' she whispers, ' blindly run;
 A web is wov'n across the sky;
 From out waste places comes a cry,
And murmurs from the dying sun :

' And all the phantom, Nature, stands—
 With all the music in her tone,   *10*
 A hollow echo of my own,—
A hollow form with empty hands.'

And shall I take a thing so blind,
 Embrace her as my natural good;
 Or crush her, like a vice of blood,
Upon the threshold of the mind?

IV

To Sleep I give my powers away;
 My will is bondsman to the dark;
 I sit within a helmless bark,
And with my heart I muse and say :

O heart, how fares it with thee now,
 That thou should'st fail from thy desire,
 Who scarcely darest to inquire,
' What is it makes me beat so low? '

Something it is which thou hast lost,
 Some pleasure from thine early years. *10*
 Break, thou deep vase of chilling tears,
That grief hath shaken into frost !

Such clouds of nameless trouble cross
 All night below the darken'd eyes;
 With morning wakes the will, and cries,
' Thou shalt not be the fool of loss.'

V

I sometimes hold it half a sin
　　To put in words the grief I feel;
　　For words, like Nature, half reveal
And half conceal the Soul within.

But, for the unquiet heart and brain,
　　A use in measured language lies;
　　The sad mechanic exercise,
Like dull narcotics, numbing pain.

In words, like weeds, I'll wrap me o'er,
　　Like coarsest clothes against the cold:　　　*10*
　　But that large grief which these enfold
Is given in outline and no more.

VI

One writes, that ' Other friends remain,'
　　That ' Loss is common to the race '—
　　And common is the commonplace,
And vacant chaff well meant for grain.

That loss is common would not make
　　My own less bitter, rather more:
　　Too common! Never morning wore
To evening, but some heart did break.

O father, whereso'er thou be,
　　Who pledgest now thy gallant son;　　　*10*
　　A shot, ere half thy draught be done,
Hath still'd the life that beat from thee.

O mother, praying God will save
　　Thy sailor,—while thy head is bow'd,
　　His heavy-shotted hammock-shroud
Drops in his vast and wandering grave.

Ye know no more than I who wrought
　　At that last hour to please him well;
　　Who mused on all I had to tell,
And something written, something thought;　　　*20*

Expecting still his advent home;
　　And ever met him on his way
　　With wishes, thinking, ' here to-day,'
Or ' here to-morrow will he come.'

O somewhere, meek, unconscious dove,
    That sittest ranging golden hair;
    And glad to find thyself so fair,
Poor child, that waitest for thy love!

For now her father's chimney glows
    In expectation of a guest;   *30*
    And thinking ' this will please him best,'
She takes a riband or a rose;

For he will see them on to-night;
    And with the thought her colour burns;
    And, having left the glass, she turns
Once more to set a ringlet right;

And, even when she turn'd, the curse
    Had fallen, and her future Lord
    Was drown'd in passing thro' the ford,
Or kill'd in falling from his horse.   *40*

O what to her shall be the end?
    And what to me remains of good?
    To her, perpetual maidenhood,
And unto me no second friend.

VII

Dark house, by which once more I stand
    Here in the long unlovely street,
    Doors, where my heart was used to beat
So quickly, waiting for a hand,

A hand that can be clasp'd no more—
    Behold me, for I cannot sleep,
    And like a guilty thing I creep
At earliest morning to the door.

He is not here; but far away
    The noise of life begins again,   *10*
    And ghastly thro' the drizzling rain
On the bald street breaks the blank day.

VIII

A happy lover who has come
    To look on her that loves him well, ,
    Who 'lights and rings the gateway bell,
And learns her gone and far from home;

He saddens, all the magic light
    Dies off at once from bower and hall,
    And all the place is dark, and all
The chambers emptied of delight:

So find I every pleasant spot
    In which we two were wont to meet,   *10*
    The field, the chamber and the street,
For all is dark where thou art not.

Yet as that other, wandering there
    In those deserted walks, may find
    A flower beat with rain and wind,
Which once she foster'd up with care;

So seems it in my deep regret,
    O my forsaken heart, with thee
    And this poor flower of poesy
Which little cared for fades not yet.   *20*

But since it pleased a vanish'd eye,
    I go to plant it on his tomb,
    That if it can it there may bloom,
Or dying, there at least may die.

IX

Fair ship, that from the Italian shore
    Sailest the placid ocean-plains
    With my lost Arthur's loved remains,
Spread thy full wings, and waft him o'er.

So draw him home to those that mourn
    In vain; a favourable speed
    Ruffle thy mirror'd mast, and lead
Thro' prosperous floods his holy urn.

All night no ruder air perplex
    Thy sliding keel, till Phosphor, bright   *10*
    As our pure love, thro' early light
Shall glimmer on the dewy decks.

Sphere all your lights around, above;
    Sleep, gentle heavens, before the prow;
    Sleep, gentle winds, as he sleeps now,
My friend, the brother of my love;

My Arthur, whom I shall not see
    Till all my widow'd race be run;
    Dear as the mother to the son,
More than my brothers are to me.   *20*

x

I hear the noise about thy keel;
    I hear the bell struck in the night:
    I see the cabin-window bright;
I see the sailor at the wheel.

Thou bring'st the sailor to his wife,
    And travell'd men from foreign lands;
    And letters unto trembling hands;
And, thy dark freight, a vanish'd life.

So bring him: we have idle dreams:
    This look of quiet flatters thus   *10*
    Our home-bred fancies: O to us,
The fools of habit, sweeter seems

To rest beneath the clover sod,
    That takes the sunshine and the rains,
    Or where the kneeling hamlet drains
The chalice of the grapes of God;

Than if with thee the roaring wells
    Should gulf him fathom-deep in brine;
    And hands so often clasp'd in mine,
Should toss with tangle and with shells.   *20*

XI

Calm is the morn without a sound,
    Calm as to suit a calmer grief,
    And only thro' the faded leaf
The chestnut pattering to the ground:

Calm and deep peace on this high wold,
    And on these dews that drench the furze,
    And all the silvery gossamers
That twinkle into green and gold:

Calm and still light on yon great plain
    That sweeps with all its autumn bowers,   *10*
    And crowded farms and lessening towers,
To mingle with the bounding main:

Calm and deep peace in this wide air,
    These leaves that redden to the fall;
    And in my heart, if calm at all,
If any calm, a calm despair:

Calm on the seas, and silver sleep,
    And waves that sway themselves in rest,
    And dead calm in that noble breast   20
Which heaves but with the heaving deep.

XII

Lo, as a dove when up she springs
    To bear thro' Heaven a tale of woe,
    Some dolorous message knit below
The wild pulsation of her wings;

Like her I go; I cannot stay;
    I leave this mortal ark behind,
    A weight of nerves without a mind,
And leave the cliffs, and haste away

O'er ocean-mirrors rounded large,   10
    And reach the glow of southern skies,
    And see the sails at distance rise,
And linger weeping on the marge,

And saying; ' Comes he thus, my friend?
    Is this the end of all my care?'
    And circle moaning in the air:
' Is this the end? Is this the end?'

And forward dart again, and play
    About the prow, and back return
    To where the body sits, and learn   20
That I have been an hour away.

XIII

Tears of the widower, when he sees
    A late-lost form that sleep reveals,
    And moves his doubtful arms, and feels
Her place is empty, fall like these;

Which weep a loss for ever new,
    A void where heart on heart reposed;
    And, where warm hands have prest and closed,
Silence, till I be silent too.

Which weep the comrade of my choice,
 An awful thought, a life removed,
  The human-hearted man I loved,   *10*
A Spirit, not a breathing voice.

Come Time, and teach me, many years,
 I do not suffer in a dream;
  For now so strange do these things seem,
Mine eyes have leisure for their tears;

My fancies time to rise on wing,
 And glance about the approaching sails,
  As tho' they brought but merchants' bales,
And not the burthen that they bring.   *20*

XIV

If one should bring me this report,
 That thou hadst touch'd the land to-day,
  And I went down unto the quay,
And found thee lying in the port;

And standing, muffled round with woe,
 Should see thy passengers in rank
  Come stepping lightly down the plank,
And beckoning unto those they know;

And if along with these should come
 The man I held as half-divine;   *10*
  Should strike a sudden hand in mine,
And ask a thousand things of home;

And I should tell him all my pain,
 And how my life had droop'd of late,
  And he should sorrow o'er my state
And marvel what possess'd my brain;

And I perceived no touch of change,
 No hint of death in all his frame,
  But found him all in all the same,
I should not feel it to be strange.   *20*

XV

To-night the winds begin to rise
 And roar from yonder dropping day:
  The last red leaf is whirl'd away,
The rooks are blown about the skies;

The forest crack'd, the waters curl'd,
    The cattle huddled on the lea;
    And wildly dash'd on tower and tree
The sunbeam strikes along the world:

And but for fancies, which aver
    That all thy motions gently pass   *10*
    Athwart a plane of molten glass,
I scarce could brook the strain and stir

That makes the barren branches loud;
    And but for fear it is not so,
    The wild unrest that lives in woe
Would dote and pore on yonder cloud

That rises upward always higher,
    And onward drags a labouring breast,
    And topples round the dreary west,
A looming bastion fringed with fire.   *20*

XVI

What words are these have fall'n from me?
    Can calm despair and wild unrest
    Be tenants of a single breast,
Or sorrow such a changeling be?

Or doth she only seem to take
    The touch of change in calm or storm;
    But knows no more of transient form
In her deep self, than some dead lake

That holds the shadow of a lark
    Hung in the shadow of a heaven?   *10*
    Or has the shock, so harshly given,
Confused me like the unhappy bark

That strikes by night a craggy shelf,
    And staggers blindly ere she sink?
    And stunn'd me from my power to think
And all my knowledge of myself;

And made me that delirious man
    Whose fancy fuses old and new,
    And flashes into false and true,
And mingles all without a plan?   *20*

XVII

Thou comest, much wept for: such a breeze
    Compell'd thy canvas, and my prayer
    Was as the whisper of an air
To breathe thee over lonely seas.

For I in spirit saw thee move
    Thro' circles of the bounding sky,
    Week after week: the days go by:
Come quick, thou bringest all I love.

Henceforth, wherever thou may'st roam,
    My blessing, like a line of light,   *10*
    Is on the waters day and night,
And like a beacon guards thee home.

So may whatever tempest mars
    Mid-ocean, spare thee, sacred bark;
    And balmy drops in summer dark
Slide from the bosom of the stars.

So kind an office hath been done,
    Such precious relics brought by thee;
    The dust of him I shall not see
Till all my widow'd race be run.   *20*

XVIII

'Tis well; 'tis something; we may stand
    Where he in English earth is laid,
    And from his ashes may be made
The violet of his native land.

'Tis little; but it looks in truth
    As if the quiet bones were blest
    Among familiar names to rest
And in the places of his youth.

Come then, pure hands, and bear the head
    That sleeps or wears the mask of sleep,   *10*
    And come, whatever loves to weep,
And hear the ritual of the dead.

Ah yet, ev'n yet, if this might be,
    I, falling on his faithful heart,
    Would breathing thro' his lips impart
The life that almost dies in me;

That dies not, but endures with pain,
    And slowly forms the firmer mind,
    Treasuring the look it cannot find,
The words that are not heard again.   *20*

XIX

The Danube to the Severn gave
    The darken'd heart that beat no more;
    They laid him by the pleasant shore,
And in the hearing of the wave.

There twice a day the Severn fills;
    The salt sea-water passes by,
    And hushes half the babbling Wye,
And makes a silence in the hills.

The Wye is hush'd nor moved along,
    And hush'd my deepest grief of all,   *10*
    When fill'd with tears that cannot fall,
I brim with sorrow drowning song.

The tide flows down, the wave again
    Is vocal in its wooded walls;
    My deeper anguish also falls,
And I can speak a little then.

XX

The lesser griefs that may be said,
    That breathe a thousand tender vows,
    Are but as servants in a house
Where lies the master newly dead;

Who speak their feeling as it is,
    And weep the fullness from the mind:
    ' It will be hard,' they say, ' to find
Another service such as this.'

My lighter moods are like to these,
    That out of words a comfort win;   *10*
    But there are other griefs within,
And tears that at their fountain freeze;

For by the hearth the children sit
    Cold in that atmosphere of Death,
    And scarce endure to draw the breath,
Or like to noiseless phantoms flit:

But open converse is there none,
    So much the vital spirits sink
    To see the vacant chair, and think,
'How good! how kind! and he is gone.'   *20*

XXI

I sing to him that rests below,
    And, since the grasses round me wave,
    I take the grasses of the grave,
And make them pipes whereon to blow.

The traveller hears me now and then,
    And sometimes harshly will he speak:
    ' This fellow would make weakness weak,
And melt the waxen hearts of men.'

Another answers, ' Let him be,
    He loves to make parade of pain,   *10*
    That with his piping he may gain
The praise that comes to constancy.'

A third is wroth: ' Is this an hour
    For private sorrow's barren song,
    When more and more the people throng
The chairs and thrones of civil power?

' A time to sicken and to swoon,
    When Science reaches forth her arms
    To feel from world to world, and charms
Her secret from the latest moon?'   *20*

Behold, ye speak an idle thing:
    Ye never knew the sacred dust:
    I do but sing because I must,
And pipe but as the linnets sing:

And one is glad; her note is gay,
    For now her little ones have ranged;
    And one is sad; her note is changed,
Because her brood is stol'n away.

XXII

The path by which we twain did go,
    Which led by tracts that pleased us well,
    Thro' four sweet years arose and fell,
From flower to flower, from snow to snow:

And we with singing cheer'd the way,
 And, crown'd with all the season lent,
 From April on to April went,
And glad at heart from May to May:

But where the path we walk'd began
 To slant the fifth autumnal slope,   *10*
 As we descended following Hope,
There sat the Shadow fear'd of man;

Who broke our fair companionship,
 And spread his mantle dark and cold,
 And wrapt thee formless in the fold,
And dull'd the murmur on thy lip,

And bore thee where I could not see
 Nor follow, tho' I walk in haste,
 And think, that somewhere in the waste
The Shadow sits and waits for me.   *20*

XXIII

Now, sometimes in my sorrow shut,
 Or breaking into song by fits,
 Alone, alone, to where he sits,
The Shadow cloak'd from head to foot,

Who keeps the keys of all the creeds,
 I wander, often falling lame,
 And looking back to whence I came,
Or on to where the pathway leads;

And crying, How changed from where it ran
 Thro' lands where not a leaf was dumb;   *10*
 But all the lavish hills would hum
The murmur of a happy Pan:

When each by turns was guide to each,
 And Fancy light from Fancy caught,
 And Thought leapt out to wed with Thought
Ere Thought could wed itself with Speech;

And all we met was fair and good,
 And all was good that Time could bring,
 And all the secret of the Spring
Moved in the chambers of the blood;   *20*

And many an old philosophy
    On Argive heights divinely sang,
    And round us all the thicket rang
To many a flute of Arcady.

XXIV

And was the day of my delight
    As pure and perfect as I say?
    The very source and fount of Day
Is dash'd with wandering isles of night.

If all was good and fair we met,
    This earth had been the Paradise
    It never look'd to human eyes
Since our first Sun arose and set.

And is it that the haze of grief
    Makes former gladness loom so great?   *10*
    The lowness of the present state,
That sets the past in this relief?

Or that the past will always win
    A glory from its being far;
    And orb into the perfect star
We saw not, when we moved therein?

XXV

I know that this was Life,—the track
    Whereon with equal feet we fared;
    And then, as now, the day prepared
The daily burden for the back.

But this it was that made me move
    As light as carrier-birds in air;
    I loved the weight I had to bear,
Because it needed help of Love:

Nor could I weary, heart or limb,
    When mighty Love would cleave in twain   *10*
    The lading of a single pain,
And part it, giving half to him.

XXVI

Still onward winds the dreary way;
    I with it; for I long to prove
    No lapse of moons can canker Love,
Whatever fickle tongues may say.

And if that eye which watches guilt
    And goodness, and hath power to see
    Within the green the moulder'd tree,
And towers fall'n as soon as built—

Oh, if indeed that eye foresee
    Or see (in Him is no before)   *10*
    In more of life true life no more
And Love the indifference to be,

Then might I find, ere yet the morn
    Breaks hither over Indian seas,
    That Shadow waiting with the keys,
To shroud me from my proper scorn.

XXVII

I envy not in any moods
    The captive void of noble rage,
    The linnet born within the cage,
That never knew the summer woods:

I envy not the beast that takes
    His license in the field of time,
    Unfetter'd by the sense of crime,
To whom a conscience never wakes;

Nor, what may count itself as blest,
    The heart that never plighted troth   *10*
    But stagnates in the weeds of sloth;
Nor any want-begotten rest.

I hold it true, whate'er befall;
    I feel it, when I sorrow most;
    'Tis better to have loved and lost
Than never to have loved at all.

XXVIII

The time draws near the birth of Christ:
    The moon is hid; the night is still;
    The Christmas bells from hill to hill
Answer each other in the mist.

Four voices of four hamlets round,
    From far and near, on mead and moor,
    Swell out and fail, as if a door
Were shut between me and the sound:

Each voice four changes on the wind,
    That now dilate, and now decrease,   *10*
    Peace and goodwill, goodwill and peace,
Peace and goodwill, to all mankind.

This year I slept and woke with pain,
    I almost wish'd no more to wake,
    And that my hold on life would break
Before I heard those bells again:

But they my troubled spirit rule,
    For they controll'd me when a boy;
    They bring me sorrow touch'd with joy,
The merry merry bells of Yule.   *20*

XXIX

With such compelling cause to grieve
    As daily vexes household peace,
    And chains regret to his decease,
How dare we keep our Christmas-eve;

Which brings no more a welcome guest
    To enrich the threshold of the night
    With shower'd largess of delight
In dance and song and game and jest?

Yet go, and while the holly boughs
    Entwine the cold baptismal font,   *10*
    Make one wreath more for Use and Wont,
That guard the portals of the house;

Old sisters of a day gone by,
    Gray nurses, loving nothing new;
    Why should they miss their yearly due
Before their time? They too will die.

XXX

With trembling fingers did we weave
    The holly round the Christmas hearth;
    A rainy cloud possess'd the earth,
And sadly fell our Christmas-eve.

At our old pastimes in the hall
    We gambol'd, making vain pretence
    Of gladness, with an awful sense
Of one mute Shadow watching all.

We paused: the winds were in the beech:
    We heard them sweep the winter land;   *10*
    And in a circle hand-in-hand
Sat silent, looking each at each.

Then echo-like our voices rang;
    We sung, tho' every eye was dim,
    A merry song we sang with him
Last year: impetuously we sang:

We ceased: a gentler feeling crept
    Upon us: surely rest is meet:
    ' They rest,' we said, ' their sleep is sweet,'
And silence follow'd, and we wept.   *20*

Our voices took a higher range;
    Once more we sang: ' They do not die
    Nor lose their mortal sympathy,
Nor change to us, although they change;

' Rapt from the fickle and the frail
    With gather'd power, yet the same,
    Pierces the keen seraphic flame
From orb to orb, from veil to veil.'

Rise, happy morn, rise, holy morn,
    Draw forth the cheerful day from night: *30*
    O Father, touch the east, and light
The light that shone when Hope was born.

XXXI

When Lazarus left his charnel-cave,
    And home to Mary's house return'd,
    Was this demanded—if he yearn'd
To hear her weeping by his grave?

' Where wert thou, brother, those four days?'
    There lives no record of reply,
    Which telling what it is to die
Had surely added praise to praise.

From every house the neighbours met,
    The streets were fill'd with joyful sound,   *10*
    A solemn gladness even crown'd
The purple brows of Olivet.

Behold a man raised up by Christ!
    The rest remaineth unreveal'd;
    He told it not; or something seal'd
The lips of that Evangelist.

XXXII

Her eyes are homes of silent prayer,
    Nor other thought her mind admits
    But, he was dead, and there he sits,
And he that brought him back is there.

Then one deep love doth supersede
    All other, when her ardent gaze
    Roves from the living brother's face,
And rests upon the Life indeed.

All subtle thought, all curious fears,
    Borne down by gladness so complete,   *10*
    She bows, she bathes the Saviour's feet
With costly spikenard and with tears.

Thrice blest whose lives are faithful prayers,
    Whose loves in higher love endure;
    What souls possess themselves so pure,
Or is there blessedness like theirs?

XXXIII

O thou that after toil and storm
    Mayst seem to have reach'd a purer air,
    Whose faith has centre everywhere,
Nor cares to fix itself to form,

Leave thou thy sister when she prays,
    Her early Heaven, her happy views;
    Nor thou with shadow'd hint confuse
A life that leads melodious days.

Her faith thro' form is pure as thine,
    Her hands are quicker unto good: *10*
    Oh, sacred be the flesh and blood
To which she links a truth divine!

See thou, that countest reason ripe
    In holding by the law within,
    Thou fail not in a world of sin,
And ev'n for want of such a type.

XXXIV

My own dim life should teach me this,
    That life shall live for evermore,
    Else earth is darkness at the core,
And dust and ashes all that is;

This round of green, this orb of flame,
    Fantastic beauty; such as lurks
    In some wild Poet, when he works
Without a conscience or an aim.

What then were God to such as I?
    'Twere hardly worth my while to choose   *10*
    Of things all mortal, or to use
A little patience ere I die;

'Twere best at once to sink to peace,
    Like birds the charming serpent draws,
    To drop head-foremost in the jaws
Of vacant darkness and to cease.

XXXV

Yet if some voice that man could trust
    Should murmur from the narrow house,
    ' The cheeks drop in; the body bows;
Man dies: nor is there hope in dust:'

Might I not say? ' Yet even here,
    But for one hour, O Love, I strive
    To keep so sweet a thing alive:'
But I should turn mine ears and hear

The moanings of the homeless sea,
    The sound of streams that swift or slow   *10*
    Draw down Æonian hills, and sow
The dust of continents to be;

And Love would answer with a sigh,
    ' The sound of that forgetful shore
    Will change my sweetness more and more,
Half-dead to know that I shall die.'

O me, what profits it to put
    An idle case? If Death were seen
    At first as Death, Love had not been,   *20*
Or been in narrowest working shut,

Mere fellowship of sluggish moods,
　　Or in his coarsest Satyr-shape
　　Had bruised the herb and crush'd the grape,
And bask'd and batten'd in the woods.

XXXVI

Tho' truths in manhood darkly join,
　　Deep-seated in our mystic frame,
　　We yield all blessing to the name
Of Him that made them current coin;

For Wisdom dealt with mortal powers,
　　Where truth in closest words shall fail,
　　When truth embodied in a tale
Shall enter in at lowly doors.

And so the Word had breath, and wrought
　　With human hands the creed of creeds　　　　*10*
　　In loveliness of perfect deeds,
More strong than all poetic thought;

Which he may read that binds the sheaf,
　　Or builds the house, or digs the grave,
　　And those wild eyes that watch the wave
In roarings round the coral reef.

XXXVII

Urania speaks with darken'd brow:
　　' Thou pratest here where thou art least;
　　This faith has many a purer priest,
And many an abler voice than thou.

' Go down beside thy native rill,
　　On thy Parnassus set thy feet,
　　And hear thy laurel whisper sweet
About the ledges of the hill.'

And my Melpomene replies,
　　A touch of shame upon her cheek:　　　　*10*
　　' I am not worthy ev'n to speak
Of thy prevailing mysteries;

' For I am but an earthly Muse,
　　And owning but a little art
　　To lull with song an aching heart,
And render human love his dues;

' But brooding on the dear one dead,
    And all he said of things divine,
    (And dear to me as sacred wine
To dying lips is all he said)   *20*

' I murmur'd, as I came along,
    Of comfort clasp'd in truth reveal'd;
    And loiter'd in the master's field,
And darken'd sanctities with song.'

XXXVIII

With weary steps I loiter on,
    Tho' always under alter'd skies
    The purple from the distance dies,
My prospect and horizon gone.

No joy the blowing season gives,
    The herald melodies of spring,
    But in the songs I love to sing
A doubtful gleam of solace lives.

If any care for what is here
    Survive in spirits render'd free,   *10*
    Then are these songs I sing of thee
Not all ungrateful to thine ear.

XXXIX

Old warder of these buried bones,
    And answering now my random stroke
    With fruitful cloud and living smoke,
Dark yew, that graspest at the stones

And dippest toward the dreamless head,
    To thee too comes the golden hour
    When flower is feeling after flower;
But Sorrow—fixt upon the dead,

And darkening the dark graves of men,—
    What whisper'd from her lying lips?   *10*
    Thy gloom is kindled at the tips,
And passes into gloom again.

XL

Could we forget the widow'd hour
    And look on Spirits breathed away,
    As on a maiden in the day
When first she wears her orange-flower !

When crown'd with blessing she doth rise
    To take her latest leave of home,
    And hopes and light regrets that come
Make April of her tender eyes;

And doubtful joys the father move,
    And tears are on the mother's face,   *10*
    As parting with a long embrace
She enters other realms of love;

Her office there to rear, to teach,
    Becoming as is meet and fit
    A link among the days, to knit
The generations each with each;

And, doubtless, unto thee is given
    A life that bears immortal fruit
    In those great offices that suit
The full-grown energies of heaven.   *20*

Ay me, the difference I discern!
    How often shall her old fireside
    Be cheer'd with tidings of the bride,
How often she herself return,

And tell them all they would have told,
    And bring her babe, and make her boast,
    Till even those that miss'd her most
Shall count new things as dear as old:

But thou and I have shaken hands,
    Till growing winters lay me low;   *30*
    My paths are in the fields I know,
And thine in undiscover'd lands.

XLI

Thy spirit ere our fatal loss
    Did ever rise from high to higher;
    As mounts the heavenward altar-fire,
As flies the lighter thro' the gross.

But thou art turn'd to something strange,
    And I have lost the links that bound
    Thy changes; here upon the ground,
No more partaker of thy change.

Deep folly! yet that this could be—
    That I could wing my will with might   *10*
    To leap the grades of life and light,
And flash at once, my friend, to thee.

For tho' my nature rarely yields
    To that vague fear implied in death;
    Nor shudders at the gulfs beneath,
The howlings from forgotten fields;

Yet oft when sundown skirts the moor
    An inner trouble I behold,
    A spectral doubt which makes me cold,
That I shall be thy mate no more,   *20*

Tho' following with an upward mind
    The wonders that have come to thee,
    Thro' all the secular to-be,
But evermore a life behind.

XLII

I vex my heart with fancies dim:
    He still outstript me in the race;
    It was but unity of place
That made me dream I rank'd with him.

And so may Place retain us still,
    And he the much-beloved again,
    A lord of large experience, train
To riper growth the mind and will:

And what delights can equal those
    That stir the spirit's inner deeps,   *10*
    When one that loves but knows not, reaps
A truth from one that loves and knows?

XLIII

If Sleep and Death be truly one,
    And every spirit's folded bloom
    Thro' all its intervital gloom
In some long trance should slumber on;

Unconscious of the sliding hour,
    Bare of the body, might it last,
    And silent traces of the past
Be all the colour of the flower:

So then were nothing lost to man;
    So that still garden of the souls   *10*
    In many a figured leaf enrolls
The total world since life began;

And love will last as pure and whole
    As when he loved me here in Time,
    And at the spiritual prime
Rewaken with the dawning soul.

XLIV

How fares it with the happy dead?
    For here the man is more and more;
    But he forgets the days before
God shut the doorways of his head.

The days have vanish'd, tone and tint,
    And yet perhaps the hoarding sense
    Gives out at times (he knows not whence)
A little flash, a mystic hint;

And in the long harmonious years
    (If Death so taste Lethean springs),   *10*
    May some dim touch of earthly things
Surprise thee ranging with thy peers.

If such a dreamy touch should fall,
    O turn thee round, resolve the doubt;
    My guardian angel will speak out
In that high place, and tell thee all.

XLV

The baby new to earth and sky,
    What time his tender palm is prest
    Against the circle of the breast,
Has never thought that ' this is I : '

But as he grows he gathers much,
    And learns the use of ' I,' and ' me,'
    And finds ' I am not what I see,
And other than the things I touch.'

So rounds he to a separate mind
    From whence clear memory may begin,   *10*
    As thro' the frame that binds him in
His isolation grows defined.

This use may lie in blood and breath,
    Which else were fruitless of their due,
    Had man to learn himself anew
Beyond the second birth of Death.

XLVI

We ranging down this lower track,
    The path we came by, thorn and flower,
    Is shadow'd by the growing hour,
Lest life should fail in looking back.

So be it: there no shade can last
    In that deep dawn behind the tomb,
    But clear from marge to marge shall bloom
The eternal landscape of the past;

A lifelong tract of time reveal'd;
    The fruitful hours of still increase;   *10*
    Days order'd in a wealthy peace,
And those five years its richest field.

O Love, thy province were not large,
    A bounded field, nor stretching far;
    Look also, Love, a brooding star,
A rosy warmth from marge to marge.

XLVII

That each, who seems a separate whole,
    Should move his rounds, and fusing all
    The skirts of self again, should fall
Remerging in the general Soul,

Is faith as vague as all unsweet:
    Eternal form shall still divide
    The eternal soul from all beside;
And I shall know him when we meet:

And we shall sit at endless feast,
    Enjoying each the other's good: *10*
    What vaster dream can hit the mood
Of Love on earth? He seeks at least

Upon the last and sharpest height,
    Before the spirits fade away,
    Some landing-place, to clasp and say,
'Farewell! We lose ourselves in light.'

XLVIII

If these brief lays, of Sorrow born,
    Were taken to be such as closed
    Grave doubts and answers here proposed,
Then these were such as men might scorn:

Her care is not to part and prove;
    She takes, when harsher moods remit,
    What slender shade of doubt may flit,
And makes it vassal unto love:

And hence, indeed, she sports with words,
    But better serves a wholesome law,   *10*
    And holds it sin and shame to draw
The deepest measure from the chords:

Nor dare she trust a larger lay,
    But rather loosens from the lip
    Short swallow-flights of song, that dip
Their wings in tears, and skim away.

XLIX

From art, from nature, from the schools,
    Let random influences glance,
    Like light in many a shiver'd lance
That breaks about the dappled pools:

The lightest wave of thought shall lisp,
    The fancy's tenderest eddy wreathe,
    The slightest air of song shall breathe
To make the sullen surface crisp.

And look thy look, and go thy way,
    But blame not thou the winds that make   *10*
    The seeming-wanton ripple break,
The tender-pencil'd shadow play.

Beneath all fancied hopes and fears
    Ay me, the sorrow deepens down,
    Whose muffled motions blindly drown
The bases of my life in tears.

L

Be near me when my light is low,
    When the blood creeps, and the nerves prick
    And tingle; and the heart is sick,
And all the wheels of Being slow.

Be near me when the sensuous frame
  Is rack'd with pangs that conquer trust;
  And Time, a maniac scattering dust,
And Life, a Fury slinging flame.

Be near me when my faith is dry,
  And men the flies of latter spring,   *10*
  That lay their eggs, and sting and sing
And weave their petty cells and die.

Be near me when I fade away,
  To point the term of human strife,
  And on the low dark verge of life
The twilight of eternal day.

      LI

Do we indeed desire the dead
  Should still be near us at our side?
  Is there no baseness we would hide?
No inner vileness that we dread?

Shall he for whose applause I strove,
  I had such reverence for his blame,
  See with clear eye some hidden shame
And I be lessen'd in his love?

I wrong the grave with fears untrue:
  Shall love be blamed for want of faith? *10*
  There must be wisdom with great Death:
The dead shall look me thro' and thro'.

Be near us when we climb or fall:
  Ye watch, like God, the rolling hours
  With larger other eyes than ours,
To make allowance for us all.

      LII

I cannot love thee as I ought,
  For love reflects the thing beloved;
  My words are only words, and moved
Upon the topmost froth of thought.

' Yet blame not thou thy plaintive song,'
  The Spirit of true love replied;
  ' Thou canst not move me from thy side,
Nor human frailty do me wrong.

' What keeps a spirit wholly true
　　To that ideal which he bears?
　　What record? not the sinless years
That breathed beneath the Syrian blue:

' So fret not, like an idle girl,
　　That life is dash'd with flecks of sin.
　　Abide: thy wealth is gather'd in,
When Time hath sunder'd shell from pearl.'

10

LIII

How many a father have I seen,
　　A sober man, among his boys,
　　Whose youth was full of foolish noise,
Who wears his manhood hale and green:

And dare we to this fancy give,
　　That had the wild oat not been sown,
　　The soil, left barren, scarce had grown
The grain by which a man may live?

Or, if we held the doctrine sound
　　For life outliving heats of youth,
　　Yet who would preach it as a truth
To those that eddy round and round?

10

Hold thou the good: define it well:
　　For fear divine Philosophy
　　Should push beyond her mark, and be
Procuress to the Lords of Hell.

LIV

Oh yet we trust that somehow good
　　Will be the final goal of ill,
　　To pangs of nature, sins of will,
Defects of doubt, and taints of blood;

That nothing walks with aimless feet;
　　That not one life shall be destroy'd,
　　Or cast as rubbish to the void,
When God hath made the pile complete;

That not a worm is cloven in vain;
　　That not a moth with vain desire
　　Is shrivell'd in a fruitless fire,
Or but subserves another's gain.

10

Behold, we know not anything;
    I can but trust that good shall fall
    At last—far off—at last, to all,
And every winter change to spring.

So runs my dream: but what am I?
    An infant crying in the night:
    An infant crying for the light:
And with no language but a cry.   20

LV

The wish, that of the living whole
    No life may fail beyond the grave,
    Derives it not from what we have
The likest God within the soul?

Are God and Nature then at strife,
    That Nature lends such evil dreams?
    So careful of the type she seems,
So careless of the single life;

That I, considering everywhere
    Her secret meaning in her deeds,   10
    And finding that of fifty seeds
She often brings but one to bear,

I falter where I firmly trod,
    And falling with my weight of cares
    Upon the great world's altar-stairs
That slope thro' darkness up to God,

I stretch lame hands of faith, and grope,
    And gather dust and chaff, and call
    To what I feel is Lord of all,
And faintly trust the larger hope.   20

LVI

' So careful of the type?' but no.
    From scarped cliff and quarried stone
    She cries, ' A thousand types are gone:
I care for nothing, all shall go.

' Thou makest thine appeal to me:
    I bring to life, I bring to death:
    The spirit does but mean the breath:
I know no more.'   And he, shall he,

Man, her last work, who seem'd so fair,
    Such splendid purpose in his eyes,   *10*
    Who roll'd the psalm to wintry skies,
Who built him fanes of fruitless prayer,

Who trusted God was love indeed
    And love Creation's final law—
    Tho' Nature, red in tooth and claw
With ravine, shriek'd against his creed—

Who loved, who suffer'd countless ills,
    Who battled for the True, the Just,
    Be blown about the desert dust,
Or seal'd within the iron hills?   *20*

No more?   A monster then, a dream,
    A discord.   Dragons of the prime,
    That tare each other in their slime,
Were mellow music match'd with him.

O life as futile, then, as frail!
    O for thy voice to soothe and bless!
    What hope of answer, or redress?
Behind the veil, behind the veil.

LVII

Peace; come away: the song of woe
    Is after all an earthly song:
    Peace; come away: we do him wrong
To sing so wildly: let us go.

Come; let us go: your cheeks are pale;
    But half my life I leave behind:
    Methinks my friend is richly shrined;
But I shall pass; my work will fail.

Yet in these ears, till hearing dies,
    One set slow bell will seem to toll   *10*
    The passing of the sweetest soul
That ever look'd with human eyes.

I hear it now, and o'er and o'er,
    Eternal greetings to the dead;
    And ' Ave, Ave, Ave,' said,
' Adieu, adieu ' for evermore.

LVIII

In those sad words I took farewell:
    Like echoes in sepulchral halls,
    As drop by drop the water falls
In vaults and catacombs, they fell;

And, falling, idly broke the peace
    Of hearts that beat from day to day,
    Half-conscious of their dying clay,
And those cold crypts where they shall cease.

The high Muse answer'd: ' Wherefore grieve
    Thy brethren with a fruitless tear?   *10*
    Abide a little longer here,
And thou shalt take a nobler leave.'

LIX

O Sorrow, wilt thou live with me
    No casual mistress, but a wife,
    My bosom-friend and half of life;
As I confess it needs must be;

O Sorrow, wilt thou rule my blood,
    Be sometimes lovely like a bride,
    And put thy harsher moods aside,
If thou wilt have me wise and good.

My centred passion cannot move,
    Nor will it lessen from to-day;   *10*
    But I'll have leave at times to play
As with the creature of my love;

And set thee forth, for thou art mine,
    With so much hope for years to come,
    That, howsoe'er I know thee, some
Could hardly tell what name were thine.

LX

He past; a soul of nobler tone:
    My spirit loved and loves him yet,
    Like some poor girl whose heart is set
On one whose rank exceeds her own.

He mixing with his proper sphere,
    She finds the baseness of her lot,
    Half jealous of she knows not what,
And envying all that meet him there.

The little village looks forlorn;
    She sighs amid her narrow days,   *10*
    Moving about the household ways,
In that dark house where she was born.

The foolish neighbours come and go,
    And tease her till the day draws by:
    At night she weeps, ' How vain am I !
How should he love a thing so low?'

LXI

If, in thy second state sublime,
    Thy ransom'd reason change replies
    With all the circle of the wise,
The perfect flower of human time;

And if thou cast thine eyes below,
    How dimly character'd and slight,
    How dwarf'd a growth of cold and night,
How blanch'd with darkness must I grow!

Yet turn thee to the doubtful shore,
    Where thy first form was made a man;   *10*
    I loved thee, Spirit, and love, nor can
The soul of Shakspeare love thee more.

LXII

Tho' if an eye that's downward cast
    Could make thee somewhat blench or fail,
    Then be my love an idle tale,
And fading legend of the past;

And thou, as one that once declined,
    When he was little more than boy,
    On some unworthy heart with joy,
But lives to wed an equal mind;

And breathes a novel world, the while
    His other passion wholly dies,   *10*
    Or in the light of deeper eyes
Is matter for a flying smile.

LXIII

Yet pity for a horse o'er-driven,
    And love in which my hound has part,
    Can hang no weight upon my heart
In its assumptions up to heaven;

And I am so much more than these,
    As thou, perchance, art more than I,
    And yet I spare them sympathy,
And I would set their pains at ease.

So mayst thou watch me where I weep,
    As, unto vaster motions bound,   *10*
    The circuits of thine orbit round
A higher height, a deeper deep.

LXIV

Dost thou look back on what hath been,
    As some divinely gifted man,
    Whose life in low estate began
And on a simple village green;

Who breaks his birth's invidious bar,
    And grasps the skirts of happy chance,
    And breasts the blows of circumstance,
And grapples with his evil star;

Who makes by force his merit known
    And lives to clutch the golden keys,   *10*
    To mould a mighty state's decrees,
And shape the whisper of the throne;

And moving up from high to higher,
    Becomes on Fortune's crowning slope
    The pillar of a people's hope,
The centre of a world's desire;

Yet feels, as in a pensive dream,
    When all his active powers are still,
    A distant dearness in the hill,
A secret sweetness in the stream,   *20*

The limit of his narrower fate,
    While yet beside its vocal springs
    He play'd at counsellors and kings,
With one that was his earliest mate;

Who ploughs with pain his native lea
    And reaps the labour of his hands,
    Or in the furrow musing stands;
' Does my old friend remember me? '

LXV

Sweet soul, do with me as thou wilt;
    I lull a fancy trouble-tost
      With 'Love's too precious to be lost,
A little grain shall not be spilt.'

And in that solace can I sing,
    Till out of painful phases wrought
      There flutters up a happy thought,
Self-balanced on a lightsome wing:

Since we deserved the name of friends,
    And thine effect so lives in me,   *10*
      A part of mine may live in thee
And move thee on to noble ends.

LXVI

You thought my heart too far diseased;
    You wonder when my fancies play
      To find me gay among the gay,
Like one with any trifle pleased.

The shade by which my life was crost,
    Which makes a desert in the mind,
      Has made me kindly with my kind,
And like to him whose sight is lost;

Whose feet are guided thro' the land,
    Whose jest among his friends is free,   *10*
      Who takes the children on his knee,
And winds their curls about his hand:

He plays with threads, he beats his chair
    For pastime, dreaming of the sky;
      His inner day can never die,
His night of loss is always there.

LXVII

When on my bed the moonlight falls,
    I know that in thy place of rest
      By that broad water of the west,
There comes a glory on the walls:

Thy marble bright in dark appears,
    As slowly steals a silver flame
      Along the letters of thy name,
And o'er the number of thy years.

The mystic glory swims away;
    From off my bed the moonlight dies;   *10*
    And closing eaves of wearied eyes
I sleep till dusk is dipt in gray:

And then I know the mist is drawn
    A lucid veil from coast to coast,
    And in the dark church like a ghost
Thy tablet glimmers to the dawn.

LXVIII

When in the down I sink my head,
    Sleep, Death's twin-brother, times my breath;
    Sleep, Death's twin-brother, knows not Death,
Nor can I dream of thee as dead:

I walk as ere I walk'd forlorn,
    When all our path was fresh with dew,
    And all the bugle breezes blew
Reveillée to the breaking morn.

But what is this? I turn about,
    I find a trouble in thine eye,   *10*
    Which makes me sad I know not why,
Nor can my dream resolve the doubt:

But ere the lark hath left the lea
    I wake, and I discern the truth;
    It is the trouble of my youth
That foolish sleep transfers to thee.

LXIX

I dream'd there would be Spring no more,
    That Nature's ancient power was lost:
    The streets were black with smoke and frost,
They chatter'd trifles at the door:

I wander'd from the noisy town,
    I found a wood with thorny boughs:
    I took the thorns to bind my brows,
I wore them like a civic crown:

I met with scoffs, I met with scorns
    From youth and babe and hoary hairs: *10*
    They call'd me in the public squares
The fool that wears a crown of thorns:

They call'd me fool, they call'd me child:
    I found an angel of the night;
    The voice was low, the look was bright;
He look'd upon my crown and smiled:

He reach'd the glory of a hand,
    That seem'd to touch it into leaf:
    The voice was not the voice of grief,
The words were hard to understand.   *20*

LXX

I cannot see the features right,
    When on the gloom I strive to paint
    The face I know; the hues are faint
And mix with hollow masks of night;

Cloud-towers by ghostly masons wrought,
    A gulf that ever shuts and gapes,
    A hand that points, and palled shapes
In shadowy thoroughfares of thought;

And crowds that stream from yawning doors,
    And shoals of pucker'd faces drive;   *10*
    Dark bulks that tumble half alive,
And lazy lengths on boundless shores;

Till all at once beyond the will
    I hear a wizard music roll,
    And thro' a lattice on the soul
Looks thy fair face and makes it still.

LXXI

Sleep, kinsman thou to death and trance
    And madness, thou hast forged at last
    A night-long Present of the Past
In which we went thro' summer France.

Hadst thou such credit with the soul?
    Then bring an opiate trebly strong,
    Drug down the blindfold sense of wrong
That so my pleasure may be whole;

While now we talk as once we talk'd
    Of men and minds, the dust of change,   *10*
    The days that grow to something strange,
In walking as of old we walk'd

Beside the river's wooded reach,
    The fortress, and the mountain ridge,
    The cataract flashing from the bridge,
The breaker breaking on the beach.

LXXII

Risest thou thus, dim dawn, again,
    And howlest, issuing out of night,
    With blasts that blow the poplar white,
And lash with storm the streaming pane?

Day, when my crown'd estate begun
    To pine in that reverse of doom,
    Which sicken'd every living bloom,
And blurr'd the splendour of the sun;

Who usherest in the dolorous hour
    With thy quick tears that make the rose   10
    Pull sideways, and the daisy close
Her crimson fringes to the shower;

Who might'st have heaved a windless flame
    Up the deep East, or, whispering, play'd
    A chequer-work of beam and shade
Along the hills, yet look'd the same.

As wan, as chill, as wild as now;
    Day, mark'd as with some hideous crime,
    When the dark hand struck down thro' time,
And cancell'd nature's best: but thou,   20

Lift as thou may'st thy burthen'd brows
    Thro' clouds that drench the morning star,
    And whirl the ungarner'd sheaf afar,
And sow the sky with flying boughs,

And up thy vault with roaring sound
    Climb thy thick noon, disastrous day;
    Touch thy dull goal of joyless gray,
And hide thy shame beneath the ground.

LXXIII

So many worlds, so much to do,
    So little done, such things to be,
    How know I what had need of thee,
For thou wert strong as thou wert true?

The fame is quench'd that I foresaw,
    The head hath miss'd an earthly wreath:
    I curse not nature, no, nor death;
For nothing is that errs from law.

We pass; the path that each man trod
    Is dim, or will be dim, with weeds: *10*
    What fame is left for human deeds
In endless age?   It rests with God.

O hollow wraith of dying fame,
    Fade wholly, while the soul exults,
    And self-infolds the large results
Of force that would have forged a name.

LXXIV

As sometimes in a dead man's face,
    To those that watch it more and more,
    A likeness, hardly seen before,
Comes out—to some one of his race:

So, dearest, now thy brows are cold,
    I see thee what thou art, and know
    Thy likeness to the wise below,
Thy kindred with the great of old.

But there is more than I can see,
    And what I see I leave unsaid,   *10*
    Nor speak it, knowing Death has made
His darkness beautiful with thee.

LXXV

I leave thy praises unexpress'd
    In verse that brings myself relief,
    And by the measure of my grief
I leave thy greatness to be guess'd;

What practice howsoe'er expert
    In fitting aptest words to things,
    Or voice the richest-toned that sings,
Hath power to give thee as thou wert?

I care not in these fading days
    To raise a cry that lasts not long,   *10*
    And round thee with the breeze of song
To stir a little dust of praise.

Thy leaf has perish'd in the green,
    And, while we breathe beneath the sun,
    The world which credits what is done
Is cold to all that might have been.

So here shall silence guard thy fame;
    But somewhere, out of human view,
    Whate'er thy hands are set to do
Is wrought with tumult of acclaim.   20

LXXVI

Take wings of fancy, and ascend,
    And in a moment set thy face
    Where all the starry heavens of space
Are sharpen'd to a needle's end;

Take wings of foresight; lighten thro'
    The secular abyss to come,
    And lo, thy deepest lays are dumb
Before the mouldering of a yew;

And if the matin songs, that woke
    The darkness of our planet, last,   10
    Thine own shall wither in the vast,
Ere half the lifetime of an oak.

Ere these have clothed their branchy bowers
    With fifty Mays, thy songs are vain;
    And what are they when these remain
The ruin'd shells of hollow towers?

LXXVII

What hope is here for modern rhyme
    To him, who turns a musing eye
    On songs, and deeds, and lives, that lie
Foreshorten'd in the tract of time?

These mortal lullabies of pain
    May bind a book, may line a box,
    May serve to curl a maiden's locks,
Or when a thousand moons shall wane

A man upon a stall may find,
    And, passing, turn the page that tells   10
    A grief, then changed to something else,
Sung by a long-forgotten mind.

But what of that?   My darken'd ways
    Shall ring with music all the same;
    To breathe my loss is more than fame,
To utter love more sweet than praise.

LXXVIII

Again at Christmas did we weave
    The holly round the Christmas hearth;
    The silent snow possess'd the earth,
And calmly fell our Christmas-eve:

The yule-clog sparkled keen with frost,
    No wing of wind the region swept,
    But over all things brooding slept
The quiet sense of something lost.

As in the winters left behind,
    Again our ancient games had place,   *10*
    The mimic picture's breathing grace,
And dance and song and hoodman-blind.

Who show'd a token of distress?
    No single tear, no mark of pain:
    O sorrow, then can sorrow wane?
O grief, can grief be changed to less?

O last regret, regret can die!
    No—mixt with all this mystic frame,
    Her deep relations are the same,
But with long use her tears are dry.   *20*

LXXIX

' More than my brothers are to me,'—
    Let this not vex thee, noble heart!
    I know thee of what force thou art
To hold the costliest love in fee.

But thou and I are one in kind,
    As moulded like in Nature's mint;
    And hill and wood and field did print
The same sweet forms in either mind.

For us the same cold streamlet curl'd
    Thro' all his eddying coves; the same   *10*
    All winds that roam the twilight came
In whispers of the beauteous world.

At one dear knee we proffer'd vows,
    One lesson from one book we learn'd,
    Ere childhood's flaxen ringlet turn'd
To black and brown on kindred brows.

And so my wealth resembles thine,
    But he was rich where I was poor,
    And he supplied my want the more
As his unlikeness fitted mine.   *20*

LXXX

If any vague desire should rise,
    That holy Death ere Arthur died
    Had moved me kindly from his side,
And dropt the dust on tearless eyes;

Then fancy shapes, as fancy can
    The grief my loss in him had wrought,
    A grief as deep as life or thought,
But stay'd in peace with God and man.

I make a picture in the brain;
    I hear the sentence that he speaks;   *10*
    He bears the burthen of the weeks
But turns his burthen into gain.

His credit thus shall set me free;
    And, influence-rich to soothe and save,
    Unused example from the grave
Reach out dead hands to comfort me.

LXXXI

Could I have said while he was here,
    ' My love shall now no further range;
    There cannot come a mellower change,
For now is love mature in ear.'

Love, then, had hope of richer store:
    What end is here to my complaint?
    This haunting whisper makes me faint,
' More years had made me love thee more.'

But Death returns an answer sweet:
    ' My sudden frost was sudden gain,   *10*
    And gave all ripeness to the grain,
It might have drawn from after-heat.'

LXXXII

I wage not any feud with Death
    For changes wrought on form and face;
    No lower life that earth's embrace
May breed with him, can fright my faith.

Eternal process moving on,
    From state to state the spirit walks;
    And these are but the shatter'd stalks,
Or ruin'd chrysalis of one.

Nor blame I Death, because he bare
    The use of virtue out of earth: *10*
    I know transplanted human worth
Will bloom to profit, otherwhere.

For this alone on Death I wreak
    The wrath that garners in my heart;
    He put our lives so far apart
We cannot hear each other speak.

LXXXIII

Dip down upon the northern shore,
    O sweet new-year delaying long;
    Thou doest expectant nature wrong;
Delaying long, delay no more.

What stays thee from the clouded noons,
    Thy sweetness from its proper place?
    Can trouble live with April days,
Or sadness in the summer moons?

Bring orchis, bring the foxglove spire,
    The little speedwell's darling blue,   *10*
    Deep tulips dash'd with fiery dew,
Laburnums, dropping-wells of fire.

O thou, new-year, delaying long,
    Delayest the sorrow in my blood,
    That longs to burst a frozen bud
And flood a fresher throat with song.

LXXXIV

When I contemplate all alone
    The life that had been thine below,
    And fix my thoughts on all the glow
To which thy crescent would have grown;

I see thee sitting crown'd with good,
    A central warmth diffusing bliss
    In glance and smile, and clasp and kiss,
On all the branches of thy blood;

Thy blood, my friend, and partly mine;
    For now the day was drawing on,   *10*
    When thou should'st link thy life with one
Of mine own house, and boys of thine

Had babbled ' Uncle ' on my knee;
    But that remorseless iron hour
    Made cypress of her orange flower,
Despair of Hope, and earth of thee.

I seem to meet their least desire,
    To clap their cheeks, to call them mine.
    I see their unborn faces shine
Beside the never-lighted fire.   *20*

I see myself an honour'd guest,
    Thy partner in the flowery walk
    Of letters, genial table-talk,
Or deep dispute, and graceful jest;

While now thy prosperous labour fills
    The lips of men with honest praise,
    And sun by sun the happy days
Descend below the golden hills

With promise of a morn as fair;
    And all the train of bounteous hours   *30*
    Conduct by paths of growing powers,
To reverence and the silver hair;

Till slowly worn her earthly robe,
    Her lavish mission richly wrought,
    Leaving great legacies of thought,
Thy spirit should fail from off the globe;

What time mine own might also flee,
    As link'd with thine in love and fate,
    And, hovering o'er the dolorous strait
To the other shore, involved in thee,   *40*

Arrive at last the blessed goal,
    And He that died in Holy Land
    Would reach us out the shining hand,
And take us as a single soul.

What reed was that on which I leant?
    Ah, backward fancy, wherefore wake
    The old bitterness again, and break
The low beginnings of content.

LXXXV

This truth came borne with bier and pall,
    I felt it, when I sorrow'd most,
    'Tis better to have loved and lost,
Than never to have loved at all——

O true in word, and tried in deed,
    Demanding, so to bring relief
    To this which is our common grief,
What kind of life is that I lead;

And whether trust in things above
    Be dimm'd of sorrow, or sustain'd;   *10*
    And whether love for him have drain'd
My capabilities of love;

Your words have virtue such as draws
    A faithful answer from the breast,
    Thro' light reproaches, half exprest
And loyal unto kindly laws.

My blood an even tenor kept,
    Till on mine ear this message falls,
    That in Vienna's fatal walls
God's finger touch'd him, and he slept.   *20*

The great Intelligences fair
    That range above our mortal state,
    In circle round the blessed gate,
Received and gave him welcome there;

And led him thro' the blissful climes,
    And show'd him in the fountain fresh
    All knowledge that the sons of flesh
Shall gather in the cycled times.

But I remain'd, whose hopes were dim,
    Whose life, whose thoughts were little worth,   *30*
    To wander on a darken'd earth,
Where all things round me breathed of him.

O friendship, equal-poised control,
    O heart, with kindliest motion warm,
    O sacred essence, other form,
O solemn ghost, O crowned soul!

Yet none could better know than I,
    How much of act at human hands
    The sense of human will demands
By which we dare to live or die.   *40*

Whatever way my days decline,
    I felt and feel, tho' left alone,
    His being working in mine own,
The footsteps of his life in mine;

A life that all the Muses deck'd
    With gifts of grace, that might express
    All-comprehensive tenderness,
All-subtilising intellect:

And so my passion hath not swerved
    To works of weakness, but I find   *50*
    An image comforting the mind,
And in my grief a strength reserved.

Likewise the imaginative woe,
    That loved to handle spiritual strife,
    Diffused the shock thro' all my life,
But in the present broke the blow.

My pulses therefore beat again
    For other friends that once I met;
    Nor can it suit me to forget
The mighty hopes that make us men.   *60*

I woo your love: I count it crime
    To mourn for any overmuch;
    I, the divided half of such
A friendship as had master'd Time;

Which masters Time indeed, and is
    Eternal, separate from fears:
    The all-assuming months and years
Can take no part away from this:

But Summer on the steaming floods,
    And Spring that swells the narrow brooks,   *70*
    And Autumn, with a noise of rooks,
That gather in the waning woods,

And every pulse of wind and wave
    Recalls, in change of light or gloom,
    My old affection of the tomb,
And my prime passion in the grave:

My old affection of the tomb,
    A part of stillness, yearns to speak:
    ' Arise, and get thee forth and seek
A friendship for the years to come.   *80*

' I watch thee from the quiet shore;
    Thy spirit up to mine can reach;
    But in dear words of human speech
We two communicate no more.'

And I, ' Can clouds of nature stain
    The starry clearness of the free?
    How is it? Canst thou feel for me
Some painless sympathy with pain?'

And lightly does the whisper fall;
    ' 'Tis hard for thee to fathom this;   *90*
    I triumph in conclusive bliss,
And that serene result of all.'

So hold I commerce with the dead;
    Or so methinks the dead would say;
    Or so shall grief with symbols play
And pining life be fancy-fed.

Now looking to some settled end,
    That these things pass, and I shall prove
    A meeting somewhere, love with love,
I crave your pardon, O my friend;   *100*

If not so fresh, with love as true,
    I, clasping brother-hands, aver
    I could not, if I would, transfer
The whole I felt for him to you.

For which be they that hold apart
    The promise of the golden hours?
    First love, first friendship, equal powers,
That marry with the virgin heart.

Still mine, that cannot but deplore,
    That beats within a lonely place,   *110*
    That yet remembers his embrace,
But at his footstep leaps no more,

My heart, tho' widow'd, may not rest
    Quite in the love of what is gone,
    But seeks to beat in time with one
That warms another living breast.

Ah, take the imperfect gift I bring,
    Knowing the primrose yet is dear,
    The primrose of the later year,
As not unlike to that of Spring.   *120*

LXXXVI

Sweet after showers, ambrosial air,
    That rollest from the gorgeous gloom
    Of evening over brake and bloom
And meadow, slowly breathing bare

The round of space, and rapt below
    Thro' all the dewy-tassell'd wood,
    And shadowing down the horned flood
In ripples, fan my brows and blow

The fever from my cheek, and sigh
    The full new life that feeds thy breath   *10*
    Throughout my frame, till Doubt and Death,
Ill brethren, let the fancy fly

From belt to belt of crimson seas
    On leagues of odour streaming far,
    To where in yonder orient star
A hundred spirits whisper ' Peace.'

LXXXVII

I past beside the reverend walls
    In which of old I wore the gown;
    I roved at random thro' the town,
And saw the tumult of the halls;

And heard once more in college fanes
    The storm their high-built organs make,
    And thunder-music, rolling, shake
The prophet blazon'd on the panes;

And caught once more the distant shout,
 The measured pulse of racing oars   *10*
 Among the willows; paced the shores
And many a bridge, and all about

The same gray flats again, and felt
 The same, but not the same; and last
 Up that long walk of limes I past
To see the rooms in which he dwelt.

Another name was on the door:
 I linger'd; all within was noise
 Of songs, and clapping hands, and boys
That crash'd the glass and beat the floor;   *20*

Where once we held debate, a band
 Of youthful friends, on mind and art,
 And labour, and the changing mart,
And all the framework of the land;

When one would aim an arrow fair,
 But send it slackly from the string;
 And one would pierce an outer ring,
And one an inner, here and there;

And last the master-bowman, he,
 Would cleave the mark. A willing ear   *30*
 We lent him. Who, but hung to hear
The rapt oration flowing free

From point to point, with power and grace
 And music in the bounds of law,
 To those conclusions when we saw
The God within him light his face,

And seem to lift the form, and glow
 In azure orbits heavenly-wise;
 And over those ethereal eyes
The bar of Michael Angelo.   *40*

LXXXVIII

Wild bird, whose warble, liquid sweet,
 Rings Eden thro' the budded quicks,
 O tell me where the senses mix,
O tell me where the passions meet,

Whence radiate: fierce extremes employ
 Thy spirits in the darkening leaf,
 And in the midmost heart of grief
Thy passion clasps a secret joy:

And I—my harp would prelude woe—
    I cannot all command the strings;   *10*
    The glory of the sum of things
Will flash along the chords and go.

LXXXIX

Witch-elms that counterchange the floor
    Of this flat lawn with dusk and bright;
    And thou, with all thy breadth and height
Of foliage, towering sycamore;

How often, hither wandering down,
    My Arthur found your shadows fair,
    And shook to all the liberal air
The dust and din and steam of town:

He brought an eye for all he saw;
    He mixt in all our simple sports;   *10*
    They pleased him, fresh from brawling courts
And dusty purlieus of the law.

O joy to him in this retreat,
    Immantled in ambrosial dark,
    To drink the cooler air, and mark
The landscape winking thro' the heat:

O sound to rout the brood of cares,
    The sweep of scythe in morning dew,
    The gust that round the garden flew,
And tumbled half the mellowing pears!   *20*

O bliss, when all in circle drawn
    About him, heart and ear were fed
    To hear him, as he lay and read
The Tuscan poets on the lawn:

Or in the all-golden afternoon
    A guest, or happy sister, sung,
    Or here she brought the harp and flung
A ballad to the brightening moon:

Nor less it pleased in livelier moods,
    Beyond the bounding hill to stray,   *30*
    And break the livelong summer day
With banquet in the distant woods;

Whereat we glanced from theme to theme,
 Discuss'd the books to love or hate,
 Or touch'd the changes of the state,
Or threaded some Socratic dream;

But if I praised the busy town,
 He loved to rail against it still,
 For ' ground in yonder social mill
We rub each other's angles down,   *40*

' And merge ' he said ' in form and gloss
 The picturesque of man and man.'
 We talk'd : the stream beneath us ran,
The wine-flask lying couch'd in moss,

Or cool'd within the glooming wave;
 And last, returning from afar,
 Before the crimson-circled star
Had fall'n into her father's grave,

And brushing ankle-deep in flowers,
 We heard behind the woodbine veil   *50*
 The milk that bubbled in the pail,
And buzzings of the honied hours.

XC

He tasted love with half his mind,
 Nor ever drank the inviolate spring
 Where nighest heaven, who first could fling
This bitter seed among mankind;

That could the dead, whose dying eyes
 Were closed with wail, resume their life,
 They would but find in child and wife
An iron welcome when they rise;

'Twas well, indeed, when warm with wine,
 To pledge them with a kindly tear,   *10*
 To talk them o'er, to wish them here,
To count their memories half divine;

But if they came who past away,
 Behold their brides in other hands;
 The hard heir strides about their lands,
And will not yield them for a day.

Yea, tho' their sons were none of these,
 Not less the yet-loved sire would make
 Confusion worse than death, and shake
The pillars of domestic peace.   *20*

Ah dear, but come thou back to me :
    Whatever change the years have wrought,
    I find not yet one lonely thought
That cries against my wish for thee.

XCI

When rosy plumelets tuft the larch,
    And rarely pipes the mounted thrush;
    Or underneath the barren bush
Flits by the sea-blue bird of March;

Come, wear the form by which I know
    Thy spirit in time among thy peers;
    The hope of unaccomplish'd years
Be large and lucid round thy brow.

When summer's hourly-mellowing change
    May breathe, with many roses sweet,   *10*
    Upon the thousand waves of wheat,
That ripple round the lonely grange;

Come : not in watches of the night,
    But where the sunbeam broodeth warm,
    Come, beauteous in thine after form,
And like a finer light in light.

XCII

If any vision should reveal
    Thy likeness, I might count it vain
    As but the canker of the brain;
Yea, tho' it spake and made appeal

To chances where our lots were cast
    Together in the days behind,
    I might but say, I hear a wind
Of memory murmuring the past.

Yea, tho' it spake and bared to view
    A fact within the coming year;   *10*
    And tho' the months, revolving near,
Should prove the phantom-warning true,

They might not seem thy prophecies,
    But spiritual presentiments,
    And such refraction of events
As often rises ere they rise.

XCIII

I shall not see thee.   Dare I say
    No spirit ever brake the band
    That stays him from the native land
Where first he walk'd when claspt in clay?

No visual shade of some one lost,
    But he, the Spirit himself, may come
    Where all the nerve of sense is numb;
Spirit to Spirit, Ghost to Ghost.

O, therefore from thy sightless range
    With gods in unconjectured bliss,   *10*
    O, from the distance of the abyss
Of tenfold-complicated change,

Descend, and touch, and enter; hear
    The wish too strong for words to name;
    That in this blindness of the frame
My Ghost may feel that thine is near.

XCIV

How pure at heart and sound in head,
    With what divine affections bold
    Should be the man whose thought would hold
An hour's communion with the dead.

In vain shalt thou, or any, call
    The spirits from their golden day,
    Except, like them, thou too canst say,
My spirit is at peace with all.

They haunt the silence of the breast,
    Imaginations calm and fair,   *10*
    The memory like a cloudless air,
The conscience as a sea at rest:

But when the heart is full of din,
    And doubt beside the portal waits,
    They can but listen at the gates,
And hear the household jar within.

XCV

By night we linger'd on the lawn,
    For underfoot the herb was dry;
    And genial warmth; and o'er the sky
The silvery haze of summer drawn;

And calm that let the tapers burn
    Unwavering: not a cricket chirr'd:
    The brook alone far-off was heard,
And on the board the fluttering urn:

And bats went round in fragrant skies,
    And wheel'd or lit the filmy shapes   *10*
    That haunt the dusk, with ermine capes
And woolly breasts and beaded eyes;

While now we sang old songs that peal'd
    From knoll to knoll, where, couch'd at ease,
    The white kine glimmer'd, and the trees
Laid their dark arms about the field.

But when those others, one by one,
    Withdrew themselves from me and night,
    And in the house light after light
Went out, and I was all alone,   *20*

A hunger seized my heart; I read
    Of that glad year which once had been,
    In those fall'n leaves which kept their green,
The noble letters of the dead:

And strangely on the silence broke
    The silent-speaking words, and strange
    Was love's dumb cry defying change
To test his worth; and strangely spoke

The faith, the vigour, bold to dwell
    On doubts that drive the coward back,   *30*
    And keen thro' wordy snares to track
Suggestion to her inmost cell.

So word by word, and line by line,
    The dead man touch'd me from the past,
    And all at once it seem'd at last
The living soul was flash'd on mine,

And mine in this was wound, and whirl'd
    About empyreal heights of thought,
    And came on that which is, and caught
The deep pulsations of the world.   *40*

Æonian music measuring out
    The steps of Time—the shocks of Chance—
    The blows of Death.   At length my trance
Was cancell'd, stricken thro' with doubt.

Vague words! but ah, how hard to frame
 In matter-moulded forms of speech,
 Or ev'n for intellect to reach
Thro' memory that which I became:

Till now the doubtful dusk reveal'd
 The knolls once more where, couch'd at ease, *50*
 The white kine glimmer'd, and the trees
Laid their dark arms about the field:

And suck'd from out the distant gloom
 A breeze began to tremble o'er
 The large leaves of the sycamore,
And fluctuate all the still perfume,

And gathering freshlier overhead,
 Rock'd the full-foliaged elms, and swung
 The heavy-folded rose, and flung
The lilies to and fro, and said   *60*

' The dawn, the dawn,' and died away;
 And East and West, without a breath,
 Mixt their dim lights, like life and death,
To broaden into boundless day.

XCVI

You say, but with no touch of scorn,
 Sweet-hearted, you whose light-blue eyes
 Are tender over drowning flies,
You tell me, doubt is Devil-born.

I know not: one indeed I knew
 In many a subtle question versed,
 Who touch'd a jarring lyre at first,
But ever strove to make it true:

Perplext in faith, but pure in deeds,
 At last he beat his music out,   *10*
 There lives more faith in honest doubt,
Believe me, than in half the creeds.

He fought his doubts and gather'd strength,
 He would not make his judgment blind,
 He faced the spectres of the mind
And laid them: thus he came at length

To find a stronger faith his own;
    And Power was with him in the night,
    Which makes the darkness and the light,
And dwells not in the light alone,   *20*

But in the darkness and the cloud,
    As over Sinaï's peaks of old,
    While Israel made their gods of gold,
Altho' the trumpet blew so loud.

XCVII

My love has talk'd with rocks and trees;
    He finds on misty mountain-ground
    His own vast shadow glory-crown'd;
He sees himself in all he sees.

Two partners of a married life—
    I look'd on these and thought of thee
    In vastness and in mystery,
And of my spirit as of a wife.

These two—they dwelt with eye on eye,
    Their hearts of old have beat in tune,   *10*
    Their meetings made December June
Their every parting was to die.

Their love has never past away;
    The days she never can forget
    Are earnest that he loves her yet,
Whate'er the faithless people say.

Her life is lone, he sits apart,
    He loves her yet, she will not weep,
    Tho' rapt in matters dark and deep
He seems to slight her simple heart.   *20*

He thrids the labyrinth of the mind,
    He reads the secret of the star,
    He seems so near and yet so far,
He looks so cold: she thinks him kind.

She keeps the gift of years before,
    A wither'd violet is her bliss:
    She knows not what his greatness is,
For that, for all, she loves him more.

For him she plays, to him she sings
 Of early faith and plighted vows;   *30*
 She knows but matters of the house,
And he, he knows a thousand things.

Her faith is fixt and cannot move,
 She darkly feels him great and wise,
 She dwells on him with faithful eyes,
' I cannot understand : I love.'

XCVIII

You leave us : you will see the Rhine,
 And those fair hills I sail'd below,
 When I was there with him; and go
By summer belts of wheat and vine

To where he breathed his latest breath,
 That City. All her splendour seems
 No livelier than the wisp that gleams
On Lethe in the eyes of Death.

Let her great Danube rolling fair
 Enwind her isles, unmark'd of me :   *10*
 I have not seen, I will not see
Vienna; rather dream that there,

A treble darkness, Evil haunts
 The birth, the bridal; friend from friend
 Is oftener parted, fathers bend
Above more graves, a thousand wants

Gnarr at the heels of men, and prey
 By each cold hearth, and sadness flings
 Her shadow on the blaze of kings :
And yet myself have heard him say,   *20*

That not in any mother town
 With statelier progress to and fro
 The double tides of chariots flow
By park and suburb under brown

Of lustier leaves; nor more content,
 He told me, lives in any crowd,
 When all is gay with lamps, and loud
With sport and song, in booth and tent,

Imperial halls, or open plain;
 And wheels the circled dance, and breaks *30*
 The rocket molten into flakes
Of crimson or in emerald rain.

XCIX

Risest thou thus, dim dawn, again,
 So loud with voices of the birds,
 So thick with lowings of the herds,
Day, when I lost the flower of men;

Who tremblest thro' thy darkling red
 On yon swoll'n brook that bubbles fast
 By meadows breathing of the past,
And woodlands holy to the dead;

Who murmurest in the foliaged eaves
 A song that slights the coming care, *10*
 And Autumn laying here and there
A fiery finger on the leaves;

Who wakenest with thy balmy breath
 To myriads on the genial earth,
 Memories of bridal, or of birth,
And unto myriads more, of death.

O wheresoever those may be,
 Betwixt the slumber of the poles,
 To-day they count as kindred souls;
They know me not, but mourn with me. *20*

C

I climb the hill: from end to end
 Of all the landscape underneath,
 I find no place that does not breathe
Some gracious memory of my friend;

No gray old grange, or lonely fold,
 Or low morass and whispering reed,
 Or simple stile from mead to mead,
Or sheepwalk up the windy wold;

Nor hoary knoll of ash and haw
 That hears the latest linnet trill, *10*
 Nor quarry trench'd along the hill
And haunted by the wrangling daw;

Nor runlet tinkling from the rock;
 Nor pastoral rivulet that swerves
 To left and right thro' meadowy curves,
That feed the mothers of the flock;

But each has pleased a kindred eye,
 And each reflects a kindlier day;
 And, leaving these, to pass away,
I think once more he seems to die.   *20*

CI

Unwatch'd, the garden bough shall sway,
 The tender blossom flutter down,
 Unloved, that beech will gather brown,
This maple burn itself away;

Unloved, the sun-flower, shining fair,
 Ray round with flames her disk of seed,
 And many a rose-carnation feed
With summer spice the humming air;

Unloved, by many a sandy bar,
 The brook shall babble down the plain,   *10*
 At noon or when the lesser wain
Is twisting round the polar star;

Uncared for, gird the windy grove,
 And flood the haunts of hern and crake;
 Or into silver arrows break
The sailing moon in creek and cove;

Till from the garden and the wild
 A fresh association blow,
 And year by year the landscape grow
Familiar to the stranger's child;   *20*

As year by year the labourer tills
 His wonted glebe, or lops the glades;
 And year by year our memory fades
From all the circle of the hills.

CII

We leave the well-beloved place
 Where first we gazed upon the sky;
 The roofs, that heard our earliest cry,
Will shelter one of stranger race.

We go, but ere we go from home,
 As down the garden-walks I move,
 Two spirits of a diverse love
Contend for loving masterdom.

One whispers, ' Here thy boyhood sung
    Long since its matin song, and heard   *10*
    The low love-language of the bird
In native hazels tassel-hung.'

The other answers, ' Yea, but here
    Thy feet have stray'd in after hours
    With thy lost friend among the bowers,
And this hath made them trebly dear.'

These two have striven half the day,
    And each prefers his separate claim,
    Poor rivals in a losing game,
That will not yield each other way.   *20*

I turn to go : my feet are set
    To leave the pleasant fields and farms;
    They mix in one another's arms
To one pure image of regret.

CIII

On that last night before we went
    From out the doors where I was bred,
    I dream'd a vision of the dead,
Which left my after-morn content.

Methought I dwelt within a hall,
    And maidens with me : distant hills
    From hidden summits fed with rills
A river sliding by the wall.

The hall with harp and carol rang.
    They sang of what is wise and good   *10*
    And graceful.   In the centre stood
A statue veil'd, to which they sang;

And which, tho' veil'd, was known to me,
    The shape of him I loved, and love
    For ever : then flew in a dove
And brought a summons from the sea :

And when they learnt that I must go
    They wept and wail'd, but led the way
    To where a little shallop lay
At anchor in the flood below;   *20*

And on by many a level mead,
    And shadowing bluff that made the banks,
    We glided winding under ranks
Of iris, and the golden reed;

And still as vaster grew the shore
 And roll'd the floods in grander space,
 The maidens gather'd strength and grace
And presence, lordlier than before;

And I myself, who sat apart
 And watch'd them, wax'd in every limb; *30*
 I felt the thews of Anakim,
The pulses of a Titan's heart;

As one would sing the death of war,
 And one would chant the history
 Of that great race, which is to be,
And one the shaping of a star;

Until the forward-creeping tides
 Began to foam, and we to draw
 From deep to deep, to where we saw
A great ship lift her shining sides. *40*

The man we loved was there on deck,
 But thrice as large as man he bent
 To greet us.   Up the side I went,
And fell in silence on his neck:

Whereat those maidens with one mind
 Bewail'd their lot; I did them wrong:
 'We served thee here,' they said, 'so long,
And wilt thou leave us now behind?'

So rapt I was, they could not win
 An answer from my lips, but he *50*
 Replying, 'Enter likewise ye
And go with us': they enter'd in.

And while the wind began to sweep
 A music out of sheet and shroud,
 We steer'd her toward a crimson cloud
That landlike slept along the deep.

CIV

The time draws near the birth of Christ;
 The moon is hid, the night is still;
 A single church below the hill
Is pealing, folded in the mist.

A single peal of bells below,
　　That wakens at this hour of rest
　　A single murmur in the breast,
That these are not the bells I know.

Like strangers' voices here they sound,
　　In lands where not a memory strays,   *10*
　　Nor landmark breathes of other days,
But all is new unhallow'd ground.

CV

To-night ungather'd let us leave
　　This laurel, let this holly stand :
　　We live within the stranger's land,
And strangely falls our Christmas-eve.

Our father's dust is left alone
　　And silent under other snows :
　　There in due time the woodbine blows,
The violet comes, but we are gone.

No more shall wayward grief abuse
　　The genial hour with mask and mime ;   *10*
　　For change of place, like growth of time,
Has broke the bond of dying use.

Let cares that petty shadows cast,
　　By which our lives are chiefly proved,
　　A little spare the night I loved,
And hold it solemn to the past.

But let no footstep beat the floor,
　　Nor bowl of wassail mantle warm ;
　　For who would keep an ancient form
Thro' which the spirit breathes no more ?   *20*

Be neither song, nor game, nor feast ;
　　Nor harp be touch'd, nor flute be blown ;
　　No dance, no motion, save alone
What lightens in the lucid east

Of rising worlds by yonder wood.
　　Long sleeps the summer in the seed ;
　　Run out your measured arcs, and lead
The closing cycle rich in good.

CVI

Ring out, wild bells, to the wild sky,
  The flying cloud, the frosty light:
  The year is dying in the night;
Ring out, wild bells, and let him die.

Ring out the old, ring in the new,
  Ring, happy bells, across the snow:
  The year is going, let him go;
Ring out the false, ring in the true.

Ring out the grief that saps the mind,
  For those that here we see no more;   *10*
  Ring out the feud of rich and poor,
Ring in redress to all mankind.

Ring out a slowly dying cause,
  And ancient forms of party strife;
  Ring in the nobler modes of life,
With sweeter manners, purer laws.

Ring out the want, the care, the sin,
  The faithless coldness of the times;
  Ring out, ring out my mournful rhymes,
But ring the fuller minstrel in.   *20*

Ring out false pride in place and blood,
  The civic slander and the spite;
  Ring in the love of truth and right,
Ring in the common love of good.

Ring out old shapes of foul disease;
  Ring out the narrowing lust of gold;
  Ring out the thousand wars of old,
Ring in the thousand years of peace.

Ring in the valiant man and free,
  The larger heart, the kindlier hand;   *30*
  Ring out the darkness of the land,
Ring in the Christ that is to be.

CVII

It is the day when he was born,
  A bitter day that early sank
  Behind a purple-frosty bank
Of vapour, leaving night forlorn.

The time admits not flowers or leaves
  To deck the banquet.   Fiercely flies
  The blast of North and East, and ice
Makes daggers at the sharpen'd eaves,

And bristles all the brakes and thorns
    To yon hard crescent, as she hangs   *10*
    Above the wood which grides and clangs
Its leafless ribs and iron horns

Together, in the drifts that pass
    To darken on the rolling brine
    That breaks the coast.   But fetch the wine,
Arrange the board and brim the glass;

Bring in great logs and let them lie,
    To make a solid core of heat;
    Be cheerful-minded, talk and treat
Of all things ev'n as he were by;   *20*

We keep the day.   With festal cheer,
    With books and music, surely we
    Will drink to him, whate'er he be,
And sing the songs he loved to hear.

CVIII

I will not shut me from my kind,
    And, lest I stiffen into stone,
    I will not eat my heart alone,
Nor feed with sighs a passing wind:

What profit lies in barren faith,
    And vacant yearning, tho' with might
    To scale the heaven's highest height,
Or dive below the wells of Death?

What find I in the highest place,
    But mine own phantom chanting hymns?   *10*
    And on the depths of death there swims
The reflex of a human face.

I'll rather take what fruit may be
    Of sorrow under human skies:
    'Tis held that sorrow makes us wise,
Whatever wisdom sleep with thee.

CIX

Heart-affluence in discursive talk
    From household fountains never dry;
    The critic clearness of an eye,
That saw thro' all the Muses' walk;

Seraphic intellect and force
  To seize and throw the doubts of man;
  Impassion'd logic, which outran
The hearer in its fiery course;

High nature amorous of the good,
  But touch'd with no ascetic gloom;   *10*
  And passion pure in snowy bloom
Thro' all the years of April blood;

A love of freedom rarely felt,
  Of freedom in her regal seat
  Of England; not the schoolboy heat,
The blind hysterics of the Celt;

And manhood fused with female grace
  In such a sort, the child would twine
  A trustful hand, unask'd, in thine,
And find his comfort in thy face;   *20*

All these have been, and thee mine eyes
  Have look'd on: if they look'd in vain,
  My shame is greater who remain,
Nor let thy wisdom make me wise.

CX

Thy converse drew us with delight,
  The men of rathe and riper years:
  The feeble soul, a haunt of fears,
Forgot his weakness in thy sight.

On thee the loyal-hearted hung,
  The proud was half disarm'd of pride,
  Nor cared the serpent at thy side
To flicker with his double tongue.

The stern were mild when thou wert by,
  The flippant put himself to school   *10*
  And heard thee, and the brazen fool
Was soften'd, and he knew not why;

While I, thy nearest, sat apart,
  And felt thy triumph was as mine;
  And loved them more, that they were thine,
The graceful tact, the Christian art;

Nor mine the sweetness or the skill,
  But mine the love that will not tire,
  And, born of love, the vague desire
That spurs an imitative will.   *20*

CXI

The churl in spirit, up or down
　　Along the scale of ranks, thro' all,
　　To him who grasps a golden ball,
By blood a king, at heart a clown;

The churl in spirit, howe'er he veil
　　His want in forms for fashion's sake,
　　Will let his coltish nature break
At seasons thro' the gilded pale:

For who can always act? but he,
　　To whom a thousand memories call,　　*10*
　　Not being less but more than all
The gentleness he seem'd to be,

Best seem'd the thing he was, and join'd
　　Each office of the social hour
　　To noble manners, as the flower
And native growth of noble mind;

Nor ever narrowness or spite,
　　Or villain fancy fleeting by,
　　Drew in the expression of an eye,
Where God and Nature met in light;　　*20*

And thus he bore without abuse
　　The grand old name of gentleman,
　　Defamed by every charlatan,
And soil'd with all ignoble use.

CXII

High wisdom holds my wisdom less,
　　That I, who gaze with temperate eyes
　　On glorious insufficiencies,
Set light by narrower perfectness.

But thou, that fillest all the room
　　Of all my love, art reason why
　　I seem to cast a careless eye
On souls, the lesser lords of doom.

For what wert thou? some novel power
　　Sprang up for ever at a touch,　　*10*
　　And hope could never hope too much,
In watching thee from hour to hour,

Large elements in order brought,
    And tracts of calm from tempest made,
    And world-wide fluctuation sway'd
In vassal tides that follow'd thought.

CXIII

'Tis held that sorrow makes us wise;
    Yet how much wisdom sleeps with thee
    Which not alone had guided me,
But served the seasons that may rise;

For can I doubt, who knew thee keen
    In intellect, with force and skill
    To strive, to fashion, to fulfil—
I doubt not what thou wouldst have been:

A life in civic action warm,
    A soul on highest mission sent,   *10*
    A potent voice of Parliament,
A pillar steadfast in the storm,

Should licensed boldness gather force,
    Becoming, when the time has birth,
    A lever to uplift the earth
And roll it in another course,

With thousand shocks that come and go,
    With agonies, with energies,
    With overthrowings, and with cries,
And undulations to and fro.   *20*

CXIV

Who loves not Knowledge? Who shall rail
    Against her beauty? May she mix
    With men and prosper! Who shall fix
Her pillars? Let her work prevail.

But on her forehead sits a fire:
    She sets her forward countenance
    And leaps into the future chance,
Submitting all things to desire.

Half-grown as yet, a child, and vain—
    She cannot fight the fear of death.   *10*
    What is she, cut from love and faith,
But some wild Pallas from the brain

Of Demons? fiery-hot to burst
    All barriers in her onward race
    For power.   Let her know her place;
She is the second, not the first.

A higher hand must make her mild,
    If all be not in vain; and guide
    Her footsteps, moving side by side
With wisdom, like the younger child :   *20*

For she is earthly of the mind,
    But Wisdom heavenly of the soul.
    O, friend, who camest to thy goal
So early, leaving me behind,

I would the great world grew like thee,
    Who grewest not alone in power
    And knowledge, but by year and hour
In reverence and in charity.

CXV

Now fades the last long streak of snow,
    Now burgeons every maze of quick
    About the flowering squares, and thick
By ashen roots the violets blow.

Now rings the woodland loud and long,
    The distance takes a lovelier hue,
    And drown'd in yonder living blue
The lark becomes a sightless song.

Now dance the lights on lawn and lea,
    The flocks are whiter down the vale,   *10*
    And milkier every milky sail
On winding stream or distant sea;

Where now the seamew pipes, or dives
    In yonder greening gleam, and fly
    The happy birds, that change their sky
To build and brood; that live their lives

From land to land; and in my breast
    Spring wakens too; and my regret
    Becomes an April violet,
And buds and blossoms like the rest.   *20*

CXVI

Is it, then, regret for buried time
    That keenlier in sweet April wakes,
    And meets the year, and gives and takes
The colours of the crescent prime?

Not all : the songs, the stirring air,
    The life re-orient out of dust,
    Cry thro' the sense to hearten trust
In that which made the world so fair.

Not all regret : the face will shine
    Upon me, while I muse alone;   *10*
    And that dear voice, I once have known,
Still speak to me of me and mine :

Yet less of sorrow lives in me
    For days of happy commune dead;
    Less yearning for the friendship fled,
Than some strong bond which is to be.

CXVII

O days and hours, your work is this
    To hold me from my proper place,
    A little while from his embrace,
For fuller gain of after bliss :

That out of distance might ensue
    Desire of nearness doubly sweet;
    And unto meeting when we meet,
Delight a hundredfold accrue,

For every grain of sand that runs,
    And every span of shade that steals,   *10*
    And every kiss of toothed wheels,
And all the courses of the suns.

CXVIII

Contemplate all this work of Time,
    The giant labouring in his youth;
    Nor dream of human love and truth,
As dying Nature's earth and lime;

But trust that those we call the dead
    Are breathers of an ampler day
    For ever nobler ends.   They say,
The solid earth whereon we tread

In tracts of fluent heat began,
  And grew to seeming-random forms,   *10*
  The seeming prey of cyclic storms,
Till at the last arose the man;

Who throve and branch'd from clime to clime,
  The herald of a higher race,
  And of himself in higher place,
If so he type this work of time

Within himself, from more to more;
  Or, crown'd with attributes of woe
  Like glories, move his course, and show
That life is not as idle ore,   *20*

But iron dug from central gloom,
  And heated hot with burning fears,
  And dipt in baths of hissing tears,
And batter'd with the shocks of doom

To shape and use. Arise and fly
  The reeling Faun, the sensual feast;
  Move upward, working out the beast,
And let the ape and tiger die.

CXIX

Doors, where my heart was used to beat
  So quickly, not as one that weeps
  I come once more; the city sleeps;
I smell the meadow in the street;

I hear a chirp of birds; I see
  Betwixt the black fronts long-withdrawn
  A light-blue lane of early dawn,
And think of early days and thee,

And bless thee, for thy lips are bland,
  And bright the friendship of thine eye;   *10*
  And in my thoughts, with scarce a sigh
I take the pressure of thine hand.

CXX

I trust I have not wasted breath:
  I think we are not wholly brain,
  Magnetic mockeries; not in vain,
Like Paul with beasts, I fought with Death;

Not only cunning casts in clay:
    Let Science prove we are, and then
    What matters Science unto men,
At least to me? I would not stay.

Let him, the wiser man who springs
    Hereafter, up from childhood shape   *10*
    His action like the greater ape,
But I was *born* to other things.

CXXI

Sad Hesper o'er the buried sun
    And ready, thou, to die with him,
    Thou watchest all things ever dim
And dimmer, and a glory done:

The team is loosen'd from the wain,
    The boat is drawn upon the shore;
    Thou listenest to the closing door,
And life is darken'd in the brain.

Bright Phosphor, fresher for the night,
    By thee the world's great work is heard   *10*
    Beginning, and the wakeful bird;
Behind thee comes the greater light:

The market boat is on the stream,
    And voices hail it from the brink;
    Thou hear'st the village hammer clink,
And see'st the moving of the team.

Sweet Hesper-Phosphor, double name
    For what is one, the first, the last,
    Thou, like my present and my past,
Thy place is changed; thou art the same.   *20*

CXXII

Oh, wast thou with me, dearest, then,
    While I rose up against my doom,
    And yearn'd to burst the folded gloom,
To bare the eternal Heavens again,

To feel once more, in placid awe,
    The strong imagination roll
    A sphere of stars about my soul.
In all her motion one with law;

If thou wert with me, and the grave
 Divide us not, be with me now,
 And enter in at breast and brow,
Till all my blood, a fuller wave,

Be quicken'd with a livelier breath,
 And like an inconsiderate boy,
 As in the former flash of joy,
I slip the thoughts of life and death;

And all the breeze of Fancy blows,
 And every dew-drop paints a bow,
 The wizard lightnings deeply glow,
And every thought breaks out a rose.

CXXIII

There rolls the deep where grew the tree.
 O earth, what changes hast thou seen!
 There where the long street roars, hath been
The stillness of the central sea.

The hills are shadows, and they flow
 From form to form, and nothing stands;
 They melt like mist, the solid lands,
Like clouds they shape themselves and go.

But in my spirit will I dwell,
 And dream my dream, and hold it true;
 For tho' my lips may breathe adieu,
I cannot think the thing farewell.

CXXIV

That which we dare invoke to bless;
 Our dearest faith; our ghastliest doubt;
 He, They, One, All; within, without;
The Power in darkness whom we guess;

I found Him not in world or sun,
 Or eagle's wing, or insect's eye;
 Nor thro' the questions men may try,
The petty cobwebs we have spun:

If e'er when faith had fall'n asleep,
 I heard a voice 'believe no more'
 And heard an ever-breaking shore
That tumbled in the Godless deep;

A warmth within the breast would melt
    The freezing reason's colder part,
    And like a man in wrath the heart
Stood up and answer'd ' I have felt.'

No, like a child in doubt and fear:
    But that blind clamour made me wise;
    Then was I as a child that cries,
But, crying, knows his father near;   *20*

And what I am beheld again
    What is, and no man understands;
    And out of darkness came the hands
That reach thro' nature, moulding men.

CXXV

Whatever I have said or sung,
    Some bitter notes my harp would give,
    Yea, tho' there often seem'd to live
A contradiction on the tongue,

Yet Hope had never lost her youth;
    She did but look through dimmer eyes;
    Or Love but play'd with gracious lies,
Because he felt so fix'd in truth:

And if the song were full of care,
    He breathed the spirit of the song;   *10*
    And if the words were sweet and strong
He set his royal signet there;

Abiding with me till I sail
    To seek thee on the mystic deeps,
    And this electric force, that keeps
A thousand pulses dancing, fail.

CXXVI

Love is and was my Lord and King,
    And in his presence I attend
    To hear the tidings of my friend,
Which every hour his couriers bring.

Love is and was my King and Lord,
    And will be, tho' as yet I keep
    Within his court on earth, and sleep
Encompass'd by his faithful guard,

And hear at times a sentinel
    Who moves about from place to place,   *10*
    And whispers to the worlds of space,
In the deep night, that all is well.

CXXVII

And all is well, tho' faith and form
    Be sunder'd in the night of fear;
    Well roars the storm to those that hear
A deeper voice across the storm,

Proclaiming social truth shall spread,
    And justice, ev'n tho' thrice again
    The red fool-fury of the Seine
Should pile her barricades with dead.

But ill for him that wears a crown,
    And him, the lazar, in his rags: *10*
    They tremble, the sustaining crags;
The spires of ice are toppled down,

And molten up, and roar in flood;
    The fortress crashes from on high,
    The brute earth lightens to the sky,
And the great Æon sinks in blood,

And compass'd by the fires of Hell;
    While thou, dear spirit, happy star,
    O'erlook'st the tumult from afar,
And smilest, knowing all is well.   *20*

CXXVIII

The love that rose on stronger wings,
    Unpalsied when he met with Death,
    Is comrade of the lesser faith
That sees the course of human things.

No doubt vast eddies in the flood
    Of onward time shall yet be made,
    And throned races may degrade;
Yet O ye mysteries of good,

Wild Hours that fly with Hope and Fear,
    If all your office had to do   *10*
    With old results that look like new;
If this were all your mission here,

To draw, to sheathe a useless sword,
    To fool the crowd with glorious lies,
    To cleave a creed in sects and cries,
To change the bearing of a word,

To shift an arbitrary power,
    To cramp the student at his desk,
    To make old bareness picturesque
And tuft with grass a feudal tower;   *20*

Why then my scorn might well descend
    On you and yours.   I see in part
    That all, as in some piece of art,
Is toil cöoperant to an end.

CXXIX

Dear friend, far off, my lost desire,
    So far, so near in woe and weal;
    O loved the most, when most I feel
There is a lower and a higher;

Known and unknown; human, divine;
    Sweet human hand and lips and eye;
    Dear heavenly friend that canst not die,
Mine, mine, for ever, ever mine;

Strange friend, past, present, and to be;
    Loved deeplier, darklier understood;   *10*
    Behold, I dream a dream of good,
And mingle all the world with thee.

CXXX

Thy voice is on the rolling air;
    I hear thee where the waters run;
    Thou standest in the rising sun,
And in the setting thou art fair.

What art thou then?   I cannot guess;
    But tho' I seem in star and flower
    To feel thee some diffusive power,
I do not therefore love thee less:

My love involves the love before;
    My love is vaster passion now;   *10*
    Tho' mix'd with God and Nature thou,
I seem to love thee more and more.

Far off thou art, but ever nigh;
   I have thee still, and I rejoice;
   I prosper, circled with thy voice;
I shall not lose thee tho' I die.

CXXXI

O living will that shalt endure
   When all that seems shall suffer shock,
   Rise in the spiritual rock,
Flow thro' our deeds and make them pure,

That we may lift from out of dust
   A voice as unto him that hears,
   A cry above the conquer'd years
To one that with us works, and trust,

With faith that comes of self-control,
   The truths that never can be proved   *10*
   Until we close with all we loved,
And all we flow from, soul in soul.

———

O true and tried, so well and long,
   Demand not thou a marriage lay;
   In that it is thy marriage day
Is music more than any song.

Nor have I felt so much of bliss
   Since first he told me that he loved
   A daughter of our house; nor proved
Since that dark day a day like this;

Tho' I since then have number'd o'er
   Some thrice three years: they went and came, *10*
   Remade the blood and changed the frame,
And yet is love not less, but more;

No longer caring to embalm
   In dying songs a dead regret,
   But like a statue solid-set,
And moulded in colossal calm.

Regret is dead, but love is more
   Than in the summers that are flown,
   For I myself with these have grown
To something greater than before;   *20*

Which makes appear the songs I made
   As echoes out of weaker times,
   As half but idle brawling rhymes,
The sport of random sun and shade.

But where is she, the bridal flower,
　　That must be made a wife ere noon?
　　She enters, glowing like the moon
Of Eden on its bridal bower:

On me she bends her blissful eyes
　　And then on thee; they meet thy look　　*30*
　　And brighten like the stars that shook
Betwixt the palms of paradise.

O when her life was yet in bud,
　　He too foretold the perfect rose.
　　For thee she grew, for thee she grows
For ever, and as fair as good.

And thou art worthy; full of power;
　　As gentle; liberal-minded, great,
　　Consistent; wearing all that weight
Of learning lightly like a flower.　　*40*

But now set out: the noon is near,
　　And I must give away the bride;
　　She fears not, or with thee beside
And me behind her, will not fear.

For I that danced her on my knee,
　　That watch'd her on her nurse's arm,
　　That shielded all her life from harm
At last must part with her to thee;

Now waiting to be made a wife,
　　Her feet, my darling, on the dead;　　*50*
　　Their pensive tablets round her head,
And the most living words of life

Breathed in her ear. The ring is on,
　　The ' wilt thou ' answer'd, and again
　　The ' wilt thou ' ask'd, till out of twain
Her sweet ' I will ' has made you one.

Now sign your names, which shall be read,
　　Mute symbols of a joyful morn,
　　By village eyes as yet unborn;
The names are sign'd, and overhead　　*60*

Begins the clash and clang that tells
　　The joy to every wandering breeze;
　　The blind wall rocks, and on the trees
The dead leaf trembles to the bells.

O happy hour, and happier hours
 Await them. Many a merry face
 Salutes them—maidens of the place,
That pelt us in the porch with flowers.

O happy hour, behold the bride
 With him to whom her hand I gave.   70
 They leave the porch, they pass the grave
That has to-day its sunny side.

To-day the grave is bright for me,
 For them the light of life increased,
 Who stay to share the morning feast,
Who rest to-night beside the sea.

Let all my genial spirits advance
 To meet and greet a whiter sun;
 My drooping memory will not shun
The foaming grape of eastern France.   80

It circles round, and fancy plays,
 And hearts are warm'd and faces bloom,
 As drinking health to bride and groom
We wish them store of happy days.

Nor count me all to blame if I
 Conjecture of a stiller guest,
 Perchance, perchance, among the rest,
And, tho' in silence, wishing joy.

But they must go, the time draws on,
 And those white-favour'd horses wait;   90
 They rise, but linger; it is late;
Farewell, we kiss, and they are gone.

A shade falls on us like the dark
 From little cloudlets on the grass,
 But sweeps away as out we pass
To range the woods, to roam the park,

Discussing how their courtship grew,
 And talk of others that are wed,
 And how she look'd, and what he said,
And back we come at fall of dew.   100

Again, the feast, the speech, the glee,
 The shade of passing thought, the wealth
 Of words and wit, the double health,
The crowning cup, the three-times-three,

And last the dance;—till I retire:
    Dumb is that tower which spake so loud,
    And high in heaven the streaming cloud,
And on the downs a rising fire:

And rise, O moon, from yonder down,
    Till over down and over dale   *110*
    All night the shining vapour sail
And pass the silent-lighted town,

The white-faced halls, the glancing rills,
    And catch at every mountain head,
    And o'er the friths that branch and spread
Their sleeping silver thro' the hills;

And touch with shade the bridal doors,
    With tender gloom the roof, the wall;
    And breaking let the splendour fall
To spangle all the happy shores   *120*

By which they rest, and ocean sounds,
    And, star and system rolling past,
    A soul shall draw from out the vast
And strike his being into bounds,

And, moved thro' life of lower phase,
    Result in man, be born and think,
    And act and love, a closer link
Betwixt us and the crowning race

Of those that, eye to eye, shall look
    On knowledge; under whose command   *130*
    Is Earth and Earth's, and in their hand
Is Nature like an open book;

No longer half-akin to brute,
    For all we thought and loved and did,
    And hoped, and suffer'd, is but seed
Of what in them is flower and fruit;

Whereof the man, that with me trod
    This planet, was a noble type
    Appearing ere the times were ripe,
That friend of mine who lives in God,   *140*

That God, which ever lives and loves,
    One God, one law, one element,
    And one far-off divine event
To which the whole creation moves.

THE CHARGE OF THE LIGHT BRIGADE

HALF a league, half a league,
  Half a league onward,
All in the valley of Death
  Rode the six hundred.
' Forward, the Light Brigade !
Charge for the guns ! ' he said :
Into the valley of Death
  Rode the six hundred.

' Forward, the Light Brigade ! '
Was there a man dismay'd ?   *10*
Not tho' the soldier knew
  Some one had blunder'd :
Their's not to make reply,
Their's not to reason why,
Their's but to do and die :
Into the valley of Death
  Rode the six hundred.

Cannon to right of them,
Cannon to left of them,
Cannon in front of them   *20*
  Volley'd and thunder'd ;
Storm'd at with shot and shell,
Boldly they rode and well,
Into the jaws of Death,
Into the mouth of Hell
  Rode the six hundred.

Flash'd all their sabres bare,
Flash'd as they turn'd in air
Sabring the gunners there,
Charging an army, while   *30*
  All the world wonder'd :
Plunged in the battery smoke
Right thro' the line they broke ;
Cossack and Russian
Reel'd from the sabre-stroke
  Shatter'd and sunder'd.
Then they rode back, but not
  Not the six hundred.

Cannon to right of them,
Cannon to left of them,   *40*
Cannon behind them
  Volley'd and thunder'd;
Storm'd at with shot and shell,
While horse and hero fell,
They that had fought so well
Came thro' the jaws of Death,
Back from the mouth of Hell,
All that was left of them,
  Left of six hundred.

When can their glory fade?   *50*
O the wild charge they made!
  All the world wonder'd.
Honour the charge they made!
Honour the Light Brigade,
  Noble six hundred!

MAUD: A MONODRAMA

PART I

I

I HATE the dreadful hollow behind the little wood,
Its lips in the field above are dabbled with blood-red heath,
The red-ribb'd ledges drip with a silent horror of blood,
And Echo there, whatever is ask'd her, answers ' Death.'

For there in the ghastly pit long since a body was found,
His who had given me life—O father ! O God ! was it well ?—
Mangled, and flatten'd, and crush'd, and dinted into the ground :
There yet lies the rock that fell with him when he fell.

Did he fling himself down? who knows? for a vast speculation had
    fail'd,
And ever he mutter'd and madden'd, and ever wann'd with despair,   **10**
And out he walk'd when the wind like a broken worldling wail'd,
And the flying gold of the ruin'd woodlands drove thro' the air.

I remember the time, for the roots of my hair were stirr'd
By a shuffled step, by a dead weight trail'd, by a whisper'd fright,
And my pulses closed their gates with a shock on my heart as I
    heard
The shrill-edged shriek of a mother divide the shuddering night.

Villainy somewhere ! whose? One says, we are villains all.
Not he : his honest fame should at least by me be maintained :
But that old man, now lord of the broad estate and the Hall,
Dropt off gorged from a scheme that had left us flaccid and drain'd.   **20**

Why do they prate of the blessings of Peace? we have made them a
    curse,
Pickpockets, each hand lusting for all that is not its own;
And lust of gain, in the spirit of Cain, is it better or worse
Than the heart of the citizen hissing in war on his own hearthstone?

But these are the days of advance, the works of the men of mind,
When who but a fool would have faith in a tradesman's ware or his
    word?
Is it peace or war? Civil war, as I think, and that of a kind
The viler, as underhand, not openly bearing the sword.

Sooner or later I too may passively take the print
Of the golden age—why not?   I have neither hope nor trust;   *30*
May make my heart as a millstone, set my face as a flint,
Cheat and be cheated, and die : who knows? we are ashes and dust.

Peace sitting under her olive, and slurring the days gone by,
When the poor are hovell'd and hustled together, each sex, like swine,
When only the ledger lives, and when only not all men lie;
Peace in her vineyard—yes !—but a company forges the wine.

And the vitriol madness flushes up in the ruffian's head,
Till the filthy by-lane rings to the yell of the trampled wife,
And chalk and alum and plaster are sold to the poor for bread,
And the spirit of murder works in the very means of life,   *40*

And Sleep must lie down arm'd, for the villainous centre-bits
Grind on the wakeful ear in the hush of the moonless nights,
While another is cheating the sick of a few last gasps, as he sits
To pestle a poison'd poison behind his crimson lights.

When a Mammonite mother kills her babe for a burial fee,
And Timour-Mammon grins on a pile of children's bones,
Is it peace or war? better, war! loud war by land and by sea,
War with a thousand battles, and shaking a hundred thrones.

For I trust if an enemy's fleet came yonder round by the hill,
And the rushing battle-bolt sang from the three-decker out of the foam, *50*
That the smooth-faced snubnosed rogue would leap from his counter
    and till,
And strike, if he could, were it but with his cheating yardwand,
    home.——

What ! am I raging alone as my father raged in his mood?
Must *I* too creep to the hollow and dash myself down and die
Rather than hold by the law that I made, nevermore to brood
On a horror of shatter'd limbs and a wretched swindler's lie?

Would there be sorrow for *me* ? there was *love* in the passionate shriek,
Love for the silent thing that had made false haste to the grave—
Wrapt in a cloak, as I saw him, and thought he would rise and speak
And rave at the lie and the liar, ah God, as he used to rave.   *60*

I am sick of the Hall and the hill, I am sick of the moor and the main.
Why should I stay? can a sweeter chance ever come to me here?
O, having the nerves of motion as well as the nerves of pain,
Were it not wise if I fled from the place and the pit and the fear?

Workmen up at the Hall!—they are coming back from abroad;
The dark old place will be gilt by the touch of a millionaire:
I have heard, I know not whence, of the singular beauty of Maud;
I play'd with the girl when a child; she promised then to be fair.

Maud with her venturous climbings and tumbles and childish escapes,
Maud the delight of the village, the ringing joy of the Hall,   70
Maud with her sweet purse-mouth when my father dangled the grapes,
Maud the beloved of my mother, the moon-faced darling of all,—

What is she now? My dreams are bad. She may bring me a curse.
No, there is fatter game on the moor; she will let me alone.
Thanks, for the fiend best knows whether woman or man be the worse.
I will bury myself in myself, and the Devil may pipe to his own.

II

Long have I sigh'd for a calm: God grant I may find it at last!
It will never be broken by Maud, she has neither savour nor salt,
But a cold and clear-cut face, as I found when her carriage past,
Perfectly beautiful: let it be granted her: where is the fault?
All that I saw (for her eyes were downcast, not to be seen)
Faultily faultless, icily regular, splendidly null,
Dead perfection, no more; nothing more, if it had not been
For a chance of travel, a paleness, an hour's defect of the rose,
Or an underlip, you may call it a little too ripe, too full,
Or the least little delicate aquiline curve in a sensitive nose,   10
From which I escaped heart-free, with the least little touch of spleen.

III

Cold and clear-cut face, why come you so cruelly meek,
Breaking a slumber in which all spleenful folly was drown'd,
Pale with the golden beam of an eyelash dead on the cheek,
Passionless, pale, cold face, star-sweet on a gloom profound;
Womanlike, taking revenge too deep for a transient wrong
Done but in thought to your beauty, and ever as pale as before
Growing and fading and growing upon me without a sound,
Luminous, gemlike, ghostlike, deathlike, half the night long
Growing and fading and growing, till I could bear it no more,   10
But arose, and all by myself in my own dark garden ground,
Listening now to the tide in its broad-flung shipwrecking roar,
Now to the scream of a madden'd beach dragg'd down by the wave,
Walk'd in a wintry wind by a ghastly glimmer, and found
The shining daffodil dead, and Orion low in his grave.

IV

A million emeralds break from the ruby-budded lime
In the little grove where I sit—ah, wherefore cannot I be
Like things of the season gay, like the bountiful season bland,
When the far-off sail is blown by the breeze of a softer clime,
Half-lost in the liquid azure bloom of a crescent of sea,
The silent sapphire-spangled marriage ring of the land?

Below me, there, is the village, and looks how quiet and small!
And yet bubbles o'er like a city, with gossip, scandal, and spite;
And Jack on his ale-house bench has as many lies as a Czar;
And here on the landward side, by a red rock, glimmers the Hall;   10
And up in the high Hall-garden I see her pass like a light;
But sorrow seize me if ever that light be my leading star!

When have I bow'd to her father, the wrinkled head of the race?
I met her to-day with her brother, but not to her brother I bow'd:
I bow'd to his lady-sister as she rode by on the moor;
But the fire of a foolish pride flash'd over her beautiful face.
O child, you wrong your beauty, believe it, in being so proud;
Your father has wealth well-gotten, and I am nameless and poor.

I keep but a man and a maid, ever ready to slander and steal;
I know it, and smile a hard-set smile, like a stoic, or like   20
A wiser epicurean, and let the world have its way:
For nature is one with rapine, a harm no preacher can heal;
The Mayfly is torn by the swallow, the sparrow spear'd by the shrike,
And the whole little wood where I sit is a world of plunder and prey.

We are puppets, Man in his pride, and Beauty fair in her flower;
Do we move ourselves, or are moved by an unseen hand at a game
That pushes us off from the board, and others ever succeed?
Ah yet, we cannot be kind to each other here for an hour;
We whisper, and hint, and chuckle, and grin at a brother's shame;
However we brave it out, we men are a little breed.   30

A monstrous eft was of old the Lord and Master of Earth,
For him did his high sun flame, and his river billowing ran,
And he felt himself in his force to be Nature's crowning race.
As nine months go to the shaping an infant ripe for his birth,
So many a million of ages have gone to the making of man:
He now is first, but is he the last? is he not too base?

The man of science himself is fonder of glory, and vain,
An eye well-practised in nature, a spirit bounded and poor;
The passionate heart of the poet is whirl'd into folly and vice.

I would not marvel at either, but keep a temperate brain;   **40**
For not to desire or admire, if a man could learn it, were more
Than to walk all day like the sultan of old in a garden of spice.

For the drift of the Maker is dark, an Isis hid by the veil.
Who knows the ways of the world, how God will bring them about?
Our planet is one, the suns are many, the world is wide.
Shall I weep if a Poland fall? shall I shriek if a Hungary fail?
Or an infant civilisation be ruled with rod or with knout?
I have not made the world, and He that made it will guide.

Be mine a philosopher's life in the quiet woodland ways,
Where if I cannot be gay let a passionless peace be my lot,   **50**
Far-off from the clamour of liars belied in the hubbub of lies;
From the long-neck'd geese of the world that are ever hissing dispraise
Because their natures are little, and, whether he heed it or not,
Where each man walks with his head in a cloud of poisonous flies.

And most of all would I flee from the cruel madness of love,
The honey of poison-flowers and all the measureless ill.
Ah Maud, you milkwhite fawn, you are all unmeet for a wife.
Your mother is mute in her grave as her image in marble above;
Your father is ever in London, you wander about at your will;
You have but fed on the roses and lain in the lilies of life.   **60**

V

A voice by the cedar tree
In the meadow under the Hall!
She is singing an air that is known to me,
A passionate ballad gallant and gay,
A martial song like a trumpet's call!
Singing alone in the morning of life,
In the happy morning of life and of May,
Singing of men that in battle array,
Ready in heart and ready in hand,
March with banner and bugle and fife   **10**
To the death, for their native land.

Maud with her exquisite face,
And wild voice pealing up to the sunny sky,
And feet like sunny gems on an English green,
Maud in the light of her youth and her grace,
Singing of Death, and of Honour that cannot die,
Till I well could weep for a time so sordid and mean,
And myself so languid and base.

Silence, beautiful voice!
Be still, for you only trouble the mind   *20*
With a joy in which I cannot rejoice,
A glory I shall not find.
Still! I will hear you no more,
For your sweetness hardly leaves me a choice
But to move to the meadow and fall before
Her feet on the meadow grass, and adore,
Not her, who is neither courtly nor kind,
Not her, not her, but a voice.

VI

Morning arises stormy and pale,
No sun, but a wannish glare
In fold upon fold of hueless cloud,
And the budded peaks of the wood are bow'd
Caught and cuff'd by the gale:
I had fancied it would be fair.

Whom but Maud should I meet
Last night, when the sunset burn'd
On the blossom'd gable-ends
At the head of the village street,   *10*
Whom but Maud should I meet?
And she touch'd my hand with a smile so sweet
She made me divine amends
For a courtesy not return'd.

And thus a delicate spark
Of glowing and growing light
Thro' the livelong hours of the dark
Kept itself warm in the heart of my dreams,
Ready to burst in a coloured flame;
Till at last when the morning came   *20*
In a cloud, it faded, and seems
But an ashen-gray delight.

What if with her sunny hair,
And smile as sunny as cold,
She meant to weave me a snare
Of some coquettish deceit,
Cleopatra-like as of old
To entangle me when we met,
To have her lion roll in a silken net
And fawn at a victor's feet.   *30*

Ah, what shall I be at fifty
Should Nature keep me alive,
If I find the world so bitter
When I am but twenty-five?
Yet, if she were not a cheat,
If Maud were all that she seem'd,
And her smile were all that I dream'd,
Then the world were not so bitter
But a smile could make it sweet.

What if tho' her eye seem'd full   40
Of a kind intent to me,
What if that dandy-despot, he,
That jewell'd mass of millinery,
That oil'd and curl'd Assyrian Bull
Smelling of musk and of insolence,
Her brother, from whom I keep aloof,
Who wants the finer politic sense
To mask, tho' but in his own behoof,
With a glassy smile his brutal scorn—
What if he had told her yestermorn   50
How prettily for his own sweet sake
A face of tenderness might be feign'd,
And a moist mirage in desert eyes,
That so, when the rotten hustings shake
In another month to his brazen lies,
A wretched vote may be gain'd.

For a raven ever croaks, at my side,
Keep watch and ward, keep watch and ward,
Or thou wilt prove their tool.
Yea, too, myself from myself I guard,   60
For often a man's own angry pride
Is cap and bells for a fool.

Perhaps the smile and tender tone
Came out of her pitying womanhood,
For am I not, am I not, here alone
So many a summer since she died,
My mother, who was so gentle and good?
Living alone in an empty house,
Here half-hid in the gleaming wood,
Where I hear the dead at midday moan,   70
And the shrieking rush of the wainscot mouse,
And my own sad name in corners cried,
When the shiver of dancing leaves is thrown
About its echoing chambers wide,

Till a morbid hate and horror have grown
Of a world in which I have hardly mixt,
And a morbid eating lichen fixt
On a heart half-turn'd to stone.

O heart of stone, are you flesh, and caught
By that you swore to withstand?   *80*
For what was it else within me wrought
But, I fear, the new strong wine of love,
That made my tongue so stammer and trip
When I saw the treasured splendour, her hand,
Come sliding out of her sacred glove,
And the sunlight broke from her lip?

I have play'd with her when a child;
She remembers it now we meet.
Ah well, well, well, I *may* be beguiled
By some coquettish deceit.   *90*
Yet, if she were not a cheat,
If Maud were all that she seem'd,
And her smile had all that I dream'd,
Then the world were not so bitter
But a smile could make it sweet.

VII

Did I hear it half in a doze
    Long since, I know not where?
Did I dream it an hour ago,
    When asleep in this arm-chair?

Men were drinking together,
    Drinking and talking of me;
' Well, if it prove a girl, the boy
    Will have plenty: so let it be.'

Is it an echo of something
    Read with a boy's delight,   *10*
Viziers nodding together
    In some Arabian night?

Strange, that I hear two men,
    Somewhere, talking of me;
' Well, if it prove a girl, my boy
    Will have plenty: so let it be.'

VIII

She came to the village church
And sat by a pillar alone;
An angel watching an urn
Wept over her, carved in stone;
And once, but once, she lifted her eyes,
And suddenly, sweetly, strangely blush'd
To find they were met by my own;
And suddenly, sweetly, my heart beat stronger
And thicker, until I heard no longer
The snowy-banded, dilettante,   *10*
Delicate-handed priest intone;
And thought, is it pride, and mused and sigh'd
' No surely, now it cannot be pride.'

IX

I was walking a mile,
More than a mile from the shore,
The sun look'd out with a smile
Betwixt the cloud and the moor
And riding at set of day
Over the dark moor land,
Rapidly riding far away,
She waved to me with her hand.
There were two at her side,
Something flash'd in the sun,   *10*
Down by the hill I saw them ride,
In a moment they were gone:
Like a sudden spark
Struck vainly in the night,
Then returns the dark
With no more hope of light.

X

Sick, am I sick of a jealous dread?
Was not one of the two at her side
This new-made lord, whose splendour plucks
The slavish hat from the villager's head?
Whose old grandfather has lately died,
Gone to a blacker pit, for whom
Grimy nakedness dragging his trucks
And laying his trams in a poison'd gloom
Wrought, till he crept from a gutted mine
Master of half a servile shire,   *10*

And left his coal all turn'd into gold
To a grandson, first of his noble line,
Rich in the grace all women desire,
Strong in the power that all men adore,
And simper and set their voices lower,
And soften as if to a girl, and hold
Awe-stricken breaths at a work divine,
Seeing his gewgaw castle shine,
New as his title, built last year,
There amid perky larches and pine,   20
And over the sullen-purple moor
(Look at it) pricking a cockney ear.

What, has he found my jewel out?
For one of the two that rode at her side
Bound for the Hall, I am sure was he:
Bound for the Hall, and I think for a bride.
Blithe would her brother's acceptance be.
Maud could be gracious too, no doubt
To a lord, a captain, a padded shape,
A bought commission, a waxen face,   30
A rabbit mouth that is ever agape—
Bought? what is it he cannot buy?
And therefore splenetic, personal, base,
A wounded thing with a rancorous cry,
At war with myself and a wretched race,
Sick, sick to the heart of life, am I.

Last week came one to the county town,
To preach our poor little army down,
And play the game of the despot kings,
Tho' the state has done it and thrice as well: 40
This broad-brimm'd hawker of holy things,
Whose ear is cramm'd with his cotton, and rings
Even in dreams to the chink of his pence,
This huckster put down war! can he tell
Whether war be a cause or a consequence?
Put down the passions that make earth Hell!
Down with ambition, avarice, pride,
Jealousy, down! cut off from the mind
The bitter springs of anger and fear;
Down too, down at your own fireside,   50
With the evil tongue and the evil ear,
For each is at war with mankind.

I wish I could hear again
The chivalrous battle-song
That she warbled alone in her joy!

I might persuade myself then
She would not do herself this great wrong,
To take a wanton dissolute boy
For a man and leader of men.

Ah God, for a man with heart, head, hand,   *60*
Like some of the simple great ones gone
For ever and ever by,
One still strong man in a blatant land,
Whatever they call him, what care I,
Aristocrat, democrat, autocrat—one
Who can rule and dare not lie.

And ah for a man to arise in me,
That the man I am may cease to be!

XI

O let the solid ground
    Not fail beneath my feet
Before my life has found
    What some have found so sweet;
Then let come what come may,
What matter if I go mad,
I shall have had my day.

Let the sweet heavens endure,
    Not close and darken above me
Before I am quite quite sure   *10*
    That there is one to love me;
Then let come what come may
To a life that has been so sad,
I shall have had my day.

XII

Birds in the high Hall-garden
    When twilight was falling,
Maud, Maud, Maud, Maud,
    They were crying and calling.

Where was Maud? in our wood;
    And I, who else, was with her,
Gathering woodland lilies,
    Myriads blow together.

Birds in our wood sang
  Ringing thro' the valleys,   *10*
Maud is here, here, here
  In among the lilies.

I kiss'd her slender hand,
  She took the kiss sedately;
Maud is not seventeen,
  But she is tall and stately.

I to cry out on pride
  Who have won her favour!
O Maud were sure of Heaven
  If lowliness could save her.   *20*

I know the way she went
  Home with her maiden posy,
For her feet have touch'd the meadows
  And left the daisies rosy.

Birds in the high Hall-garden
  Were crying and calling to her,
Where is Maud, Maud, Maud?
  One is come to woo her.

Look, a horse at the door,
  And little King Charley snarling,   *30*
Go back, my lord, across the moor,
  You are not her darling.

XIII

Scorn'd, to be scorn'd by one that I scorn,
Is that a matter to make me fret?
That a calamity hard to be borne?
Well, he may live to hate me yet.
Fool that I am to be vext with his pride!
I past him, I was crossing his lands;
He stood on the path a little aside;
His face, as I grant, in spite of spite,
Has a broad-blown comeliness, red and white,
And six feet two, as I think, he stands;   *10*
But his essences turn'd the live air sick,
And barbarous opulence jewel-thick
Sunn'd itself on his breast and his hands.

Who shall call me ungentle, unfair,
I long'd so heartily then and there
To give him the grasp of fellowship;
But while I past he was humming an air,
Stopt, and then with a riding whip
Leisurely tapping a glossy boot,
And curving a contumelious lip,   20
Gorgonised me from head to foot
With a stony British stare.

Why sits he here in his father's chair?
That old man never comes to his place:
Shall I believe him ashamed to be seen?
For only once, in the village street,
Last year, I caught a glimpse of his face,
A gray old wolf and a lean,
Scarcely, now, would I call him a cheat;
For then, perhaps, as a child of deceit,   30
She might by a true descent be untrue;
And Maud is as true as Maud is sweet:
Tho' I fancy her sweetness only due
To the sweeter blood by the other side;
Her mother has been a thing complete,
However she came to be so allied.
And fair without, faithful within,
Maud to him is nothing akin:
Some peculiar mystic grace
Made her only the child of her mother,   40
And heap'd the whole inherited sin
On that huge scapegoat of the race,
All, all upon the brother.

Peace, angry spirit, and let him be!
Has not his sister smiled on me?

XIV

Maud has a garden of roses
And lilies fair on a lawn;
There she walks in her state
And tends upon bed and bower,
And thither I climb'd at dawn
And stood by her garden-gate;
A lion ramps at the top,
He is claspt by a passion-flower.

Maud's own little oak-room
(Which Maud, like a precious stone   *10*
Set in the heart of the carven gloom,
Lights with herself, when alone
She sits by her music and books
And her brother lingers late
With a roystering company) looks
Upon Maud's own garden-gate:
And I thought as I stood, if a hand, as white
As ocean-foam in the moon, were laid
On the hasp of the window, and my Delight
Had a sudden desire, like a glorious ghost, to glide,   *20*
Like a beam of the seventh Heaven, down to my side,
There were but a step to be made.

The fancy flatter'd my mind,
And again seem'd overbold;
Now I thought that she cared for me,
Now I thought she was kind
Only because she was cold.

I heard no sound where I stood
But the rivulet on from the lawn
Running down to my own dark wood;   *30*
Or the voice of the long sea-wave as it swell'd
Now and then in the dim-gray dawn;
But I look'd, and round, all round the house I beheld
The death-white curtain drawn;
Felt a horror over me creep,
Prickle my skin and catch my breath,
Knew that the death-white curtain meant but sleep,
Yet I shudder'd and thought like a fool of the sleep of death.

XV

So dark a mind within me dwells,
    And I make myself such evil cheer,
That if *I* be dear to some one else,
    Then some one else may have much to fear;
But if *I* be dear to some one else,
    Then I should be to myself more dear.
Shall I not take care of all that I think,
Yea ev'n of wretched meat and drink,
If I be dear,
If I be dear to someone else.   *10*

XVI

This lump of earth has left his estate
The lighter by the loss of his weight;
And so that he find what he went to seek,
And fulsome Pleasure clog him, and drown
His heart in the gross mud-honey of town,
He may stay for a year who has gone for a week:
But this is the day when I must speak,
And I see my Oread coming down,
O this is the day!
O beautiful creature, what am I   *10*
That I dare to look her way;
Think I may hold dominion sweet,
Lord of the pulse that is lord of her breast,
And dream of her beauty with tender dread,
From the delicate Arab arch of her feet
To the grace that, bright and light as the crest
Of a peacock, sits on her shining head,
And she knows it not: O, if she knew it,
To know her beauty might half undo it.
I know it the one bright thing to save   *20*
My yet young life in the wilds of Time,
Perhaps from madness, perhaps from crime,
Perhaps from a selfish grave.

What, if she be fasten'd to this fool lord,
Dare I bid her abide by her word?
Should I love her so well if she
Had given her word to a thing so low?
Shall I love her as well if she
Can break her word were it even for me?
I trust that it is not so.   *30*

Catch not my breath, O clamorous heart,
Let not my tongue be a thrall to my eye,
For I must tell her before we part,
I must tell her, or die.

XVII

Go not, happy day,
    From the shining fields,
Go not, happy day,
    Till the maiden yields.
Rosy is the West,

Rosy is the South,
Roses are her cheeks,
    And a rose her mouth
When the happy Yes
    Falters from her lips,   *10*
Pass and blush the news
    Over glowing ships;
Over blowing seas,
    Over seas at rest,
Pass the happy news,
    Blush it thro' the West:
Till the red man dance
    By his red cedar-tree,
And the red man's babe
    Leap, beyond the sea.   *20*
Blush from West to East,
    Blush from East to West,
Till the West is East,
    Blush it thro' the West.
Rosy is the West,
    Rosy is the South,
Roses are her cheeks,
    And a rose her mouth.

XVIII

I have led her home, my love, my only friend.
There is none like her, none.
And never yet so warmly ran my blood
And sweetly, on and on
Calming itself to the long-wish'd-for end,
Full to the banks, close on the promised good.

None like her, none.
Just now the dry-tongued laurels' pattering talk
Seem'd her light foot along the garden walk,
And shook my heart to think she comes once more;   *10*
But even then I heard her close the door,
The gates of Heaven are closed, and she is gone.

There is none like her, none.
Nor will be when our summers have deceased.
O, art thou sighing for Lebanon
In the long breeze that streams to thy delicious East,
Sighing for Lebanon,
Dark cedar, tho' thy limbs have here increased,

Upon a pastoral slope as fair,
And looking to the South, and fed   20
With honey'd rain and delicate air,
And haunted by the starry head
Of her whose gentle will has changed my fate,
And made my life a perfumed altar-flame;
And over whom thy darkness must have spread
With such delight as theirs of old, thy great
Forefathers of the thornless garden, there
Shadowing the snow-limb'd Eve from whom she came.

Here will I lie, while these long branches sway,
And you fair stars that crown a happy day   30
Go in and out as if at merry play,
Who am no more so all forlorn,
As when it seem'd far better to be born
To labour and the mattock-harden'd hand,
Than nursed at ease and brought to understand
A sad astrology, the boundless plan
That makes you tyrants in your iron skies,
Innumerable, pitiless, passionless eyes,
Cold fires, yet with power to burn and brand
His nothingness into man.   40

But now shine on, and what care I,
Who in this stormy gulf have found a pearl
The countercharm of space and hollow sky,
And do accept my madness, and would die
To save from some slight shame one simple girl.

Would die; for sullen-seeming Death may give
More life to Love than is or ever was
In our low world, where yet 'tis sweet to live.
Let no one ask me how it came to pass;
It seems that I am happy, that to me   50
A livelier emerald twinkles in the grass,
A purer sapphire melts into the sea.

Not die; but live a life of truest breath,
And teach true life to fight with mortal wrongs,
O, why should Love, like men in drinking-songs,
Spice his fair banquet with the dust of death?
Make answer, Maud my bliss,
Maud made my Maud by that long loving kiss,
Life of my life, wilt thou not answer this?
' The dusky strand of Death inwoven here   60
With dear Love's tie, makes Love himself more dear.'

Is that enchanted moan only the swell
Of the long waves that roll in yonder bay?
And hark the clock within, the silver knell
Of twelve sweet hours that past in bridal white,
And died to live, long as my pulses play;
But now by this my love has closed her sight
And given false death her hand, and stol'n away
To dreamful wastes where footless fancies dwell
Among the fragments of the golden day.   *70*
May nothing there her maiden grace affright!
Dear heart, I feel with thee the drowsy spell.
My bride to be, my evermore delight,
My own heart's heart, my ownest own, farewell;
It is but for a little space I go:
And ye meanwhile far over moor and fell
Beat to the noiseless music of the night!
Has our whole earth gone nearer to the glow
Of your soft splendours that you look so bright?
I have climb'd nearer out of lonely Hell.   *80*
Beat, happy stars, timing with things below,
Beat with my heart more blest than heart can tell,
Blest, but for some dark undercurrent woe
That seems to draw—but it shall not be so:
Let all be well, be well.

XIX

Her brother is coming back to-night,
Breaking up my dream of delight.

My dream? do I dream of bliss?
I have walk'd awake with Truth.
O when did a morning shine
So rich in atonement as this
For my dark-dawning youth,
Darken'd watching a mother decline
And that dead man at her heart and mine:
For who was left to watch her but I?   *10*
Yet so did I let my freshness die.

I trust that I did not talk
To gentle Maud in our walk
(For often in lonely wanderings
I have cursed him even to lifeless things)
But I trust that I did not talk,
Not touch on her father's sin:
I am sure I did but speak
Of my mother's faded cheek
When it slowly grew so thin,   *20*

That I felt she was slowly dying
Vext with lawyers and harass'd with debt:
For how often I caught her with eyes all wet,
Shaking her head at her son and sighing
A world of trouble within!

And Maud too, Maud was moved
To speak of the mother she loved
As one scarce less forlorn,
Dying abroad and it seems apart
From him who had ceased to share her heart, 30
And ever mourning over the feud,
The household Fury sprinkled with blood
By which our houses are torn:
How strange was what she said,
When only Maud and the brother
Hung over her dying bed—
That Maud's dark father and mine
Had bound us one to the other,
Betrothed us over their wine,
On the day when Maud was born; 40
Seal'd her mine from her first sweet breath.
Mine, mine by a right, from birth till death.
Mine, mine—our fathers have sworn.

But the true blood spilt had in it a heat
To dissolve the precious seal on a bond,
That, if left uncancell'd, had been so sweet:
And none of us thought of a something beyond,
A desire that awoke in the heart of the child,
As it were a duty done to the tomb,
To be friends for her sake, to be reconciled; 50
And I was cursing them and my doom,
And letting a dangerous thought run wild
While often abroad in the fragrant gloom
Of foreign churches—I see her there,
Bright English lily, breathing a prayer
To be friends, to be reconciled!

But then what a flint is he!
Abroad, at Florence, at Rome,
I find whenever she touch'd on me
This brother had laugh'd her down, 60
And at last, when each came home,
He had darken'd into a frown,
Chid her, and forbid her to speak
To me, her friend of the years before;
And this was what had redden'd her cheek
When I bow'd to her on the moor.

Yet Maud, altho' not blind
To the faults of his heart and mind,
I see she cannot but love him,
And says he is rough but kind,   70
And wishes me to approve him,
And tells me, when she lay
Sick once, with a fear of worse,
That he left his wine and horses and play,
Sat with her, read to her, night and day,
And tended her like a nurse.

Kind? but the deathbed desire
Spurn'd by this heir of the liar—
Rough but kind? yet I know
He has plotted against me in this,   80
That he plots against me still.
Kind to Maud? that were not amiss.
Well, rough but kind; why let it be so:
For shall not Maud have her will?

For, Maud, so tender and true,
As long as my life endures
I feel I shall owe you a debt,
That I never can hope to pay;
And if ever I should forget
That I owe this debt to you   90
And for your sweet sake to yours;
O then, what then shall I say?—
If ever I *should* forget,
May God make me more wretched
Than ever I have been yet!

So now I have sworn to bury
All this dead body of hate,
I feel so free and so clear
By the loss of that dead weight,
That I should grow light-headed, I fear,   100
Fantastically merry;
But that her brother comes, like a blight
On my fresh hope, to the Hall to-night.

XX

Strange, that I felt so gay,
Strange, that *I* tried to-day
To beguile her melancholy;
The Sultan, as we name him,—

She did not wish to blame him—
But he vext her and perplext her
With his worldly talk and folly:
Was it gentle to reprove her
For stealing out of view
From a little lazy lover   10
Who but claims her as his due?
Or for chilling his caresses
By the coldness of her manners,
Nay, the plainness of her dresses?
Now I know her but in two,
Nor can pronounce upon it
If one should ask me whether
The habit, hat, and feather,
Or the frock and gipsy bonnet
Be the neater and completer;   20
For nothing can be sweeter
Than maiden Maud in either.

But to-morrow, if we live,
Our ponderous squire will give
A grand political dinner
To half the squirelings near;
And Maud will wear her jewels,
And the bird of prey will hover,
And the titmouse hope to win her
With his chirrup at her ear.   30

A grand political dinner
To the men of many acres,
A gathering of the Tory,
A dinner and then a dance
For the maids and marriage-makers,
And every eye but mine will glance
At Maud in all her glory.

For I am not invited,
But, with the Sultan's pardon,
I am all as well delighted,   40
For I know her own rose-garden,
And mean to linger in it
Till the dancing will be over;
And then, oh then, come out to me
For a minute, but for a minute,
Come out to your own true lover,
That your true lover may see
Your glory also, and render
All homage to his own darling,
Queen Maud in all her splendour.   50

XXI

Rivulet crossing my ground,
And bringing me down from the Hall
This garden-rose that I found,
Forgetful of Maud and me,
And lost in trouble and moving round
Here at the head of a tinkling fall,
And trying to pass to the sea;
O Rivulet, born at the Hall,
My Maud has sent it by thee
(If I read her sweet will right)　　10
On a blushing mission to me,
Saying in odour and colour, ' Ah, be
Among the roses to-night.'

XXII

Come into the garden, Maud,
　For the black bat, night, has flown,
Come into the garden, Maud,
　I am here at the gate alone;
And the woodbine spices are wafted abroad,
　And the musk of the rose is blown.

For a breeze of morning moves,
　And the planet of Love is on high,
Beginning to faint in the light that she loves
　On a bed of daffodil sky,　　10
To faint in the light of the sun she loves,
　To faint in his light, and to die.

All night have the roses heard
　The flute, violin, bassoon;
All night has the casement jessamine stirr'd
　To the dancers dancing in tune;
Till a silence fell with the waking bird,
　And a hush with the setting moon.

I said to the lily, ' There is but one
　With whom she has heart to be gay.　　20
When will the dancers leave her alone?
　She is weary of dance and play.'
Now half to the setting moon are gone,
　And half to the rising day;
Low on the sand and loud on the stone
　The last wheel echoes away.

I said to the rose, ' The brief night goes
  In babble and revel and wine.
O young lord-lover, what sighs are those,
  For one that will never be thine?   *30*
But mine, but mine,' so I sware to the rose,
  ' For ever and ever, mine.'

And the soul of the rose went into my blood,
  As the music clash'd in the hall;
And long by the garden lake I stood,
  For I heard your rivulet fall
From the lake to the meadow and on to the wood,
  Our wood, that is dearer than all;

From the meadow your walks have left so sweet
  That whenever a March-wind sighs   *40*
He sets the jewel-print of your feet
  In violets blue as your eyes,
To the woody hollows in which we meet
  And the valleys of Paradise.

The slender acacia would not shake
  One long milk-bloom on the tree;
The white lake-blossom fell into the lake
  As the pimpernel dozed on the lea;
But the rose was awake all night for your sake,
  Knowing your promise to me;   *50*
The lilies and roses were all awake,
  They sigh'd for the dawn and thee.

Queen rose of the rosebud garden of girls,
  Come hither, the dances are done,
In gloss of satin and glimmer of pearls,
  Queen lily and rose in one;
Shine out, little head, sunning over with curls,
  To the flowers, and be their sun.

There has fallen a splendid tear
  From the passion-flower at the gate.   *60*
She is coming, my dove, my dear;
  She is coming, my life, my fate;
The red rose cries, ' She is near, she is near;'
  And the white rose weeps, ' She is late;'
The larkspur listens, ' I hear, I hear;'
  And the lily whispers, ' I wait.'

She is coming, my own, my sweet;
    Were it ever so airy a tread,
My heart would hear her and beat,
    Were it earth in an earthy bed;   *70*
My dust would hear her and beat,
    Had I lain for a century dead;
Would start and tremble under her feet,
    And blossom in purple and red.

PART II

I

' THE fault was mine, the fault was mine '—
Why am I sitting here so stunn'd and still,
Plucking the harmless wild-flower on the hill?—
It is this guilty hand!—
And there rises ever a passionate cry
From underneath in the darkening land—
What is it, that has been done?
O dawn of Eden bright over earth and sky,
The fires of Hell brake out of thy rising sun,
The fires of Hell and of Hate;   *10*
For she, sweet soul, had hardly spoken a word,
When her brother ran in his rage to the gate,
He came with the babe-faced lord;
Heap'd on her terms of disgrace,
And while she wept, and I strove to be cool,
He fiercely gave me the lie,
Till I with as fierce an anger spoke,
And he struck me, madman, over the face,
Struck me before the languid fool,
Who was gaping and grinning by: *20*
Struck for himself an evil stroke;
Wrought for his house an irredeemable woe;
For front to front in an hour we stood,
And a million horrible bellowing echoes broke
From the red-ribb'd hollow behind the wood,
And thunder'd up into Heaven the Christless code,
That must have life for a blow.
Ever and ever afresh they seem'd to grow.
Was it he lay there with a fading eye?
' The fault was mine,' he whisper'd, ' fly ! '   *30*
Then glided out of the joyous wood
The ghastly Wraith of one that I know;
And there rang on a sudden a passionate cry,
A cry for a brother's blood:
It will ring in my heart and my ears, till I die, till I die.

Is it gone? my pulses beat—
What was it? a lying trick of the brain?
Yet I thought I saw her stand,
A shadow there at my feet,   40
High over the shadowy land.
It is gone; and the heavens fall in a gentle rain,
When they should burst and drown with deluging storms
The feeble vassals of wine and anger and lust,
The little hearts that know not how to forgive:
Arise, my God, and strike, for we hold Thee just,
Strike dead the whole weak race of venomous worms,
That sting each other here in the dust;
We are not worthy to live.

II

See what a lovely shell,
Small and pure as a pearl,
Lying close to my foot,
Frail, but a work divine,
Made so fairly well
With delicate spire and whorl,
How exquisitely minute,
A miracle of design!

What is it? a learned man
Could give it a clumsy name.   10
Let him name it who can,
The beauty would be the same.

The tiny cell is forlorn,
Void of the little living will
That made it stir on the shore.
Did he stand at the diamond door
Of his house in a rainbow frill?
Did he push, when he was uncurl'd,
A golden foot or a fairy horn
Thro' his dim water-world?   20

Slight, to be crush'd with a tap
Of my finger-nail on the sand,
Small, but a work divine,
Frail, but of force to withstand,
Year upon year, the shock
Of cataract seas that snap
The three decker's oaken spine
Athwart the ledges of rock,
Here on the Breton strand!

Breton, not Briton; here   *30*
Like a shipwreck'd man on a coast
Of ancient fable and fear—
Plagued with a flitting to and fro,
A disease, a hard mechanic ghost
That never came from on high
Nor ever arose from below,
But only moves with the moving eye,
Flying along the land and the main—
Why should it look like Maud?
Am I to be overawed   *40*
By what I cannot but know
Is a juggle born of the brain?

Back from the Breton coast,
Sick of a nameless fear,
Back to the dark sea-line
Looking, thinking of all I have lost;
An old song vexes my ear;
But that of Lamech is mine.

For years, a measureless ill,
For years, for ever, to part—   *50*
But she, she would love me still;
And as long, O God, as she
Have a grain of love for me,
So long, no doubt, no doubt,
Shall I nurse in my dark heart,
However weary, a spark of will
Not to be trampled out.

Strange, that the mind, when fraught
With a passion so intense
One would think that it well   *60*
Might drown all life in the eye,—
That it should, by being so overwrought,
Suddenly strike on a sharper sense
For a shell, or a flower, little things
Which else would have been past by!
And now I remember, I,
When he lay dying there,
I noticed one of his many rings
(For he had many, poor worm) and thought
It is his mother's hair.   *70*

Who knows if he be dead?
Whether I need have fled?
Am I guilty of blood?
However this may be,
Comfort her, comfort her, all things good,
While I am over the sea!
Let me and my passionate love go by,
But speak to her all things holy and high,
Whatever happen to me!
Me and my harmful love go by;   *80*
But come to her waking, find her asleep,
Powers of the height, Powers of the deep,
And comfort her tho' I die.

III

Courage, poor heart of stone!
I will not ask thee why
Thou canst not understand
That thou are left for ever alone:
Courage, poor stupid heart of stone,—
Or if I ask thee why,
Care not thou to reply:
She is but dead, and the time is at hand
When thou shalt more than die.

IV

O that 'twere possible
After long grief and pain
To find the arms of my true love
Round me once again!

When I was wont to meet her
In the silent woody places
By the home that gave me birth,
We stood tranced in long embraces
Mixt with kisses sweeter sweeter
Than anything on earth.   *10*

A shadow flits before me,
Not thou, but like to thee:
Ah Christ, that it were possible
For one short hour to see
The souls we loved, that they might tell us
What and where they be.

It leads me forth at evening,
It lightly winds and steals
In a cold white robe before me,
When all my spirit reels   *20*
At the shouts, the leagues of lights,
And the roaring of the wheels.

Half the night I waste in sighs,
Half in dreams I sorrow after
The delight of early skies;
In a wakeful doze I sorrow
For the hand, the lips, the eyes,
For the meeting of the morrow,
The delight of happy laughter,
The delight of low replies.   *30*

'Tis a morning pure and sweet,
And a dewy splendour falls
On the little flower that clings
To the turrets and the walls;
'Tis a morning pure and sweet,
And the light and shadow fleet;
She is walking in the meadow,
And the woodland echo rings;
In a moment we shall meet;
She is singing in the meadow   *40*
And the rivulet at her feet
Ripples on in light and shadow
To the ballad that she sings.

Do I hear her sing as of old,
My bird with the shining head,
My own dove with the tender eye?
But there rings on a sudden a passionate cry,
There is some one dying or dead,
And a sullen thunder is roll'd;
For a tumult shakes the city,   *50*
And I wake, my dream is fled;
In the shuddering dawn, behold,
Without knowledge, without pity,
By the curtains of my bed
That abiding phantom cold.

Get thee hence, nor come again,
Mix not memory with doubt,
Pass, thou deathlike type of pain,

Pass and cease to move about!
'Tis the blot upon the brain   60
That *will* show itself without.

Then I rise, the eavedrops fall,
And the yellow vapours choke
The great city sounding wide;
The day comes, a dull red ball
Wrapt in drifts of lurid smoke
On the misty river-tide.

Thro' the hubbub of the market
I steal, a wasted frame,
It crosses here, it crosses there,   70
Thro' all that crowd confused and loud,
The shadow still the same;
And on my heavy eyelids
My anguish hangs like shame.

Alas for her that met me,
That heard me softly call,
Came glimmering thro' the laurels
At the quiet evenfall,
In the garden by the turrets
Of the old manorial hall.   80

Would the happy spirit descend,
From the realms of light and song,
In the chamber or the street,
As she looks among the blest,
Should I fear to greet my friend
Or to say ' Forgive the wrong,'
Or to ask her, ' Take me, sweet,
To the regions of thy rest ' ?

But the broad light glares and beats,
And the shadow flits and fleets   90
And will not let me be:
And I loathe the squares and streets,
And the faces that one meets,
Hearts with no love for me:
Always I long to creep
Into some still cavern deep,
There to weep, and weep, and weep
My whole soul out to thee.

V

Dead, long dead,
Long dead!
And my heart is a handful of dust,
And the wheels go over my head,
And my bones are shaken with pain,
For into a shallow grave they are thrust,
Only a yard beneath the street,
And the hoofs of the horses beat, beat,
The hoofs of the horses beat,
Beat into my scalp and my brain,   *10*
With never an end to the stream of passing feet,
Driving, hurrying, marrying, burying,
Clamour and rumble, and ringing and clatter,
And here beneath it is all as bad,
For I thought the dead had peace, but it is not so;
To have no peace in the grave, is that not sad?
But up and down and to and fro,
Ever about me the dead men go;
And then to hear a dead man chatter
Is enough to drive one mad.   *20*

Wretchedest age, since Time began,
They cannot even bury a man;
And tho' we paid our tithes in the days that are gone,
Not a bell was rung, not a prayer was read;
It is that which makes us loud in the world of the dead;
There is none that does his work, not one;
A touch of their office might have sufficed,
But the churchmen fain would kill their church,
As the churches have kill'd their Christ.

See, there is one of us sobbing,   *30*
No limit to his distress;
And another, a lord of all things, praying
To his own great self, as I guess;
And another, a statesman there, betraying
His party-secret, fool, to the press;
And yonder a vile physician, blabbing
The case of his patient—all for what?
To tickle the maggot born in an empty head,
And wheedle a world that loves him not,
For it is but a world of the dead.   *40*

Nothing but idiot gabble!
For the prophecy given of old
And then not understood,

Has come to pass as foretold;
Not let any man think for the public good,
But babble, merely for babble.
For I never whisper'd a private affair
Within the hearing of cat or mouse,
No, not to myself in the closet alone,
But I heard it shouted at once from the top of the house;   *50*
Everything came to be known.
Who told *him* we were there?

Not that gray old wolf, for he came not back
From the wilderness, full of wolves, where he used to lie;
He has gathered the bones for his o'ergrown whelp to crack;
Crack them now for yourself, and howl, and die.

Prophet, curse me the blabbing lip,
And curse me the British vermin, the rat;
I know not whether he came in the Hanover ship,
But I know that he lies and listens mute   *60*
In an ancient mansion's crannies and holes:
Arsenic, arsenic, sure, would do it,
Except that now we poison our babes, poor souls!
It is all used up for that.

Tell him now: she is standing here at my head;
Not beautiful now, not even kind;
He may take her now; for she never speaks her mind,
But is ever the one thing silent here.
She is not *of* us, as I divine;
She comes from another stiller world of the dead,   *70*
Stiller, not fairer than mine.

But I know where a garden grows,
Fairer than aught in the world beside,
All made up of the lily and rose
That blow by night, when the season is good,
To the sound of dancing music and flutes:
It is only flowers, they had no fruits,
And I almost fear they are not roses, but blood;
For the keeper was one, so full of pride,
He linkt a dead man there to a spectral bride;   *80*
For he, if he had not been a Sultan of brutes,
Would he have that hole in his side?

But what will the old man say?
He laid a cruel snare in a pit
To catch a friend of mine one stormy day;
Yet now I could even weep to think of it;
For what will the old man say
When he comes to the second corpse in the pit?

Friend, to be struck by the public foe,
Then to strike him and lay him low,   *90*
That were a public merit, far,
Whatever the Quaker holds, from sin;
But the red life spilt for a private blow—
I swear to you, lawful and lawless war
Are scarcely even akin.

O me, why have they not buried me deep enough?
Is it kind to have made me a grave so rough,
Me, that was never a quiet sleeper?
Maybe still I am but half-dead;
Then I cannot be wholly dumb;   *100*
I will cry to the steps above my head
And somebody, surely, some kind heart will come
To bury me, bury me
Deeper, ever so little deeper.

PART III

VI

MY life has crept so long on a broken wing
Thro' cells of madness, haunts of horror and fear,
That I come to be grateful at last for a little thing:
My mood is changed, for it fell at a time of year
When the face of night is fair on the dewy downs,
And the shining daffodil dies, and the Charioteer
And starry Gemini hang like glorious crowns
Over Orion's grave low down in the west,
That like a silent lightning under the stars
She seem'd to divide in a dream from a band of the blest,   *10*
And spoke of a hope for the world in the coming wars—
' And in that hope, dear soul, let trouble have rest,
Knowing I tarry for thee,' and pointed to Mars
As he glow'd like a ruddy shield on the Lion's breast.

And it was but a dream, yet it yielded a dear delight
To have look'd, tho' but in a dream, upon eyes so fair,
That had been in a weary world my one thing bright;
And it was but a dream, yet it lighten'd my despair
When I thought that a war would arise in defence of the right,
That an iron tyranny now should bend or cease,   *20*
The glory of manhood stand on his ancient height,
Nor Britain's one sole God be the millionaire:
No more shall commerce be all in all, and Peace
Pipe on her pastoral hillock a languid note,
And watch her harvest ripen, her herd increase,

Nor the cannon-bullet rust on a slothful shore,
And the cobweb woven across the cannon's throat
Shall shake its threaded tears in the wind no more.

And as months ran on and rumour of battle grew,
' It is time, it is time, O passionate heart,' said I   *30*
(For I cleaved to a cause that I felt to be pure and true),
' It is time, O passionate heart and morbid eye,
That old hysterical mock-disease should die.'
And I stood on a giant deck and mix'd my breath
With a loyal people shouting a battle cry,
Till I saw the dreary phantom arise and fly
Far into the North, and battle, and seas of death.

Let it go or stay, so I wake to the higher aims
Of a land that has lost for a little her lust of gold,
And love of a peace that was full of wrongs and shames,   *40*
Horrible, hateful, monstrous, not to be told;
And hail once more to the banner of battle unroll'd !
Tho' many a light shall darken, and many shall weep
For those that are crush'd in the clash of jarring claims,
Yet God's just wrath shall be wreak'd on a giant liar;
And many a darkness into the light shall leap,
And shine in the sudden making of splendid names,
And noble thought be freër under the sun,
And the heart of a people beat with one desire;
For the peace, that I deem'd no peace, is over and done,   *50*
And now by the side of the Black and the Baltic deep,
And deathful-grinning mouths of the fortress, flames
The blood-red blossom of war with a heart of fire.

Let it flame or fade, and the war roll down like a wind,
We have proved we have hearts in a cause, we are noble still,
And myself have awaked, as it seems, to the better mind;
It is better to fight for the good than to rail at the ill;
I have felt with my native land, I am one with my kind,
I embrace the purpose of God, and the doom assign'd.

TITHONUS

THE woods decay, the woods decay and fall,
The vapours weep their burthen to the ground,
Man comes and tills the field and lies beneath,
And after many a summer dies the swan.
Me only cruel immortality
Consumes: I wither slowly in thine arms,
Here at the quiet limit of the world,
A white-hair'd shadow roaming like a dream
The ever-silent spaces of the East,
Far-folded mists, and gleaming halls of morn.   *10*

Alas! for this gray shadow, once a man—
So glorious in his beauty and thy choice,
Who madest him thy chosen, that he seem'd
To his great heart none other than a God!
I ask'd thee, ' Give me immortality.'
Then didst thou grant mine asking with a smile,
Like wealthy men who care not how they give.
But thy strong Hours indignant work'd their wills,
And beat me down and marr'd and wasted me,
And tho' they could not end me, left me maim'd   *20*
To dwell in presence of immortal youth,
Immortal age beside immortal youth,
And all I was, in ashes.   Can thy love,
Thy beauty, make amends, tho' even now,
Close over us, the silver star, thy guide,
Shines in those tremulous eyes that fill with tears
To hear me?   Let me go: take back thy gift:
Why should a man desire in any way
To vary from the kindly race of men,
Or pass beyond the goal of ordinance   *30*
Where all should pause, as is most meet for all?

A soft air fans the cloud apart; there comes
A glimpse of that dark world where I was born.
Once more the old mysterious glimmer steals
From thy pure brows, and from thy shoulders pure,
And bosom beating with a heart renew'd.
Thy cheek begins to redden thro' the gloom,
Thy sweet eyes brighten slowly close to mine,
Ere yet they blind the stars, and the wild team
Which love thee, yearning for thy yoke, arise,   *40*
And shake the darkness from their loosen'd manes,
And beat the twilight into flakes of fire.

Lo! ever thus thou growest beautiful
In silence, then before thine answer given
Departest, and thy tears are on my cheek.

Why wilt thou ever scare me with thy tears,
And make me tremble lest a saying learnt,
In days far-off, on that dark earth, be true?
'The Gods themselves cannot recall their gifts.'

Ay me! ay me! with what another heart   *50*
In days far-off, and with what other eyes
I used to watch—if I be he that watch'd—
The lucid outline forming round thee; saw
The dim curls kindle into sunny rings;
Changed with thy mystic change, and felt my blood
Glow with the glow that slowly crimson'd all
Thy presence and thy portals, while I lay,
Mouth, forehead, eyelids, growing dewy-warm
With kisses balmier than half-opening buds
Of April, and could hear the lips that kiss'd   *60*
Whispering I knew not what of wild and sweet,
Like that strange song I heard Apollo sing,
While Ilion like a mist rose into towers.

Yet hold me not for ever in thine East:
How can my nature longer mix with thine?
Coldly thy rosy shadows bathe me, cold
Are all thy lights, and cold my wrinkled feet
Upon thy glimmering thresholds, when the steam
Floats up from those dim fields about the homes
Of happy men that have the power to die,   *70*
And grassy barrows of the happier dead.
Release me, and restore me to the ground;
Thou seëst all things, thou wilt see my grave:
Thou wilt renew thy beauty morn by morn;
I earth in earth forget these empty courts,
And thee returning on thy silver wheels.

IN THE VALLEY OF CAUTERETZ

ALL along the valley, stream that flashest white,
Deepening thy voice with the deepening of the night,
All along the valley, where thy waters flow,
I walk'd with one I loved two and thirty years ago.
All along the valley, while I walk'd to-day,
The two and thirty years were a mist that rolls away;
For all along the valley, down thy rocky bed,
Thy living voice to me was as the voice of the dead,
And all along the valley, by rock and cave and tree,
The voice of the dead was a living voice to me.   *10*

NORTHERN FARMER

OLD STYLE

Wheer 'asta beän saw long and meä liggin' 'ere aloän?
Noorse? thourt nowt o' a noorse: whoy, Doctor's abeän an' agoän:
Says that I moänt 'a naw moor aäle: but I beänt a fool:
Git ma my aäle, fur I beänt a-gawin' to breäk my rule.

Doctors, they knaws nowt, fur a says what's nawways true:
Naw soort o' koind o' use to saäy the things that a do.
I've 'ed my point o' aäle 'ivry noight sin' I beän 'ere.
An' I've 'ed my quart ivry market-noight for foorty year.

Parson's a beän loikewoise, an' a sittin' 'ere o' my bed.
'The amoighty's a taäkin o' you to 'issén, my friend,' a said,   10
An' a towd ma my sins, an's toithe were due, an' I gied it in hond;
I done moy duty boy 'um, as I 'a done boy the lond.

Larn'd a ma' beä. I reckons I 'annot sa mooch to larn.
But a cast oop, thot a did, 'bout Bessy Marris's barne.
Thaw a knaws I hallus voäted wi' Squoire an' choorch an' staäte,
An' i' the woost o' toimes I wur niver agin the raäte.

An' I hallus coom'd to 's chooch afoor moy Sally wur deäd,
An' 'eärd 'um a bummin' awaäy loike a buzzard-clock ower my 'eäd
An' I niver knaw'd whot a meän'd but I thowt a 'ad summut to saäy,
An' I thowt a said whot a owt to 'a said an' I coom'd awaäy.   20

Bessy Marris's barne! tha knaws she laäid it to meä.
Mowt a beän, mayhap, for she wur a bad un, sheä.
'Siver, I kep 'um, I kep 'um, my lass, tha mun understond;
I done moy duty boy 'um as I 'a done boy the lond.

But Parson a cooms an' a goäs, an' a says it eäsy an' freeä
'The amoighty's a taäkin o' you to 'issén, my friend,' says 'eä.
I weänt saäy men be loiars, thaw summun said it in 'aäste:
But 'e reäds wonn sarmin a weeäk, an' I 'a stubb'd Thurnaby waäste.

D'ya moind the waäste, my lass? naw, naw, tha was not born then;
Theer wur a boggle in it, I often 'eärd 'um mysen;   30
Moäst loike a butter-bump, fur I 'eärd 'um about an' about,
But I stubb'd 'um oop wi' the lot, an' raäved an' rembled 'um out.

Keäper's it wur; fo' they fun 'um theer a-laäid of 'is faäce
Down i' the woild 'enemies afoor I coom'd to the plaäce.
Noäks or Thimbleby—toäner 'ed shot 'um as deäd as a naäil.
Noäks wur 'ang'd for it oop at 'soize—but git ma my aäle.

Dubbut loöök at the waäste : theer warn't not feeäd for a cow ;
Nowt at all but bracken an' fuzz, an' loöök at it now—
Warn't worth nowt a haäcre, an' now theer's lots o' feeäd,
Fourscoor yows upon it an' some on it down i' seeäd.   *40*

Nobbut a bit on it's left, an' I meän'd to 'a stubb'd it at fall,
Done it ta-year I meän'd an' runn'd plow thruff it an' all,
If godamoighty an' parson 'ud nobbut let ma aloän,
Meä, wi' haäte hoonderd haäcre o' Squoire's, an' lond o' my oän.

Do godamoighty knaw what a's doing a-taäkin' o' meä?
I beänt wonn as saws 'ere a beän an' yonder a peä;
An' Squoire 'ull be sa mad an' all—a' dear a' dear!
And I 'a managed for Squoire coom Michaelmas thutty year.

A mowt 'a taäen owd Joänes, as 'ant not a 'aäpoth o' sense,
Or a mowt 'a taäen young Robins—a niver mended a fence :   *50*
But godamoighty a moost taäke meä an' taäke ma now
Wi' aäf the cows to cauve an' Thurnaby hoälms to plow !

Loook 'ow quoloty smoiles when they seeäs ma a passin' boy,
Says to thessén naw doubt ' what a man a beä sewèr-loy ! '
Fur they knaws what I beän to Squoire sin fust a coom'd to the 'All;
I done moy duty by Squoire an' I done moy duty boy hall.

Squoire's i' Lunnon, an' summun I reckons 'ull 'a to wroite,
For whoä's to howd the lond ater meä thot muddles ma quoit;
Sartin-sewer I beä, thot a weänt niver give it to Joänes,
Naw, nor a moänt to Robins—a niver rembles the stoäns.   *60*

But summun 'ull come ater meä mayhap wi' 'is kittle o' steäm
Huzzin' an' maäzin' the blessed feälds wi' the Divil's oän teäm.
Sin' I mun doy I mun doy, thaw loife they says is sweet,
But sin' I mun doy I mun doy, for I couldn abeär to see it.

What atta stannin' theer fur, an' doesn bring ma the aäle?
Doctor's a 'toättler, lass, an a's hallus i' the owd taäle;
I weänt breäk rules fur Doctor, a knaws naw moor nor a floy;
Git ma my aäle I tell tha, an' if I mun doy I mun doy.

NORTHERN FARMER

NEW STYLE

Dosn't thou 'ear my 'erse's legs, as they canters awaäy?
Proputty, proputty, proputty—that's what I 'ears 'em saäy.
Proputty, proputty, proputty—Sam, thou's an ass for thy paaïns:
Theer's moor sense i' one o' 'is legs nor in all thy braaïns.

Woä—theer's a craw to pluck wi' tha, Sam: yon's parson's 'ouse—
Dosn't thou knaw that a man mun be eäther a man or a mouse?
Time to think on it then; for thou'll be twenty to weeäk.
Proputty, proputty—woä then woä—let ma 'ear mysén speäk.

Me an' thy muther, Sammy, 'as beän a-talkin' o' thee;
Thou's beän talkin' to muther, an' she beän a tellin' it me.   _10_
Thou'll not marry for munny—thou's sweet upo' parson's lass—
Noä—thou'll marry for luvv—an' we boäth on us thinks tha an ass.

Seeä'd her todaäy goä by—Saäint's-daäy—they was ringing the bells.
She's a beauty thou thinks—an' soä is scoors o' gells,
Them as 'as munny an' all—wot's a beauty?—the flower as blaws.
But proputty, proputty sticks, an' proputty, proputty graws.

Do'ant be stunt: taäke time: I knaws what maäkes tha sa mad.
Warn't I craäzed fur the lasses mysén when I wur a lad?
But I knaw'd a Quaäker feller as often 'as towd ma this:
'Doänt thou marry for munny, but goä wheer munny is!'   _20_

An' I went wheer munny war: an' thy muther coom to 'and,
Wi' lots o' munny laaïd by, an' a nicetish bit o' land.
Maäybe she warn't a beauty:—I niver give it a thowt—
But warn't she as good to cuddle an' kiss as a lass as 'ant nowt?

Parson's lass 'ant nowt, an' she weänt 'a nowt when 'e's deäd,
Mun be a guvness, lad, or summut, and addle her breäd:
Why? fur 'e's nobbut a curate, an' weänt niver git hissen clear,
An' 'e maäde the bed as 'e ligs on afoor 'e coom'd to the shere.

An' thin 'e coom'd to the parish wi' lots o' Varsity debt,
Stook to his taaïl they did, an' 'e 'ant got shut on 'em yet.   _30_
An' 'e ligs on 'is back i' the grip, wi' noän to lend 'im a shuvv,
Woorse nor a far-welter'd yowe: fur, Sammy, 'e married fur luvv.

Luvv? what's luvv? thou can luvv thy lass an' 'er munny too,
Maakin' 'em goä togither as they've good right to do.
Could'n I luvv thy muther by cause o' 'er munny laaïd by?
Naäy—fur I luvv'd 'er a vast sight moor fur it : reäson why.

Ay an' thy muther says thou wants to marry the lass,
Cooms of a gentleman burn : an' we boäth on us thinks tha an ass.
Woä then, proputty, wiltha?—an ass as near as mays nowt —
Woa then, wiltha? dangtha !—the bees is as fell as owt.   *40*

Breäk me a bit o' the esh for his 'eäd, lad, out o' the fence !
Gentleman burn ! what's gentleman burn? is it shillins an' pence?
Proputty, proputty's ivrything 'ere, an', Sammy, I'm blest
If it isn't the saäme oop yonder, fur them as 'as it's the best.

Tis'n them as 'as munny as breäks into 'ouses an' steäls,
Them as 'as coäts to their backs an' taäkes their regular meäls.
Noä, but it's them as niver knaws wheer a meäl's to be 'ad.
Taäke my word for it, Sammy, the poor in a loomp is bad.

Them or thir feythers, tha sees, mun 'a beän a laäzy lot,
Fur work mun 'a gone to the gittin' whiniver munny was got.   *50*
Feyther 'ad ammost nowt; leästways 'is munny was 'id.
But 'e tued an' moil'd 'issén deäd, an 'e died a good un, 'e did.

Loook thou theer wheer Wrigglesby beck cooms out by the 'ill !
Feyther run oop to the farm, an' I runs oop to the mill;
An' I'll run oop to the brig, an' that thou'll live to see;
And if thou marries a good un I'll leäve the land to thee.

Thim's my noätions, Sammy, wheerby I means to stick;
But if thou marries a bad un, I'll leäve the land to Dick.—
Coom oop, proputty, proputty—that's what I 'ears 'im saäy
Proputty, proputty, proputty—canter an' canter awaäy.   *60*

THE COMING OF ARTHUR

LEODOGRAN, the King of Cameliard,
Had one fair daughter, and none other child;
And she was fairest of all flesh on earth,
Guinevere, and in her his one delight.

For many a petty king ere Arthur came
Ruled in this isle, and ever waging war
Each upon other, wasted all the land;
And still from time to time the heathen host
Swarm'd overseas, and harried what was left.
And so there grew great tracts of wilderness,   10
Wherein the beast was ever more and more,
But man was less and less, till Arthur came.
For first Aurelius lived and fought and died,
And after him King Uther fought and died,
But either fail'd to make the kingdom one.
And after these King Arthur for a space,
And thro' the puissance of his Table Round,
Drew all their petty princedoms under him,
Their king and head, and made a realm, and reign'd.

And thus the land of Cameliard was waste,   20
Thick with wet woods, and many a beast therein,
And none or few to scare or chase the beast;
So that wild dog, and wolf and boar and bear
Came night and day, and rooted in the fields,
And wallow'd in the gardens of the King.
And ever and anon the wolf would steal
The children and devour, but now and then,
Her own brood lost or dead, lent her fierce teat
To human sucklings; and the children, housed
In her foul den, there at their meat would growl,   30
And mock their foster-mother on four feet,
Till, straighten'd, they grew up to wolf-like men,
Worse than the wolves. And King Leodogran
Groan'd for the Roman legions here again,
And Cæsar's eagle: then his brother king,
Urien, assail'd him: last a heathen horde,
Reddening the sun with smoke and earth with blood,
And on the spike that split the mother's heart
Spitting the child, brake on him, till, amazed,
He knew not whither he should turn for aid.   40

But—for he heard of Arthur newly crown'd,
Tho' not without an uproar made by those

Who cried, ' He is not Uther's son '—the King
Sent to him, saying, ' Arise, and help us thou!
For here between the man and beast we die.'

And Arthur yet had done no deed of arms,
But heard the call, and came: and Guinevere
Stood by the castle walls to watch him pass;
But since he neither wore on helm or shield
The golden symbol of his kinglihood,   50
But rode a simple knight among his knights,
And many of these in richer arms than he,
She saw him not, or mark'd not, if she saw,
One among many, tho' his face was bare.
But Arthur, looking downward as he past,
Felt the light of her eyes into his life
Smite on the sudden, yet rode on, and pitch'd
His tents beside the forest.   Then he drave
The heathen; after, slew the beast, and fell'd
The forest, letting in the sun, and made   60
Broad pathways for the hunter and the knight
And so return'd.

                    For while he linger'd there,
A doubt that ever smoulder'd in the hearts
Of those great Lords and Barons of his realm
Flash'd forth and into war: for most of these,
Colleaguing with a score of petty kings,
Made head against him, crying, ' Who is he
That he should rule us? who hath proven him
King Uther's son? for lo! we look at him,
And find nor face nor bearing, limbs nor voice,   70
Are like to those of Uther whom we knew.
This is the son of Gorloïs, not the King;
This is the son of Anton, not the King.'

And Arthur, passing thence to battle, felt
Travail, and throes and agonies of the life,
Desiring to be join'd with Guinevere;
And thinking as he rode, ' Her father said
That there between the man and beast they die.
Shall I not lift her from this land of beasts
Up to my throne, and side by side with me?   80
What happiness to reign a lonely king,
Vext—O ye stars that shudder over me,
O earth that soundest hollow under me,
Vext with waste dreams? for saving I be join'd
To her that is the fairest under heaven,
I seem as nothing in the mighty world,
And cannot will my will, nor work my work
Wholly, nor make myself in mine own realm

Victor and lord.   But were I join'd with her,
Then might we live together as one life,   *90*
And reigning with one will in everything
Have power on this dark land to lighten it,
And power on this dead world to make it live.

Thereafter—as he speaks who tells the tale—
When Arthur reach'd a field-of-battle bright
With pitch'd pavilions of his foe, the world
Was all so clear about him, that he saw
The smallest rock far on the faintest hill,
And even in high day the morning star.
So when the King had set his banner broad,   *100*
At once from either side, with trumpet-blast,
And shouts, and clarions shrilling unto blood,
The long-lanced battle let their horses run.
And now the Barons and the kings prevail'd,
And now the King, as here and there that war
Went swaying: but the Powers who walk the world
Made lightnings and great thunders over him,
And dazed all eyes, till Arthur by main might,
And mightier of his hands with every blow,
And leading all his knighthood threw the kings   *110*
Carádos, Urien, Cradlemont of Wales,
Claudias, and Clariance of Northumberland,
The King Brandagoras of Latangor,
With Anguisant of Erin, Morganore,
And Lot of Orkney.   Then, before a voice
As dreadful as the shout of one who sees
To one who sins, and deems himself alone
And all the world asleep, they swerved and brake
Flying, and Arthur call'd to stay the brands
That hack'd among the flyers, ' Ho ! they yield ! '   *120*
So like a painted battle the war stood
Silenced, the living quiet as the dead,
And in the heart of Arthur joy was lord.
He laugh'd upon his warrior whom he loved
And honour'd most.   ' Thou dost not doubt me King,
So well thine arm hath wrought for me to-day.'
' Sir and my liege,' he cried, ' the fire of God
Descends upon thee in the battle-field :
I know thee for my King ! '   Whereat the two,
For each had warded either in the fight,   *130*
Sware on the field of death a deathless love.
And Arthur said, ' Man's word is God in man :
Let chance what will, I trust thee to the death.'

Then quickly from the foughten field he sent
Ulfius, and Brastias, and Bedivere,

His new-made knights, to King Leodogran,
Saying, ' If I in aught have served thee well,
Give me thy daughter Guinevere to wife.'

Whom when he heard, Leodogran in heart
Debating—' How should I that am a king,   *140*
However much he holp me at my need,
Give my one daughter saving to a king,
And a king's son ? '—lifted his voice, and call'd
A hoary man, his chamberlain, to whom
He trusted all things, and of him required
His counsel : ' Knowest thou aught of Arthur's birth ? '

Then spake the hoary chamberlain and said,
' Sir King, there be but two old men that know :
And each is twice as old as I; and one
Is Merlin, the wise man that ever served   *150*
King Uther thro' his magic art; and one
Is Merlin's master (so they call him) Bleys,
Who taught him magic; but the scholar ran
Before the master, and so far, that Bleys
Laid magic by, and sat him down, and wrote
All things and whatsoever Merlin did
In one great annal-book, where after-years
Will learn the secret of our Arthur's birth.'

To whom the King Leodogran replied,
' O friend, had I been holpen half as well   *160*
By this King Arthur as by thee to-day,
Then beast and man had had their share of me :
But summon here before us yet once more
Ulfius, and Brastias, and Bedivere.'

Then, when they came before him, the King said,
' I have seen the cuckoo chased by lesser fowl,
And reason in the chase : but wherefore now
Do these your lords stir up the heat of war,
Some calling Arthur born of Gorloïs,
Others of Anton ?   Tell me, ye yourselves,   *170*
Hold ye this Arthur for King Uther's son ? '

And Ulfius and Brastias answer'd, ' Ay.'
Then Bedivere, the first of all his knights
Knighted by Arthur at his crowning, spake—
For bold in heart and act and word was he,
Whenever slander breathed against the King—

' Sir, there be many rumours on this head :
For there be those who hate him in their hearts,
Call him baseborn, and since his ways are sweet,

And theirs are bestial, hold him less than man :   180
And there be those who deem him more than man,
And dream he dropt from heaven : but my belief
In all this matter—so ye care to learn—
Sir, for ye know that in King Uther's time
The prince and warrior Gorloïs, he that held
Tintagil castle by the Cornish sea,
Was wedded with a winsome wife, Ygerne :
And daughters had she borne him,—one whereof
Lot's wife, the Queen of Orkney, Bellicent,
Hath ever like a loyal sister cleaved   190
To Arthur,—but a son she had not borne.
And Uther cast upon her eyes of love :
But she, a stainless wife to Gorloïs,
So loathed the bright dishonour of his love,
That Gorloïs and King Uther went to war :
And overthrown was Gorloïs and slain.
Then Uther in his wrath and heat besieged
Ygerne within Tintagil, where her men,
Seeing the mighty swarm about their walls,
Left her and fled, and Uther enter'd in,   200
And there was none to call to but himself.
So, compass'd by the power of the King,
Enforced she was to wed him in her tears,
And with a shameful swiftness : afterward,
Not many moons, King Uther died himself,
Moaning and wailing for an heir to rule
After him, lest the realm should go to wrack.
And that same night, the night of the new year,
By reason of the bitterness and grief
That vext his mother, all before his time   210
Was Arthur born, and all as soon as born
Deliver'd at a secret postern-gate
To Merlin, to be holden far apart
Until his hour should come ; because the lords
Of that fierce day were as the lords of this,
Wild beasts, and surely would have torn the child
Piecemeal among them, had they known ; for each
But sought to rule for his own self and hand,
And many hated Uther for the sake
Of Gorloïs. Wherefore Merlin took the child,   220
And gave him to Sir Anton, an old knight
And ancient friend of Uther ; and his wife
Nursed the young prince, and rear'd him with her own ;
And no man knew. And ever since the lords
Have foughten like wild beasts among themselves,
So that the realm has gone to wrack : but now,
This year, when Merlin (for his hour had come)
Brought Arthur forth, and set him in the hall,

Proclaiming, " Here is Uther's heir, your king."
A hundred voices cried, " Away with him !   *230*
No king of ours ! a son of Gorloïs he,
Or else the child of Anton, and no king,
Or else baseborn."   Yet Merlin thro' his craft,
And while the people clamour'd for a king,
Had Arthur crown'd; but after, the great lords
Banded, and so brake out in open war.'

Then while the King debated with himself
If Arthur were the child of shamefulness,
Or born the son of Gorloïs, after death,
Or Uther's son, and born before his time,   *240*
Or whether there were truth in anything
Said by these three, there came to Cameliard,
With Gawain and young Modred, her two sons,
Lot's wife, the Queen of Orkney, Bellicent;
Whom as he could, not as he would, the King
Made feast for, saying, as they sat at meat,

' A doubtful throne is ice on summer seas.
Ye come from Arthur's court.   Victor his men
Report him ! Yea, but ye—think ye this king—
So many those that hate him, and so strong,   *250*
So few his knights, however brave they be—
Hath body enow to hold his foemen down ? '

' O King,' she cried, ' and I will tell thee : few,
Few, but all brave, all of one mind with him ;
For I was near him when the savage yells
Of Uther's peerage died, and Arthur sat
Crown'd on the daïs, and his warriors cried,
" Be thou the king, and we will work thy will
Who love thee."   Then the King in low deep tones,
And simple words of great authority,   *260*
Bound them by so strait vows to his own self,
That when they rose, knighted from kneeling, some
Were pale as at the passing of a ghost,
Some flush'd, and others dazed, as one who wakes
Half-blinded at the coming of a light.

' But when he spake and cheer'd his Table Round
With large, divine, and comfortable words,
Beyond my tongue to tell thee—I beheld
From eye to eye thro' all their Order flash
A momentary likeness of the King :   *270*
And ere it left their faces, thro' the cross
And those around it and the Crucified,
Down from the casement over Arthur, smote

Flame-colour, vert and azure, in three rays,
One falling upon each of three fair queens,
Who stood in silence near his throne, the friends
Of Arthur, gazing on him, tall, with bright
Sweet faces, who will help him at his need.

' And there I saw mage Merlin, whose vast wit
And hundred winters are but as the hands   *280*
Of loyal vassals toiling for their liege.

' And near him stood the Lady of the Lake,
Who knows a subtler magic than his own—
Clothed in white samite, mystic, wonderful.
She gave the King his huge cross-hilted sword,
Whereby to drive the heathen out: a mist
Of incense curl'd about her, and her face
Wellnigh was hidden in the minster gloom;
But there was heard among the holy hymns
A voice as of the waters, for she dwells   *290*
Down in a deep; calm, whatsoever storms
May shake the world, and when the surface rolls,
Hath power to walk the waters like our Lord.

' There likewise I beheld Excalibur
Before him at his crowning borne, the sword
That rose from out the bosom of the lake,
And Arthur row'd across and took it—rich
With jewels, elfin Urim, on the hilt,
Bewildering heart and eye—the blade so bright
That men are blinded by it—on one side,   *300*
Graven in the oldest tongue of all this world,
" Take me," but turn the blade and ye shall see,
And written in the speech ye speak yourself,
" Cast me away ! "   And sad was Arthur's face
Taking it, but old Merlin counsell'd him,-
" Take thou and strike ! the time to cast away
Is yet far-off." So this great brand the King
Took, and by this will beat his foemen down.'

Thereat Leodogran rejoiced, but thought
To sift his doubtings to the last, and ask'd,   *310*
Fixing full eyes of question on her face,
' The swallow and the swift are near akin,
But thou art closer to this noble prince,
Being his own dear sister;' and she said,
' Daughter of Gorloïs and Ygerne am I;'
' And therefore Arthur's sister?' ask'd the King.
She answer'd, ' These be secret things,' and sign'd
To those two sons to pass, and let them be.

And Gawain went, and breaking into song
Sprang out, and follow'd by his flying hair   320
Ran like a colt, and leapt at all he saw:
But Modred laid his ear beside the doors,
And there half-heard; the same that afterward
Struck for the throne, and striking found his doom.

And then the Queen made answer, ' What know I?
For dark my mother was in eyes and hair,
And dark in hair and eyes am I; and dark
Was Gorloïs, yea and dark was Uther too,
Wellnigh to blackness; but this King is fair
Beyond the race of Britons and of men.   330
Moreover, always in my mind I hear
A cry from out the dawning of my life,
A mother weeping, and I hear her say,
" O that ye had some brother, pretty one,
To guard thee on the rough ways of the world." '

' Ay,' said the King, ' and hear ye such a cry?
But when did Arthur chance upon thee first?'

' O King! ' she cried, ' and I will tell thee true:
He found me first when yet a little maid:
Beaten I had been for a little fault   340
Whereof I was not guilty; and out I ran
And flung myself down on a bank of heath,
And hated this fair world and all therein,
And wept, and wish'd that I were dead; and he—
I know not whether of himself he came,
Or brought by Merlin, who, they say, can walk
Unseen at pleasure—he was at my side,
And spake sweet words, and comforted my heart,
And dried my tears, being a child with me.
And many a time he came, and evermore   350
As I grew greater grew with me; and sad
At times he seem'd, and sad with him was I,
Stern too at times, and then I loved him not,
But sweet again, and then I loved him well.
And now of late I see him less and less,
But those first days had golden hours for me,
For then I surely thought he would be king.

' But let me tell thee now another tale:
For Bleys, our Merlin's master, as they say,
Died but of late, and sent his cry to me,   360
To hear him speak before he left his life.
Shrunk like a fairy changeling lay the mage;
And when I enter'd told me that himself

And Merlin ever served about the King,
Uther, before he died; and on the night
When Uther in Tintagil past away
Moaning and wailing for an heir, the two
Left the still King, and passing forth to breathe,
Then from the castle gateway by the chasm
Descending thro' the dismal night—a night   370
In which the bounds of heaven and earth were lost—
Beheld, so high upon the dreary deeps
It seem'd in heaven, a ship, the shape thereof
A dragon wing'd, and all from stem to stern
Bright with a shining people on the decks,
And gone as soon as seen.   And then the two
Dropt to the cove, and watch'd the great sea fall,
Wave after wave, each mightier than the last,
Till last, a ninth one, gathering half the deep
And full of voices, slowly rose and plunged   380
Roaring, and all the wave was in a flame:
And down the wave and in the flame was borne
A naked babe, and rode to Merlin's feet,
Who stoopt and caught the babe, and cried " The King !
Here is an heir for Uther ! "   And the fringe
Of that great breaker, sweeping up the strand,
Lash'd at the wizard as he spake the word,
And all at once all round him rose in fire,
So that the child and he were clothed in fire.
And presently thereafter follow'd calm,   390
Free sky and stars: " And this same child," he said,
" Is he who reigns; nor could I part in peace
Till this were told."   And saying this the seer
Went thro' the strait and dreadful pass of death,
Not ever to be question'd any more
Save on the further side; but when I met
Merlin, and ask'd him if these things were truth—
The shining dragon and the naked child
Descending in the glory of the seas—
He laugh'd as is his wont, and answer'd me   400
In riddling triplets of old time, and said:

  ' " Rain, rain, and sun ! a rainbow in the sky !
A young man will be wiser by and by;
An old man's wit may wander ere he die.
  Rain, rain, and sun ! a rainbow on the lea !
And truth is this to me, and that to thee;
And truth or clothed or naked let it be.
  Rain, sun, and rain ! and the free blossom blows:
Sun, rain, and sun ! and where is he who knows?
From the great deep to the great deep he goes."   410

' So Merlin riddling anger'd me; but thou
Fear not to give this King thine only child,
Guinevere: so great bards of him will sing
Hereafter; and dark sayings from of old
Ranging and ringing thro' the minds of men,
And echo'd by old folk beside their fires
For comfort after their wage-work is done,
Speak of the King; and Merlin in our time
Hath spoken also, not in jest, and sworn
Tho' men may wound him that he will not die,   420
But pass, again to come; and then or now
Utterly smite the heathen underfoot,
Till these and all men hail him for their king.'

    She spake and King Leodogran rejoiced,
But musing ' Shall I answer yea or nay?'
Doubted, and drowsed, nodded and slept, and saw,
Dreaming, a slope of land that ever grew,
Field after field, up to a height, the peak
Haze-hidden, and thereon a phantom king,
Now looming, and now lost; and on the slope   430
The sword rose, the hind fell, the herd was driven,
Fire glimpsed; and all the land from roof and rick,
In drifts of smoke before a rolling wind,
Stream'd to the peak, and mingled with the haze
And made it thicker; while the phantom king
Sent out at times a voice; and here or there
Stood one who pointed toward the voice, the rest
Slew on and burnt, crying, ' No king of ours,
No son of Uther, and no king of ours;'
Till with a wink his dream was changed, the haze   440
Descended, and the solid earth became
As nothing, but the King stood out in heaven,
Crown'd. And Leodogran awoke, and sent
Ulfius, and Brastias and Bedivere,
Back to the court of Arthur answering yea.

    Then Arthur charged his warrior whom he loved
And honour'd most, Sir Lancelot, to ride forth
And bring the Queen;—and watch'd him from the gates;
And Lancelot past away among the flowers,
(For then was latter April) and return'd   450
Among the flowers, in May, with Guinevere.
To whom arrived, by Dubric the high saint,
Chief of the church in Britain, and before
The stateliest of her altar-shrines, the King
That morn was married, while in stainless white,
The fair beginners of a nobler time,
And glorying in their vows and him, his knights

Stood round him, and rejoicing in his joy.
Far shone the fields of May thro' open door,
The sacred altar blossom'd white with May,   *460*
The Sun of May descended on their King,
They gazed on all earth's beauty in their Queen,
Roll'd incense, and there past along the hymns
A voice as of the waters, while the two
Sware at the shrine of Christ a deathless love:
And Arthur said, ' Behold, thy doom is mine.
Let chance what will, I love thee to the death! '
To whom the Queen replied with drooping eyes,
' King and my lord, I love thee to the death! '
And holy Dubric spread his hands and spake,   *470*
' Reign ye, and live and love, and make the world
Other, and may thy Queen be one with thee,
And all this Order of thy Table Round
Fulfil the boundless purpose of their King! '

So Dubric said; but when they left the shrine
Great Lords from Rome before the portal stood,
In scornful stillness gazing as they past;
Then while they paced a city all on fire
With sun and cloth of gold, the trumpets blew,
And Arthur's knighthood sang before the King :—   *480*

' Blow trumpet, for the world is white with May;
Blow trumpet, the long night hath roll'd away!
Blow thro' the living world—" Let the King reign."

' Shall Rome or Heathen rule in Arthur's realm?
Flash brand and lance, fall battleaxe upon helm,
Fall battleaxe, and flash brand! Let the King reign.

' Strike for the King and live! his knights have heard
That God hath told the King a secret word.
Fall battleaxe, and flash brand! Let the King reign.

' Blow trumpet! he will lift us from the dust,   *490*
Blow trumpet! live the strength and die the lust!
Clang battleaxe, and clash brand! Let the King reign.

' Strike for the King and die! and if thou diest,
The King is King, and ever wills the highest.
Clang battleaxe, and clash brand! Let the King reign.

' Blow, for our Sun is mighty in his May!
Blow, for our Sun is mightier day by day!
Clang battleaxe, and clash brand! Let the King reign.

' The King will follow Christ, and we the King
In whom high God hath breathed a secret thing.   *500*
Fall battleaxe, and flash brand !   Let the King reign.'

So sang the knighthood, moving to their hall.
There at the banquet those great Lords from Rome,
The slowly-fading mistress of the world,
Strode in, and claim'd their tribute as of yore.
But Arthur spake, ' Behold, for these have sworn
To wage my wars, and worship me their King;
The old order changeth, yielding place to new;
And we that fight for our fair father Christ,
Seeing that ye be grown too weak and old   *510*
To drive the heathen from your Roman wall,
No tribute will we pay : ' so those great lords
Drew back in wrath, and Arthur strove with Rome.

And Arthur and his knighthood for a space
Were all one will, and thro' that strength the King
Drew in the petty princedoms under him,
Fought, and in twelve great battles overcame
The heathen hordes, and made a realm and reign'd.

THE REVENGE

A BALLAD OF THE FLEET

At Flores in the Azores Sir Richard Grenville lay,
And a pinnace, like a flutter'd bird, came flying from far away:
' Spanish ships of war at sea! we have sighted fifty-three!'
Then sware Lord Thomas Howard: ' 'Fore God I am no coward;
But I cannot meet them here, for my ships are out of gear,
And the half my men are sick. I must fly, but follow quick.
We are six ships of the line; can we fight with fifty-three?'

Then spake Sir Richard Grenville: ' I know you are no coward;
You fly them for a moment to fight with them again.
But I've ninety men and more that are lying sick ashore.   *10*
I should count myself the coward if I left them, my Lord Howard,
To these Inquisition dogs and the devildoms of Spain.'

So Lord Howard past away with five ships of war that day,
Till he melted like a cloud in the silent summer heaven;
But Sir Richard bore in hand all his sick men from the land
Very carefully and slow,
Men of Bideford in Devon,
And we laid them on the ballast down below;
For we brought them all aboard,
And they blest him in their pain, that they were not left to Spain,   *20*
To the thumbscrew and the stake, for the glory of the Lord.

He had only a hundred seamen to work the ship and to fight,
And he sailed away from Flores till the Spaniard came in sight,
With his huge sea-castles heaving upon the weather bow.
' Shall we fight or shall we fly?
Good Sir Richard, tell us now,
For to fight is but to die!
There'll be little of us left by the time this sun be set.'
And Sir Richard said again: ' We be all good English men.
Let us bang these dogs of Seville, the children of the devil,   *30*
For I never turn'd my back upon Don or devil yet.'

Sir Richard spoke and he laugh'd, and we roar'd a hurrah, and so
The little Revenge ran on sheer into the heart of the foe,
With her hundred fighters on deck, and her ninety sick below;

For half of their fleet to the right and half to the left were seen,
And the little Revenge ran on thro' the long sea-lane between.

Thousands of their soldiers look'd down from their decks and laugh'd,
Thousands of their seamen made mock at the mad little craft
Running on and on, till delay'd
By their mountain-like San Philip that, of fifteen hundred tons, **40**
And up-shadowing high above us with her yawning tiers of guns,
Took the breath from our sails, and we stay'd.

And while now the great San Philip hung above us like a cloud
Whence the thunderbolt will fall
Long and loud,
Four galleons drew away
From the Spanish fleet that day,
And two upon the larboard and two upon the starboard lay,
And the battle-thunder broke from them all.

But anon the great San Philip, she bethought herself and went **50**
Having that within her womb that had left her ill content;
And the rest they came aboard us, and they fought us hand to hand,
For a dozen times they came with their pikes and musqueteers,
And a dozen times we shook 'em off as a dog that shakes his ears
When he leaps from the water to the land.

And the sun went down, and the stars came out far over the summer
 sea,
But never a moment ceased the fight of the one and the fifty-three.
Ship after ship, the whole night long, their high-built galleons came,
Ship after ship, the whole night long, with her battle-thunder and flame;
Ship after ship, the whole night long, drew back with her dead and her
 shame. **60**
For some were sunk and many were shatter'd and so could fight us no
 more—
God of battles, was ever a battle like this in the world before?

For he said ' Fight on ! fight on ! '
Tho' his vessel was all but a wreck;
And it chanced that, when half of the short summer night was gone,
With a grisly wound to be drest he had left the deck,
But a bullet struck him that was dressing it suddenly dead,
And himself he was wounded again in the side and the head,
And he said ' Fight on ! fight on ! '

And the night went down, and the sun smiled out far over the summer
   sea,   70
And the Spanish fleet with broken sides lay round us all in a ring;
But they dared not touch us again, for they fear'd that we still could
   sting,
So they watch'd what the end would be.
And we had not fought them in vain,
But in perilous plight were we,
Seeing forty of our poor hundred were slain,
And half of the rest of us maim'd for life
In the crash of the cannonades and the desperate strife;
And the sick men down in the hold were most of them stark and cold,
And the pikes were all broken or bent, and the powder was all of it
   spent;   80
And the masts and the rigging were lying over the side;
But Sir Richard cried in his English pride,
' We have fought such a fight for a day and a night
As may never be fought again !
We have won great glory, my men !
And a day less or more
At sea or ashore,
We die—does it matter when?
Sink me the ship, Master Gunner—sink her, split her in twain !
Fall into the hands of God, not into the hands of Spain ! '   90

And the gunner said ' Ay, ay,' but the seamen made reply :
' We have children, we have wives,
And the Lord hath spared our lives.
We will make the Spaniard promise, if we yield, to let us go;
We shall live to fight again and to strike another blow.'
And the lion there lay dying, and they yielded to the foe.

And the stately Spanish men to their flagship bore him then,
Where they laid him by the mast, old Sir Richard caught at last,
And they praised him to his face with their courtly foreign grace;
But he rose upon their decks, and he cried :   100
' I have fought for Queen and Faith like a valiant man and true;
I have only done my duty as a man is bound to do :
With a joyful spirit I Sir Richard Grenville die ! '
And he fell upon their decks, and he died.

And they stared at the dead that had been so valiant and true,
And had holden the power and glory of Spain so cheap
That he dared her with one little ship and his English few;
Was he devil or man ?   He was devil for aught they knew,
But they sank his body with honour down into the deep,

And they mann'd the Revenge with a swarthier alien crew,
And away she sail'd with her loss and long'd for her own;
When a wind from the lands they had ruin'd awoke from sleep,
And the water began to heave and the weather to moan,
And or ever that evening ended a great gale blew
And a wave like the wave that is raised by an earthquake grew,
Till it smote on their hulls and their sails and their masts and their flags,
And the whole sea plunged and fell on the shot-shatter'd navy of Spain,
And the little Revenge herself went down by the island crags
To be lost evermore in the main.

TO E. FITZGERALD

Old Fitz, who from your suburb grange,
　Where once I tarried for a while,
Glance at the wheeling Orb of change,
　And greet it with a kindly smile;
Whom yet I see as there you sit
　Beneath your sheltering garden-tree,
And while your doves about you flit,
　And plant on shoulder, hand and knee,
Or on your head their rosy feet,
　As if they knew your diet spares   *10*
Whatever moved in that full sheet
　Let down to Peter at his prayers;
Who live on milk and meal and grass;
　And once for ten long weeks I tried
Your table of Pythagoras,
　And seem'd at first ' a thing enskied '
(As Shakespeare has it) airy-light
　To float above the ways of men,
Then fell from that half-spiritual height
　Chill'd, till I tasted flesh again   *20*
One night when earth was winter-black,
　And all the heavens flash'd in frost;
And on me, half-asleep, came back
　That wholesome heat the blood had lost,
And set me climbing icy capes
　And glaciers, over which there roll'd
To meet me long-arm'd vines with grapes
　Of Eshcol hugeness; for the cold
Without, and warmth within me, wrought
　To mould the dream; but none can say   *30*
That Lenten fare makes Lenten thought,
　Who reads your golden Eastern lay,
Than which I know no version done
　In English more divinely well;
A planet equal to the sun
　Which cast it, that large infidel
Your Omar; and your Omar drew
　Full-handed plaudits from our best
In modern letters, and from two,
　Old friends outvaluing all the rest,   *40*
Two voices heard on earth no more;
　But we old friends are still alive,
And I am nearing seventy-four,
　While you have touch'd at seventy-five,
And so I send a birthday line

Of greeting ; and my son, who dipt
In some forgotten book of mine
    With sallow scraps of manuscript,
And dating many a year ago,
    Has hit on this, which you will take   *50*
My Fitz, and welcome, as I know
    Less for its own than for the sake
Of one recalling gracious times,
    When, in our younger London days,
You found some merit in my rhymes,
    And I more pleasure in your praise.

VASTNESS

MANY a hearth upon our dark globe sighs after many a vanish'd face,
Many a planet by many a sun may roll with the dust of a vanish'd race.

Raving politics, never at rest—as this poor earth's pale history runs,—
What is it all but a trouble of ants in the gleam of a million million of
    suns?

Lies upon this side, lies upon that side, truthless violence mourn'd by the
    Wise,
Thousands of voices drowning his own in a popular torrent of lies
    upon lies;

Stately purposes, valour in battle, glorious annals of army and fleet,
Death for the right cause, death for the wrong cause, trumpets of
    victory, groans of defeat;

Innocence seethed in her mother's milk, and Charity. setting the
    martyr aflame;
Thraldom who walks with the banner of Freedom, and recks not to
    ruin a realm in her name.   *10*

Faith at her zenith, or all but lost in the gloom of doubts that darken the
    schools;
Craft with a bunch of all-heal in her hand, follow'd up by her vassal
    legion of fools;

Trade flying over a thousand seas with her spice and her vintage, her
    silk and her corn;
Desolate offing, sailorless harbours, famishing populace, wharves
    forlorn;

Star of the morning, Hope in the sunrise; gloom of the evening, Life
    at a close;
Pleasure who flaunts on her wide downway with her flying robe and her
    poison'd rose;

Pain, that has crawl'd from the corpse of Pleasure, a worm which
    writhes all day, and at night
Stirs up again in the heart of the sleeper, and stings him back to the
    curse of the light;

Wealth with his wines and his wedded harlots; honest Poverty, bare to
    the bone;
Opulent Avarice, lean as Poverty; Flattery gilding the rift in a throne; *20*

Fame blowing out from her golden trumpet a jubilant challenge to
  Time and to Fate;
Slander, her shadow, sowing the nettle on all the laurel'd graves of the
  Great;

Love for the maiden, crown'd with marriage, no regrets for aught that
  has been,
Household happiness, gracious children, debtless competence, golden
  mean;

National hatreds of whole generations, and pigmy spites of the village
  spire;
Vows that will last to the last death-ruckle, and vows that are snapt
  in a moment of fire;

He that has lived for the lust of the minute, and died in the doing it,
  flesh without mind;
He that has nail'd all flesh to the Cross, till Self died out in the love of
  his kind;

Spring and Summer and Autumn and Winter, and all these old revolu-
  tions of earth;
All new-old revolutions of Empire—change of the tide—what is all of it
  worth?   *30*

What the philosophies, all the sciences, poesy, varying voices of prayer?
All that is noblest, all that is basest, all that is filthy with all that is fair?

What is it all, if we all of us end but in being our own corpse-coffins at
  last,
Swallow'd in Vastness, lost in Silence, drown'd in the deeps of a mean-
  ingless Past?

What but a murmur of gnats in the gloom, or a moment's anger of
  bees in their hive?—

                    *   *   *   *   *

Peace, let it be! for I loved him, and love him for ever: the dead are
  not dead but alive.

CROSSING THE BAR

SUNSET and evening star,
  And one clear call for me!
And may there be no moaning of the bar,
  When I put out to sea,

But such a tide as moving seems asleep,
  Too full for sound and foam,
When that which drew from out the boundless deep
  Turns again home.

Twilight and evening bell,
  And after that the dark!   *10*
And may there be no sadness of farewell,
  When I embark;

For tho' from out our bourne of Time and Place
  The flood may bear me far,
I hope to see my Pilot face to face
  When I have crost the bar.

Finis

NOTES

Mariana (published 1830). In *Measure for Measure* the unhappy Mariana, abandoned by the man to whom she is betrothed, passes her days in a lonely grange. Tennyson had no particular country house or large farmhouse in mind; he imagined the setting in response to Shakespeare's words.

18. *trance:* throw into a trance.

40. *marish-mosses:* marsh-moss lumps floating on the water.

54. *cell:* the cave of Aeolus who controlled the winds.

Song (published 1830). Written in the garden at Somersby, this is metrically one of the most original and successful of the early lyrics.

19. *box:* a small evergreen shrub.

A Character (published 1830). According to FitzGerald, this character-study refers to a Cambridge contemporary of Tennyson's, named Thomas Sunderland, who was 'a very plausible, parliament-like, and self-satisfied speaker at the Union'. Leigh Hunt describes it well as a 'seemingly passionless exposure of its passionless object'.

11. *sleek'd:* smoothed.

15. *Pallas and Juno:* goddesses, the one associated with power and wisdom, the other regarded as the special patroness of virtuous and faithful women.

The Lady of Shalott (published 1832; much revised for 1842). Tennyson here anticipates Pre-Raphaelite poetry and provides a subject for the Pre-Raphaelite painter, W. Holman Hunt. Lines 69-72 contain the key to the symbolism of the poem. Tennyson explained: 'The new-born love for something, for some one in the wide world from which she [the Lady of Shalott] has been so long secluded, takes her out of the region of shadows into that of realities.' Her situation resembles that of an artist who forfeits his detachment only to be destroyed by the reality to which he commits himself.

3. *wold:* rolling uplands.

5. *Camelot:* legendary capital of Arthur's realm.

10. *whiten:* show the pale undersides of their leaves in the breeze.

22. *shallop:* light boat.

40. *stay:* pause.

46. *a mirror clear:* this has a technical as well as a magical function: it enables the weaver to see her work from the right side.

56. *pad:* easy-paced horse.

76. *greaves:* shin-guards.

84. *Galaxy:* Milky Way.

87. *blazon'd baldric:* heraldically decorated shoulder-belt.

The Miller's Daughter (published 1832; much revised for 1842). 'No par-
ticular mill,' declared Tennyson, 'but if I thought at all of any mill it
was that of Trumpington, near Cambridge.'
80. *beck:* brook.

Œnone (published 1832; much revised for 1842). Œnone, the daughter of a
river-god, was married to the Trojan prince Paris. Tennyson makes her
a spectator of the famous judgment by which Paris gave the apple of
discord to Aphroditè, who offered him success in love, rather than to
Herè or Pallas, who offered him power and wisdom respectively. This
judgment made Aphroditè a friend of Ilion, or Troy, the other two
goddesses its enemies. As the successful lover of Helen, Paris deserted
Œnone.
1. *Ida:* a mountain range near Troy.
2. *Ionian:* Ionia was a district on the west coast of Asia Minor.
10. *Gargarus:* the highest part of Ida.
40. *music:* that of Apollo.
51. *Simois:* one of the two rivers of the plain of Troy.
60. *foam-bow:* a rainbow-like bow, formed by sunlight upon foam.
72. *Oread:* mountain-nymph.
79. *Peleus:* the gods were celebrating his marriage to Thetis.
81. *Iris:* the messenger of the gods.
93. *smooth-swarded:* smoothly covered with a grassy turf.
102. *peacock:* sacred to Herè.
112. *champaign:* level, open country,
137. *O'erthwarted with:* crossed by.
151. *Sequel of guerdon:* addition of reward.
170-1. *Idalian . . . Paphian:* Aphroditè landed at Paphos in Cyprus after
her birth among the waves. Idalium was also sacred to her.
195. *pard:* panther or leopard.
220. *The Abominable:* Eris, the goddess of discord.
257. *the Greek woman:* Helen.
259. *Cassandra:* a sister of Paris, she prophesied that Helen would be the
ruin of Troy.

The Sisters (published 1832). Written in imitation of the border ballads.

The Lotos-Eaters (published 1832; considerably revised for 1842). In Homer's
Odyssey, ix, Odysseus tells how he landed in the country of the Lotos-
Eaters, where the natives gave the members of his reconnaisance party
some lotos to taste. As soon as they had eaten it, they lost all idea of
reporting back and wished merely to linger, feeding on the sweet fruit
without thought of returning home. Odysseus had to force them back to
the ships. Tennyson starts his poem with five Spenserian stanzas; in the
irregular 'Choric Song' that follows, the influence of *The Faerie Queene*
persists in the richly evocative suggestions of a setting in perfect harmony
with the languid mood.
1. *he:* Odysseus.
1-3. *land . . . land:* Tennyson deliberately substituted this repetition for a
previous rhyme because it seemed lazier.
11. *lawn:* a kind of fine linen.
23. *galingale:* an aromatic herb.

44. *island home:* Ithaca.

133. *amaranth and moly:* fabulous plants, the one unfading, the other possessing magical properties.

142. *acanthus:* a sacred herb.

155. *like Gods:* the Epicurean gods whose carefree existence Lucretius describes.

169–70. *Elysian valleys . . . asphodel:* the Elysian Fields, a Greek Paradise, were said to be covered with the immortal flower asphodel.

The Two Voices (published 1842). Drafted before Hallam's death. See Introduction for further details.

1. *still small voice:* but in I Kings xix.12 the 'still small voice' is that of God.

16–18. The speaker adopts a current theory reconciling scripture with science. This converted the six days of the Biblical Creation into six creative eras or cycles, the last of them witnessing the emergence of animal and human life.

39. *deficiency:* absence.

41. *peculiar difference:* individual and distinguishing quality.

87. *glebe:* soil, land.

129. *brand:* sword.

135. *mete:* measure.

192. *fold:* cloud.

195. *Ixion:* he tried to seduce the wife of Zeus, but Zeus deceived him into embracing a cloud.

219. *Stephen:* the first Christian martyr. He was stoned to death.

228. *The elements were kindlier mix'd:* he had a happier disposition.

277. *crown'd his head:* made death a king.

325. *little ducts:* as always, Tennyson aims at precision in his references to scientific matters.

350. *Lethe:* a river in the underworld which gave forgetfulness of the past to the spirits which drank from it.

436. *Æolian harp:* stringed instrument that plays in the breeze.

St. Simeon Stylites (published 1842). Tennyson wrote this poem in 1833, presumably before learning of Hallam's death. St. Simeon, a fifth-century hermit, is reputed to have spent thirty years on top of a pillar that was eventually 60 feet high; his surname, 'Stylites', is from the Greek for 'pillar'. According to FitzGerald, Tennyson would read the monologue 'with grotesque Grimness', especially at such passages as lines 13–16, 'laughing aloud at times'. Browning admired it greatly.

20. *meed:* reward. Revelation vii.9 promises the saints white robes and palms in heaven.

46. *Who may be saved?:* quoted from Matthew xix.25.

83. *cover all my sin:* quoted from Psalms lxxxv.2. The monologue contains many other echoes of scripture.

86. *Six cubits:* about nine feet.

94. *dial:* his pillar is his sundial.

165. *Pontius and Iscariot:* Judas Iscariot, who betrayed Jesus, and Pontius Pilate, who was Roman governor of Judaea at the time.

169. *Abaddon and Asmodeus:* evil spirits, the former being identified in Revelation ix.11 with Apollyon, or the Destroyer.

Ulysses (published 1842). Written shortly after Tennyson learned of Hallam's death (see Introduction). Ulysses is about to leave his island kingdom of Ithaca to his prudent and dutiful son Telemachus and to set out on a great adventure which may even reunite him with his dead comrade in the Trojan War, Achilles. Tennyson had read of Ulysses' last, mysterious voyage in Homer's *Odyssey*, xi, and Dante's *Inferno*, xxvi.

3. *mete:* administer.

4. *Unequal:* appropriate to a still 'savage' society.

7. *lees:* dregs.

10. *rainy Hyades:* the rising of these five stars simultaneously with the sun heralded the spring rains.

40. *decent:* aware of what is proper.

63. *Happy Isles:* Isles of the Blest, lying beyond the Straits of Gibraltar.

The Epic [Morte d'Arthur] (published 1842). Tennyson wrote 'Morte d'Arthur' following the blow of Hallam's death and added the apologetic frame about four years later. 'Morte d'Arthur' subsequently developed into 'The Passing of Arthur' (1869). Tennyson drew his material mainly from Malory's *Morte d'Arthur*. He acknowledges also his 'faint Homeric echoes'.

15. *church-commissioners:* an Ecclesiastical Commissioners Act was passed in 1836 and revised in 1840–1.

16. *Geology:* many Christians took offence at Sir Charles Lyell's implicit rejection of the Mosaic cosmogony in his *Principles of Geology* (1830–3).

50. According to FitzGerald, Tennyson himself read in this manner.

52. *battle:* the final battle between Arthur and his treacherous nephew Modred.

55. *Lyonnesse:* a mythical country, now supposedly submerged, off the south coast of Cornwall.

74. *Merlin:* the aged enchanter at Arthur's court.

82. *samite:* a rich silk fabric.

89. *lightly:* quickly.

94. *hest:* command.

131. *lief:* beloved.

161. *conceit:* fancy.

190. *streamer:* Aurora Borealis or nothern lights.

191. *moving isles of winter shock:* icebergs collide.

249. *Three Queens:* in Malory, one is Arthur's sister, Morgan le Fay, and the other two are the Queens of Northgalis and of the Waste Lands.

266–7. *greaves and cuisses dash'd with drops Of onset:* shin and thigh armour spattered with blood from combat.

283. *light:* Star of Bethlehem.

293. *one good custom:* for example, chivalry.

310. *Avilion:* usually Avalon, the Isle of the Blest in Celtic mythology.

'Break, break, break ...' (published 1842). Written in Lincolnshire one spring, probably 1834.

Amphion (published 1842). Amphion's music moved the stones to form the walls of Thebes. Here he has the Orphean power of making trees follow the sound of his lyre. The poet jocularly contrasts the laboriousness of his own creative achievement with the effortlessness of Amphion's.

40. *gallopaded:* the gallopade was a lively dance of Hungarian origin.
44. *Poussetting:* country dancing.
59. *flexile:* tractable.
64. *scirrhous:* morbidly hardened.
84. *Van Diemen:* Tasmania.
92. *spindlings:* spindly plants.

Locksley Hall (published 1842). Written 1837–8, about the time when Rosa Baring's marriage was being arranged. The overwrought hero denounces the materialism which has cost him the woman he loves; he toys with the thought of escape but finally determines to commit himself to the progressive movement of his day. In subject and feeling the poem anticipates *Maud.*
4. *gleams:* gleams of light.
5–6. Tennyson had the Lincolnshire coast in mind.
8. *Orion:* a constellation.
9. *Pleiads:* seven stars within the constellation Taurus.
19. *iris:* feather colours which brighten in the mating season.
41. *fathoms:* realizes.
75. *the poet:* Dante, in *Inferno,* v.
79. *he:* Amy's husband.
104. *laid:* in keeping with the belief that gunfire calms the waves.
121–4. *magic sails . . . airy navies:* balloons.
138. *process of the suns:* passage of the years.
150. *motions:* feelings.
155. *Mahratta-battle:* the Hindu race so named warred against the British until 1818.
180. *Joshua's moon:* in Joshua x. 12–13, God allows him to halt the sun and moon.
182. *ringing grooves:* Tennyson composed this line after his first railway ride. He wrongly assumed that the wheels ran in grooves.
184. *Cathay:* an old name for China.
191. *holt:* copse.

The Vision of Sin (published 1842). One of Tennyson's favourite poems. He explained it as describing 'the soul of a youth who has given himself up to pleasure and Epicureanism. He at length is worn out and wrapt in the mists of satiety. Afterwards he grows into a cynical old man afflicted with the "curse of nature", and joining in the Feast of Death. Then we see the landscape which symbolizes God, Law and the future life.'
3–4. *horse with wings . . . heavy rider:* his Pegasus-like spirit weighed down by his body.
41. *Furies . . . Graces:* respectively, three avenging goddesses, and three goddesses of beauty and grace.
96. *rouse:* drinking-bout.
141. *hue:* Tennyson several times voices his abhorrence of the violence released by the French Revolution. Here he mentions the blood-red cap worn by Liberty, whom he has just equipped with a 'civic wreath', representing her principles, and a 'human head', representing her practice.
172. *chap-fallen:* with the lower jaw hanging down, as in death.
179. *Vivat Rex!:* long live the King!
189. *Buss:* kiss.
213–4. 'The sensualist becomes worn out by his senses' (Tennyson).

SONGS AND LYRICS FROM **'The Princess'**. For *The Princess* (published 1847; extensively revised for subsequent editions), see Introduction. The three lyrics 'Tears, idle tears', 'Now sleeps the crimson petal', and 'Come down, O maid', formed part of it from the start; the other songs included here were written after 1847 and published in 1850.

'The splendour falls . . .'
'Written after hearing the echoes at Killarney in 1848. When I was there I heard a bugle blown beneath the "Eagle's Nest," and eight distinct echoes' (Tennyson).
1. *splendour:* of the sunset.
10. *Elfland:* Fairyland.
15–16. But our echoes of each other continue without end.

'Tears, idle tears . . .'
Tennyson conceived this song during an autumn visit to Tintern Abbey. It expresses his bitter-sweet longing for the life and the beauty that have passed away. Nothing in English poetry comes closer to the feeling of such Virgilian lines as the famous *sunt lacrimae rerum et mentem mortalia tangunt* (*Aeneid*, i).
7. *the underworld:* the part of the earth beyond the horizon.

'Ask me no more . . .'
Love overcomes the singer's reluctance to yield.

'Now sleeps the crimson petal . . .'
In form and in imagery, this lyric seems to owe something to Persian love-poetry. The speaker begs the loved one to yield herself.
7. *Danaë:* Zeus took the form of a shower of gold in order to have access to her.

'Come down, O maid . . .'
A pastoral appeal to the lady to forsake her aloof idealism and to join her suitor in humble love. Written in Switzerland.
12. *foxlike in the vine:* stealing the grapes. See Song of Solomon ii.15.
13. *silver horns:* snow-clad peaks.
17. *dusky:* in contrast with the snows around.
25. *azure pillars:* of rising smoke.

In Memoriam A.H.H. (published 1850). The Introduction gives some account of the composition of this poem and of its structure. Emily Sellwood, soon to become Tennyson's wife, suggested the title.
Prologue, 5. *orbs:* sun and moon.
Prologue, 17. *systems:* intellectual systems.
Prologue, 28. *before:* before the one-sided growth of knowledge wrecked the harmony of mind and soul.
i.1. *him:* Goethe.
i.8. *far-off interest of tears:* future recompense for present grief.
ii.15. *fail from out:* die away from.
iv.11–12. Tennyson explained that water on the point of freezing remains liquid if kept still but turns to ice, and may break the vase, if shaken.
v.9. *weeds:* garments.
vii.1. *house:* Hallam's London home, 67 Wimpole Street.
ix. One of the earliest lyrics in *In Memoriam*.

ix.1. *ship:* bringing home Hallam's body.

ix.10. *Phosphor:* the morning star.

x.11–16. Habit makes us think it preferable to be buried in the church-yard or in the chancel.

x.20. *tangle:* seaweed.

xii.6. *mortal ark:* body.

xiv.2. *thou:* the ship.

xv.10. *thy:* the ship's.

xv.11. *plane of molten glass:* calm sea.

xv.14–16. I should give myself up in sympathy with the storm but for the fear that it may be endangering the ship.

xvi.2. *calm despair and wild unrest:* see xi.16 and xv.15.

xviii. Refers to Hallam's burial at Clevedon in Somerset.

xviii.7. *familiar names:* those of his mother's family.

xix. Written at Tintern Abbey in the Wye Valley.

xix.1. *Danube . . . Severn:* Hallam died near the one and was buried near the other.

xix.5–8. 'Taken from my own observation—the rapids of the Wye are stilled by the incoming sea' (Tennyson).

xxi.15–16. Presumably a reference to Chartism and, ultimately, to the French Revolution.

xxii.10. *autumnal:* Hallam died 15 September 1833.

xxii.20. *the Shadow:* death.

xxiii.12. *Pan:* god of flocks and shepherds.

xxiii.22. *Argive:* Greek.

xxiii.24. *Arcady:* a district in Greece, the principal seat of the worship of Pan. Often imagined as an ideal region of rustic contentment.

xxiv.4. *isles of night:* sun-spots.

xxiv.13–16. Or does the remoteness of past experience give it a perfection that we could not perceive at the time?

xxv.1. *Life:* Tennyson explained that it was 'chequered, but the burden was shared'.

xxvi.13–16. Better sudden death than the scorn of myself that I should feel if I believed myself capable of growing indifferent.

xxix.11. *Use and Wont:* habit and custom.

xxx.8. *mute Shadow:* Hallam.

xxx.26. *yet the same:* but retaining spiritual identity.

xxx.32. *Hope was born:* with the birth of Christ.

xxxi.1. *Lazarus:* Jesus' raising of Lazarus from the dead is narrated in John xi.

xxxi.12. *Olivet:* hill near Jerusalem.

xxxii. Originally envisaged as part of xxxi. The opening lines reintroduce Mary, her brother Lazarus who 'was dead', and Jesus who 'brought him back'.

xxxiv. Without a belief in survival after death, life itself would be meaningless.

xxxv. Without such a belief, love would be impossible.

xxxv.9–12. 'The vastness of the future—the enormity of the ages to come after your little life would act against that love' (Tennyson).

xxxv.11. *Æonian hills:* hills that have outlasted whole geological ages.

xxxv.24. *bask'd and batten'd:* sprawled in the warmth and fed grossly.

xxxvi.5–8. 'For divine Wisdom had to deal with the limited powers of humanity, to which truth logically argued out would be ineffectual, whereas truth coming in the story of the Gospel can influence the poorest' (Tennyson).

xxxvi.15. *wild eyes:* of the Pacific Islanders.

xxxvii.1. *Urania:* the Muse of astronomy; here, of heavenly things.

xxxvii.6. *Parnassus:* a mountain in Greece sacred to the Muses. Its Castalian spring could be considered a poet's 'native rill'.

xxxvii.9. *Melpomene:* the Muse of tragedy; here, of elegy.

xxxvii.23. *the master's field:* God's acre, the churchyard.

xxxviii.5. *blowing:* blossoming.

xxxix. Written 1868, a late addition to *In Memoriam.*

xxxix.3. *fruitful cloud and living smoke:* 'The yew, when flowering, in a wind or if struck sends up its pollen like smoke' (Tennyson).

xxxix.11–12. Sorrow sees only the winter gloom.

xl.17. *thee:* Hallam.

xl.25. *would have told:* would wish to be told.

xli.16. *howlings from forgotten fields:* yellings of the damned, buried in oblivion.

xli.23. *secular to-be:* future ages.

xliii. Tennyson makes poetic use of the doctrine that each soul sleeps from the moment of death to the day of judgment.

xliii.3. *intervital gloom:* the darkness intervening between mortal life and eternal life.

xliii.15. *spiritual prime:* dawn of eternity.

xliv. Just as a grown man may receive faint intimations of forgotten infantile experience, so Hallam may receive faint intimations of forgotten earthly experience. Tennyson's guardian angel can tell him all.

xliv.4. *the doorways of his head:* the fontanelles of the skull, which close up when the child is about eighteen months old.

xlvi.15. 'As if Lord of the whole life' (Tennyson).

xlvii. We need to believe that we shall retain our individual identities after death. But if we are to lose ourselves in the Universal Spirit, we ask for one more parting first from those we love and have lost.

xlix.1. *schools:* of philosophy.

xlix.8. *crisp:* ripple.

l. Addressed to Hallam.

l.8. *slinging flame:* the Furies carried torches.

lii.11–12. The life of Jesus.

lii.15. *Abide:* wait in patience.

liv.1. *Oh yet:* in spite of evil, a plausible justification of which has been rejected in liii.

liv.18. *infant:* Tennyson evidently keeps in mind the Latin *infans* meaning 'unable to speak'.

lv, lvi. When he speaks of Nature's indifference both to the individual and to the species, when he describes her as 'red in tooth and claw', and when he alludes to the evidence 'seal'd within the iron hills', Tennyson is probably recalling Sir Charles Lyell's *Principles of Geology* (1830–3). Darwin's *Origin of Species* was not to appear until 1859.

lvi.2. *scarped cliff:* steep cliff-face exposing earlier layers of rock and fossilized remains.

lvi.12. *fanes:* temples.

lvi.22. *Dragons of the prime:* prehistoric monsters.

lix. This lyric pairs and contrasts with iii. The poet is now prepared to take Sorrow for a wife.

lix.9. *centred:* deep-seated.

lxiii.4. *assumptions:* ascents.

lxvi.1. *You:* an unnamed friend. (Hallam is always addressed as 'thou'.)

lxvii.2. *place of rest:* Hallam's grave.

lxvii.3. *water:* River Severn. See xix.1,5.

lxix.12. 'To write poems about death and grief is "to wear a crown of thorns", which the people say ought to be laid aside' (Tennyson).

lxix.14. 'But the Divine Thing in the gloom brought comfort' (Tennyson).

lxx.11. *bulks:* 'A word with evolutionary suggestions for Tennyson' (Ricks).

lxxi.4. *went thro' summer France:* in 1830 Tennyson travelled with Hallam in France as far as the Pyrenees.

lxxii.5. *Day:* the anniversary of Hallam's death.

lxxiii.5. *The fame . . . that I foresaw:* others foresaw it, too; Gladstone, for example.

lxxvi.8. *Before:* sooner than.

lxxvi.9. *And if the matin songs:* and even if the great works of the early poets.

lxxviii.1. *Again at Christmas:* just as in xxx. But this second Christmas falls 'calmly', whereas the first fell 'sadly'.

lxxviii.5. *yule-clog:* Christmas log.

lxxviii.11. *mimic picture's breathing grace:* tableaux vivants, representations of well-known paintings and other appropriate subjects by persons suitably dressed and posed, remaining still and silent.

lxxviii.12. *hoodman-blind:* blind man's buff.

lxxix. Addressed to Tennyson's elder brother Charles.

lxxix.1. Quoted from ix.20.

lxxix.4. *in fee:* as your absolute and rightful possession.

lxxix.18. *he:* Hallam.

lxxx.4. *dropt the dust on tearless eyes:* taken me before I had occasion to mourn for him.

lxxxi.1. *Could I:* would that I could.

lxxxiv.11. *one:* Tennyson's sister Emily.

lxxxv. Addressed to Tennyson's friend Edmund Lushington.

lxxxv.3-4. Quoted from xxvii.15-16.

lxxxv.19. *Vienna:* the place of Hallam's death.

lxxxvi.3. *brake:* thicket.

lxxxvi.7. *horned:* Tennyson explained this as meaning 'between two promontories'.

lxxxvi.13-16. 'The west wind rolling to the Eastern seas till it meets the evening star' (Tennyson).

lxxxvii. The poet visits Trinity College, Cambridge.

lxxxvii.5. *fanes:* chapels.

lxxxvii.15. *long walk of limes:* in the college grounds.

lxxxvii.21-30. 'The "Water Club",' said Tennyson, 'because there was no wine. They used to make speeches—I never did.'

lxxxvii.38. *orbits:* eyes.

lxxxvii.39–40. On reading of the prominent ridge of bone over Michael Angelo's eyes, Hallam said to Tennyson, 'Alfred, look over my eyes; surely I have the bar of Michael Angelo!'

lxxxviii.1. *bird:* according to Tennyson, a nightingale.

lxxxviii.2. *Eden:* a song as from the garden of Eden.

lxxxviii.2. *quicks:* quickset thorn.

lxxxix. Recollections of Hallam's visits to Somersby.

lxxxix.1. *counterchange:* chequer (heraldic).

lxxxix.47–8. 'Before Venus, the evening star, had dipt into the sunset. The planets, according to Laplace, were evolved from the sun' (Tennyson).

xci.4. *sea-blue bird:* kingfisher.

xciii.9. *sightless:* invisible.

xciii.12. *tenfold:* in allusion to the ten heavens of Dante.

xcv. Set in the garden at Somersby.

xcv.8. *fluttering:* the sound of the flame under the tea-urn.

xcv.10. *wheel'd or lit the filmy shapes:* the night-moths wheeled or alighted.

xcv.22. *that glad year:* a particular year of their friendship.

xcv.36–7. *The living soul . . . mine in this:* Tennyson originally had 'His living soul' and 'mine in his', which would mean that the mystical union recorded in the lyric was with Hallam alone. The revised text opens up the possibility that the poet had experienced a brief union with the Deity. But it does not exclude contact with his friend. As Tennyson himself said, 'The greater Soul may include the less'. See cxxx.11.

xcv.39. *that which is:* the ultimate reality.

xcv.41. *Æonian music:* everlasting music.

xcv.46. *matter-moulded forms of speech:* everyday speech, as shaped by practical requirements.

xcv.62–4. In the stillness, a light which seems to be that of East and West, dawn and sunset, life and death, suggests the 'boundless day' of eternal life.

xcvi.1. *You:* probably Emily Sellwood.

xcvi.5. *one:* Hallam.

xcvii. Tennyson explained: 'The relation of one on earth to one in the other and higher world. Not my relation to him here. He looked up to me as I looked up to him.

'The spirit yet in the flesh but united in love with the spirit out of the flesh resembles the wife of a great man of science. She looks up to him —but what he knows is a mystery to her.'

xcvii.3. The poet is thinking of the Spectre of the Brocken, in which an enlarged shadow of a spectator standing on a mountain is cast by the rays of the evening sun upon a bank of cloud lying opposite.

xcviii. Perhaps occasioned by the honeymoon of Tennyson's brother Charles.

xcviii.17. *Gnarr:* snarl.

xcviii.21. *mother town:* capital city.

xcix.4. *Day:* the anniversary of Hallam's death. Compare lxxii.

c–ciii. These four lyrics refer to the Tennyson's move from Somersby in 1837.

ci.11. *the lesser wain:* the Little Bear, a constellation.

cii.7. *Two spirits:* love of Somersby from early experience; and love of it as later associated with Hallam (whose visits are remembered in lxxxix).

ciii.6. *maidens:* the Muses.

ciii.7. *summits:* the divine.

ciii.8. *river:* life.

ciii.16. *sea:* eternity.

ciii.25–8. 'The progress of the Age' (Tennyson, who gave also the four preceding glosses).

ciii.31. *Anakim:* giants. See Deuteronomy ii.10.

ciii.33–6. 'The great hopes of humanity and science' (Tennyson).

ciii.52. *they enter'd in:* his 'earthly hopes and powers . . . will be still of use to him' (Tennyson).

civ.8. *not the bells I know:* from Somersby, the Tennysons moved to High Beech, Epping Forest.

cv. Compare xxx and lxxviii. This third Christmas falls 'strangely' and the 'mask and mime' lapse.

cv.5. *Our father's dust:* Dr Tennyson died six years before his family left Somersby.

cv.18. *bowl of wassail mantle:* bowl of spiced ale (customary on Christmas Eve) form a 'head' or froth.

cv.25. *worlds:* planets.

cvi.32. *Christ that is to be:* more liberal Christianity of the future.

cvii.1. *born:* Hallam was born on 1 February 1811.

cvii.11. *grides:* grates.

cvii.14. *darken:* the snow-flakes, seen in silhouette, appear darker as they fall into the foam.

cviii.3. *eat my heart:* suffer from silent grief.

cix.24. *Nor:* if I do not.

cx.2. *rathe:* early.

cxi.9. *he:* Hallam.

cxii.2–4. In that I calmly acknowledge unfulfilled greatness such as Hallam's but make light of smaller, more nearly perfect natures.

cxii.8. *the lesser lords of doom:* having free will but less intellectual power.

cxiv.12. *wild Pallas:* the true Pallas sprang from the head of Zeus. This one, born from the brain of 'Demons', exemplifies the vice of irresponsible intellectualism.

cxvi.4. *crescent prime:* growing spring.

cxvi.6. *re-orient:* rising afresh.

cxvii.9–12. For every moment measured by the hour-glass, the sundial, the clock, and the movements of the heavenly bodies.

cxviii.4. *As:* as being no more enduring than.

cxviii.7. *They:* scientists.

cxviii.9. *tracts of fluent heat:* according to the current nebular hypothesis, the earth, like the other planets and the stars, originated in the condensation of interstellar gas.

cxviii.11. *cyclic storms:* Cuvier interpreted the fossil record of the prehistory of the earth as pointing to a series of cataclysms, after each of which fresh species prevailed.

cxviii.26. *Faun:* a kind of rural deity, half-man and half-goat; reputed to be drunken and lustful.

cxix. This lyric pairs and contrasts with vii.

cxx.4. *Paul with beasts:* see 1 Corinthians xv.32.

cxx.7. If we are mechanisms, what does Science matter to us?

cxx.9–11. 'Spoken ironically against mere materialism, not against evolution' (Tennyson).

cxxi. A hymn to the planet Venus, which is both Hesper, the evening star, and Phosphor, the morning star. 'Sweet Hesper-Phosphor' evokes a dual response to death, sorrow at temporal loss and hope of eternal life.

cxxii.2. *doom:* of grief.

cxxii.18. *paints a bow:* becomes a miniature rainbow.

cxxiii. A vision of geological change as a vast insubstantial pageant.

cxxiv.5–16. *I found Him not . . . 'I have felt.':* the poet bases his belief in God not upon external evidences but upon inner experience.

cxxiv.19. *child:* contrast liv.17–20.

cxxvii. All is well, despite imminent political and social revolution.

cxxvii.7. *red fool-fury of the Seine:* revolutionary violence in Paris. Compare xxi.15–16.

cxxxi.1. *will:* 'free-will' (Tennyson).

cxxxi.3. *spiritual rock:* see 1 Corinthians x.4.

cxxxi.10. *never can be proved:* compare Prologue, 4: 'Believing where we cannot prove'.

Epilogue. Celebrates the marriage of Tennyson's sister Cecilia to his friend Edmund Lushington in 1842. Lushington has already been addressed in lxxxv.

Epilogue, 8. *dark day:* when he heard of Hallam's death.

Epilogue, 34. *He:* Hallam.

Epilogue, 115. *friths:* estuaries; arms of the sea.

Epilogue, 123–40. Tennyson looks forward to the birth of a child who will bring mankind a little nearer to the higher level of development anticipated by Hallam. The optimistic evolutionism of this lyric and of cxviii contrasts with the nightmare vision suggested by science in lv and lvi. Tennyson may have read Robert Chambers' *Vestiges of the Natural History of Creation* (1844) before writing the present passage. Chambers sees evolution as proceeding in conformity with a divine plan.

Epilogue, 125–6. Tennyson refers to the current theory that the embryo reproduces the stages of the different forms of life.

The Charge of the Light Brigade (published 1854). Written in a few minutes after reading about the Crimean charge in *The Times*.

Maud: A Monodrama (published 1855; somewhat revised for 1856; later divided into Parts). The Introduction refers to the composition of *Maud* and to its biographical relevance. Tennyson described it as 'the history of a morbid, poetic soul, under the blighting influence of a recklessly speculative age. He is the heir of madness, an egoist with the makings of a cynic, raised to a pure and holy love which elevates his whole nature, passing from the height of triumph to the lowest depth of misery, driven into madness by the loss of her whom he has loved, and, when he has at length passed through the fiery furnace, and has recovered his reason, giving himself up to work for the good of mankind through the unselfishness born of a great passion.'

PART I

I.2. *blood-red:* Tennyson considered the extravagance of the epithet an early sign of the hero's unbalance.

I.39. *chalk and alum and plaster . . . for bread:* a notorious contemporary scandal.

I.41. *centre-bits:* instruments for boring holes; here used by burglars.

I.44. *poison:* the drug which the chemist is recklessly dispensing.

I.45. *kills her babe for a burial fee:* Carlyle records such a case in *Past and Present*, I.i.

I.46. *Timour:* Timour the Lame (1336–1405), the ruthless conqueror.

III.14. *Orion:* a constellation. When low in the sky, a sign of bad weather.

IV.9. *Czar:* Nicholas I of Russia, soon to be involved in the Crimean War against England, France, and Turkey.

IV.31. *monstrous eft:* prehistoric monster. An eft is a small lizard.

IV.43. *Isis:* one of the chief Egyptian deities, she came to be looked upon as the great nature-goddess.

IV.46. Alluding to the recent suppression by the Russians and the Austrians of movements of national liberation in Poland and Hungary.

IV.47. *knout:* scourge that was used in Russia for flogging criminals. The victims often died.

VI.44. *curl'd Assyrian Bull:* 'with hair curled like that of the bulls on Assyrian sculpture' (Tennyson).

VII.1–16. 'He remembers his father and her father talking just before the birth of Maud' (Tennyson).

VII.9–12. There is indeed a similar situation in *The Story of Nourredin Ali and Bedreddin Hassan*, in the *Arabian Nights*.

VIII.13. *it cannot be pride:* in iv.15–16 her failure to return his bow was attributed to 'a foolish pride'.

X.8. *trams:* rails for the trucks.

X.37–45. Interpreted at the time as an attack on John Bright (1811–89), the advocate of free trade and peace. Bright, a Rochdale man who was currently M.P. for Manchester, represented the cotton interests; he was a Quaker. Tennyson denied that he had intended an attack on him: 'I did not even know at the time that he was a Quaker'.

X.41. *broad-brimm'd:* referring to the type of hat worn at one time by Quakers.

X.44–52. The hero sees war as a 'consequence' of passions such as Tennyson had observed and known in his own earlier life.

X.65. *Aristocrat:* accented on the second syllable, as was usual at the time.

XII.24. *left the daisies rosy:* 'because if you tread on the daisy, it turns up a rosy underside' (Tennyson).

XII.30. *little King Charley:* a spaniel.

XIII.21. *Gorgonised me:* gave me a petrifying scrutiny.

XIV.7. *ramps:* rears on its hind legs.

XVI.8. *Oread:* mountain-nymph.

XVI.15. *Arab:* alluding to an Arab horse.

XVII.1–28. Written in 1849 with a view to insertion in the 1850 edition of *The Princess*, this song has generally been considered out of keeping with *Maud*.

XVIII.15. *Lebanon:* Lebanon and its cedars were famous in Biblical times. In the Song of Solomon v.15, for example, the bride speaks of her beloved: 'his countenance is as Lebanon, excellent as the cedars'.

XVIII.34. *mattock:* farm tool used for loosening hard ground.

XVIII.36. *sad astrology:* Tennyson explained this as 'modern astronomy, for of old astrology was thought to sympathise with and rule man's fate'.

XVIII.39. *Cold fires:* 'stars are *flame of the very highest intensity*, . . . but this flame is so very far away, that not even the slightest vestige of its warmth has ever touched the human sense' (R. J. Mann, *Tennyson's 'Maud' Vindicated* (1856)).

XVIII.78–79. *the glow Of your soft splendours:* the stars seemed 'pitiless, passionless eyes' at the earlier period when he was 'all forlorn' (XVIII.32–38). Now that Maud has accepted him they 'glow' and are 'soft'.

XXII.8. *planet of Love:* Venus, the morning star.

PART II

I.1. *The fault was mine:* the words of Maud's brother after he has been shot.

I.5. *a passionate cry:* Maud's at the sight of the bloodshed.

II.1. *See what a lovely shell:* 'in Brittany. The shell undestroyed amid the storm perhaps symbolises to him his own first and highest nature preserved amid the storms of passion' (Tennyson). This lyric, like 'Go not, happy day', was written years earlier than most of *Maud*.

II.48. *Lamech:* he spoke of killing a man for wounding him, a young man for a blow (Genesis iv.23).

IV.1–98. Tennyson wrote this lyric in 1833–4 and published it in 1837. When it became the nucleus of *Maud*, it underwent further revision.

IV.11. *shadow:* a projection of the hero's guilt in the form of a 'phantom' of Maud as she appeared at the moment of uttering her 'cry for a brother's blood' (I.34). This 'phantom' is distinct from the 'happy spirit' (IV.81) of the Maud who accepted the hero as her lover.

IV.81. *Would the happy spirit descend:* if the happy spirit were to descend.

V.1. *Dead:* mad and confined, the hero fancies that he is dead and buried.

V.18. *the dead men:* the other inmates of the asylum.

V.28–9. The clergy are content to destroy their church by neglect, as the churches have already stifled Christian doctrine with formalism.

V.53. *gray old wolf:* Maud's father. See I.xiii.28.

V.56. *for yourself:* the hero believes the son to be dead.

V.58–9. He associates Hanoverian ancestry with the introduction into England of the brown Norwegian rat. The Jacobites alleged that this came over in 1714 with the new dynasty which they opposed.

V.63. *poison our babes:* recalling the social evils denounced in I.i.37–46.

V.72–82. A recollection of the Hall garden leads to one of the 'Sultan', Maud's brother, lying desperately wounded.

V.85. *a friend of mine:* the hero's father.

V.88. *the second corpse:* Maud's brother.

V.92. *the Quaker:* the 'broad-brimm'd hawker of holy things' described in I.x.37–45. The hero seeks to justify his shooting of the brother as a blow struck at a public enemy—in a just war, as it were.

PART III

'Sane, but shattered. Written when the cannon was heard booming from the battleships in the Solent before the Crimean War' (Tennyson). The present Part III was for some time the sixth and last lyric of Part II. When Tennyson made it into Part III he allowed the numeral vi to stand. This was probably an oversight, but it may express his sense that Parts II and III are more closely linked than are I and II.

VI.6–8. ¦*Charioteer . . . Gemini . . . Orion:* constellations. The season is evidently spring.

VI.10. *She:* the true spirit of Maud as distinct from the 'phantom'.

VI.13–14. *Mars . . . on the Lion's breast:* the planet Mars stands for war, the constellation Leo for Britain.

VI.20. *iron tyranny:* Czarist Russia.

VI.34. *deck:* of a troopship bound for the Crimea.

VI.45. *giant liar:* Czar Nicholas I.

VI.51. *the Black and the Baltic:* two seas where British naval power might permit operations against Russia.

Tithonus (published 1860). Written in a shorter form following the shock of Hallam's death. Tithonus was loved by Aurora, the dawn-goddess, who gave him immortality but not eternal youth. Though he grew old and shrunken, he could not die.

4. *swan:* noted for its long life.

6. *thine arms:* Aurora's.

18. *indignant:* because they cannot destroy him, though they can age him.

25. *the silver star:* Venus, the morning star.

30. *goal of ordinance:* prescribed limit.

39. *team:* the horses which draw Aurora's chariot daily from Ocean to Olympus.

62. *Apollo:* the god to whose music Troy (Ilion) arose.

In the Valley of Cauteretz (published 1864). Tennyson wrote this on re-visiting a Pyrenean valley where he had been with Hallam in 1830. 'I like the little piece as well as anything I have written', he confessed.

Northern Farmer—Old Style (published 1864). In this poem and its successor Tennyson employs a Lincolnshire dialect familiar to him from early life.

1. *liggin':* lying.

3. *'a:* have.

5. *a:* they.

10. *'issén:* himself.

10. *a said:* he said.

13. *Larn'd a ma' beä:* learned he may be.

14. *a cast oop:* he raked up and threw in my teeth.

16. *raäte:* poor-rate.

18. *bummin':* humming loudly.

18. *buzzard-clock:* cockchafer.

23. *'Siver:* howsoever.

27. *summun:* someone.

28. *stubb'd:* cleared.

29. *moind:* remember.

30. *boggle:* bogy.

31. *butter-bump:* bittern.

32. *raäved an' rembled:* pulled out and threw away.

34. *'enemies:* anemones.

35. *toäner:* one or other.

36. *'soize:* assizes.

37. *Dubbut:* just.

40. *seeäd:* clover.

41. *Nobbut:* only.

52. *hoälms:* low-lying fields.

54. *sewer-loy:* surely.
62. *Huzzin' an' maäzin':* buzzing and troubling. A scornful reference to the noise of the newly introduced steam-threshers.
66. *'toättler:* teetotaller.
66. *a's hallus i' the owd taäle:* he's always telling the same old tale, giving the same advice.

Northern Farmer—New Style (published 1869).
4. *nor:* than.
5. *Woä:* stop.
5. *a craw to pluck wi' tha:* something awkward to settle with you.
7. *to weeäk:* this week.
17. *stunt:* obstinate.
26. *addle:* earn.
32. *far-welter'd:* fow-weltered (said of a sheep lying on its back).
39. *mays nowt:* makes nothing.
40. *the bees is as fell as owt:* the flies are as fierce as anything.
52. *tued an' moil'd:* worked and slaved.

The Coming of Arthur (published 1869). The first of the *Idylls of the King* as finally arranged.
1. *Cameliard:* Tennyson located this petty kingdom in South Wales.
14. *Uther:* brother of Aurelius.
18. 'The several petty princedoms were under one head, the "pendragon" ' (Tennyson).
31. 'Imitate the wolf by going on four feet' (Tennyson).
36. *Urien:* 'King of North Wales' (Tennyson).
50. *symbol:* a dragon.
66. *Colleaguing:* joining in alliance.
103. *battle:* army.
124. *his warrior whom he loved:* Lancelot.
234. *the people:* the ordinary people, as distinct from the turbulent lords.
252. *body enow:* strength enough.
261. *strait:* rigorous.
274. *vert:* green.
275. *three fair queens:* see 'The Epic' ['Morte d'Arthur'], line 249 and note.
279. *mage:* magician.
279. *wit:* intellect, understanding.
282. *Lady of the Lake:* see 'The Epic' ['Morte d'Arthur'], lines 154-7, 193-7.
298. *Urim:* 'Urim and Thummin, those oraculous gems/On Aaron's breast' (Milton, *Paradise Regain'd*, iii, alluding to Exodus xxviii.30).
379. *a ninth one:* 'Every ninth wave is supposed by the Welsh bards to be larger than those that go before' (Hallam Tennyson).
402-10. 'The truth appears in different guise to divers persons. The one fact is that man comes from the great deep and returns to it. This is an echo of the triads of the Welsh bards' (Tennyson).
431. *hind:* farm-worker, labourer.
476. *Lords from Rome:* the Arthurian stories are set in a period when Rome, in decline, was failing to defend provinces over which it still claimed authority.
508. Compare 'The Epic' ['Morte d'Arthur'], line 291.

Notes

The Revenge (published 1878).
 112. *lands they had ruin'd:* West Indies.

To E. FitzGerald (published 1885). FitzGerald's death on 14 June 1883 meant that he never saw this charming and affectionate verse epistle. Tennyson had finished it only a week or so earlier.
 1. *suburb grange:* FitzGerald's home.
 11. *that full sheet:* see Acts x.11–16.
 15. *table of Pythagoras:* vegetarian diet.
 17. *has it:* in *Measure for Measure*, I.iv.
 28. *Eschol:* having cut a bunch of grapes there, the Israelites named it Eshcol, meaning 'bunch of grapes'. See Numbers xiii.23–4.
 32. *golden Eastern lay: The Rubáiyát of Omar Khayyám* (1859).
 40. *Old friends:* James Spedding and W. H. Brookfield.
 46. *my son:* Hallam Tennyson.
 50. *this:* 'Tiresias', which followed in 1885.

Vastness (published 1885). 'What matters anything in this world without full faith in the Immortality of the Soul and of Love?' (Tennyson).
 12. *all-heal:* that which heals all.
 14. *offing:* the part of the visible sea distant from the shore.
 26. *death-ruckle:* death-rattle.
 36. *him:* Hallam.

Crossing the Bar (published 1889). Tennyson said that he 'began and finished' this lyric in twenty minutes. A 'bar' is a bank of sand or silt across the mouth of a river or harbour; beyond it lies the open sea.
 3. *moaning:* the moaning of the sea across the bar is a sign of bad weather.
 13. *bourne:* boundary, limit.

INDEX TO FIRST LINES

INDEX TO 'IN MEMORIAM'

Index to 'In Memoriam'